Communication
at the End of Life

LIFESPAN COMMUNICATION
Children, Families, and Aging

Thomas J. Socha
GENERAL EDITOR

Vol. 6

The Lifespan Communication series
is part of the Peter Lang Media and Communication list.
Every volume is peer reviewed and meets
the highest quality standards for content and production.

PETER LANG
New York • Bern • Frankfurt • Berlin
Brussels • Vienna • Oxford • Warsaw

Communication at the End of Life

Jon F. Nussbaum, Howard Giles,
Amber K. Worthington, Editors

PETER LANG
New York • Bern • Frankfurt • Berlin
Brussels • Vienna • Oxford • Warsaw

Library of Congress Cataloging-in-Publication Data
Communication at the end of life /
edited by Jon F. Nussbaum, Howard Giles, Amber K. Worthington.
pages cm — (Lifespan communication: children, families, and aging; vol. 6)
Includes bibliographical references and index.
1. Terminally ill. 2. Palliative treatment. 3. Death—Social aspects. 4. Families.
I. Nussbaum, Jon F. II. Giles, Howard. III. Worthington, Amber K.
R726.8.C646   362.17′5—dc23   2015009641
ISBN 978-1-4331-2583-6 (hardcover)
ISBN 978-1-4331-2582-9 (paperback)
ISBN 978-1-4539-1366-6 (e-book)
ISSN 2166-6466 (print)
ISSN 2166-6474 (online)

Bibliographic information published by **Die Deutsche Nationalbibliothek**.
Die Deutsche Nationalbibliothek lists this publication in the "Deutsche
Nationalbibliografie"; detailed bibliographic data are available
on the Internet at http://dnb.d-nb.de/.

Cover photo: "La Trascendencia de los Sueños" by Amber K. Worthington

The paper in this book meets the guidelines for permanence and durability
of the Committee on Production Guidelines for Book Longevity
of the Council of Library Resources.

Dedication

This book is dedicated to the memory of
ABBY PRESTIN,
who was taken well before her time.
We honor her as a role model, given her courage, tenacity, and love for, and
loyal support of, others. She proved herself to be a stellar scholar, contributed to
the literature on communication and dying, and is sorely missed by colleagues,
friends, and family.

Contents

Series Editor Preface

Communication at the End of Life

THOMAS J. SOCHA

Communication at the End of Life represents a milestone in the history of ideas about lifespan communication and is a significant and essential addition to the *Lifespan Communication: Children, Families and Aging* book series. Together, the editors and authors provide us with a communicative lens through which to view the many sides of experiencing our final days. They enlighten us about myriad choices, provide insights into improving the quality of end of life, and offer a positive framework for use by all those sharing an end-of-life journey. Although difficult and profound on so many levels, communication during end of life is really a continuation of all the communication that has come before and will come after—something that the famous Brandeis University sociologist Morrie Schwartz (2008) understood all too well, as he reminded us that if we can learn how to die, we can learn how to live.

Like this volume, the book series invites scholars to view communication through a panoramic lens—first words to final conversations—a comprehensive communication vista that brings children, adolescents, and adults of all ages into focus for the field of communication. It is my hope that such a view will become commonplace in communication thinking and research where communication scholars take seriously the idea that all communication is developmental from its beginning to its end.

REFERENCE

Schwartz, M. (2008). *Morrie: In his own words; Life wisdom from a remarkable man*. New York, NY: Walker and Company.

Introduction: Communicating At, For, AND About THE End OF Life

MAUREEN P. KEELEY

HOWARD GILES

JON F. NUSSBAUM

Baby boomers, the largest segment of the U.S. population, are coming to the age at which they feel their own mortality and must cope with their parents' deaths and, increasingly, with their peers' deaths. Approximately 25% of our middle-aged generation (currently the largest group in our society) lives with their parents; 13 million are caregivers for ailing parents ("Baby Boomer News & Information," 2005). In addition, these same boomers have more trouble discussing end-of-life issues (their own as well as that of their family members and friends) with their parents than do their parents who are now in their 70s or beyond (Greenwald & Associates, 2005). People at times may desire to learn more about what to expect; how to talk with professional health care workers about end-of-life choices, expectations, and fears; how to be a more effective partner on this journey with a loved one; and how to better prepare themselves for dealing with their own stress and grief as they care for and deal with the immediate loss of a loved one and the aftermath (see Chapter 11 of this volume; all further references to chapters are to those in this volume).

Unfortunately, we live in a culture that removes death from our view, apart from its ubiquity in the movies and in videogames (see Chapter 5). A century ago, witnessing death was commonplace because people died at home and in the family's care. By 1992, 77% of deaths occurred in a health care facility and about 20% in a private home. Today, 80% of the 2.2 million Americans who die each year die in a hospital. While more people are entering hospice in the U.S., a mere 7%

of Americans die in hospice care, and, on average, those few die within 36 days of entering hospice care (see Chapter 10). Removal of death from everyday life leaves no models for what people should do or say to help their loved ones have a good death (see Chapter 4) and also hinders people's opportunities to use this terminal time to help them cope with their impending loss (see Chapter 12).

With medical advances in the treatment of cancer and other degenerative diseases, it is becoming likely that an ailing loved one will live longer after diagnosis than ever before ("Baby Boomers News & Information," 2005). With this trend, more people in the future may choose to die at home and/or in hospice care. The moment that a loved one is given a death notice through notification of a terminal illness, the family and friends begin their journey with their dying loved one. This journey may take days or years, but however long it is, the family and friends begin looking for answers. How do I ensure that my loved one has the best care possible at the end of life (see Chapters 2, 3, 4, 6, 7, 8, 9, and 10)? When is the right time to go into hospice or into palliative care (see Chapters 2, 10, and 12)? How do I talk with health care professionals about the dying process (see Chapters 2, 6, 7, 8, 10, and 12)? How do I deal with my anger, fears, and loss (see Chapter 11)? How can I help my mother, father, spouse, child, or sibling (see Chapter 8)? How do I say goodbye (see Chapter 7)?

Our effort in this volume—and this Introduction—is to offer one crucial recommendation: *communication*. Scholars in a wide variety of fields, such as palliative medicine (Kübler-Ross, 1969, 1997; McQuellon & Cowan, 2000), psychology (Aiken, 2001), and sociology (Moller, 1996), have examined death and dying for decades and have often suggested that communication was necessary for a good death; however, what was meant by communication was often vague. Within the past decade, communication researchers have been exploring communication among family members at the end of life (Keeley, 2007; Keeley, Generous, & Baldwin, 2014; Keeley & Yingling, 2007); communication within palliative health care teams as well as with patients (Goldsmith, Ferrell, Wittenberg-Lyles, & Ragan, 2013; Ragan, Wittenberg-Lyles, Goldsmith, & Sanchez-Reilly, 2008); and between hospice volunteers and dying individuals (Foster, 2007).

In this Introduction, we bring together recurrent themes as they unfold throughout this volume. The work represented herein is interdisciplinary, methodologically eclectic, and theoretically diverse, and, as a consequence, we contend is refreshingly varied in its recourse to data and personal narratives. Although communication research relating to end-of-life issues is, arguably, in its infancy, there is sufficient compelling extant work for us to invite chapters that span many important, albeit not all, facets of this important juncture in the lifespan.

Specifically, end-of-life communication focuses on the verbal and nonverbal communication that occurs between individuals following the diagnosis of a terminal illness (Keeley & Yingling, 2007). The approaching death creates the circumstances that affect the communication climate for the participants. For instance, the interactions will often be different depending on the stage of the dying process, whether it is in the early stages of the end-of-life journey immediately following a terminal diagnosis, or toward the end of the journey following a long fight with the illness, or coming to the decision to terminate life support, or with young children's traumatically premature demise (see Chapter 9). Many of the conversations are private, one-on-one interactions such as those that occur between the individual who is dying and his or her family and friends, often occurring within the context of home (see Chapter 8). Other conversations are conducted within small groups, such as when family members gather around their dying loved one or in the midst of palliative care teams that are focusing on the medical needs of their patient within hospitals or in-care hospice facilities.

Topics of conversations at the end of life include messages of love, identity, spirituality, everyday talk, difficult relationship talk (Keeley, 2007), instrumental talk about the illness or dying (Keeley et al., 2014), palliative care treatment (Wittenberg-Lyles, Goldsmith, & Ragan, 2010), funeral plans (Aiken, 2001), and talk about life after the death of the loved one (Keeley & Yingling, 2007; see Chapter 7). In addition, communication at the end of life is, as this volume attests, complicated because there are many communication processes that must be dealt with, including uncertainty management (Scott & Caughlin, 2014); decision making and negotiation regarding the types of and length of care (Goldsmith et al., 2013); privacy management (Petronio, 2002); communicating comfort and social support (Ragan et al., 2008); and sense-making of the death journey, the loss, and of the meaning of life, death, and the afterlife (Keeley, 2009; Keeley & Koenig Kellas, 2005; see Chapters 2 and 4).

On the one hand, some family members manage their uncertainty at the end of life by sidestepping particular conversations that are too frightening or depressing to them (Caughlin, Mikucki-Enyart, Middleton, Stone, & Brown, 2011). On the other hand, some individuals choose to face this very directly by gathering as much information as possible to reduce uncertainty as much as possible and by participating in authentic conversations (McQuellon & Cowan, 2000). While the two above-mentioned ways of dealing with uncertainty (management and reduction) are oppositional, many people at the end of life, depending on the individuals in the interaction, generally engage in open communication while simultaneously avoiding certain topics, thus protecting others and maintaining optimism (Keeley, in press).

Decision making and negotiation regarding the types of care and the length of treatment at the end of life are important communication processes because, oftentimes, making decisions about end-of-life care is one of the few things over which the dying person and the family members have any control in the midst of a terminal illness. Specifically, palliative health care specialists want to be proactive in getting patients to create an advance care plan at the end of life (Cohen & Nirenberg, 2011; see Chapters 2, 6, 7, 10, and 11). It is necessary, however, for the patient and family members to be willing to listen to and accept the terminal illness diagnosis if they are going to navigate the end-of-life journey on their own terms.

Managing privacy (physical, emotional, informational, and communicative) is challenging at best at the end of life because of the escalating needs of both the patient and the family caregivers during that period. Strangers are brought into the house (e.g., volunteers, hospice workers), thereby invading the family space. At some point (if not at many points) in time, the terminally ill patient needs help with taking care of personal needs and avoiding feeling vulnerable and exposed. In addition, medical information must be shared to ensure proper care, and roles often are drastically changed during the end-of-life process (Lynn & Harrold, 1999; see Chapters 2, 4, 6, 7, 8, 9, and 12). Managing communication privacy focuses on ownership and co-ownership of information, as well as the negotiation of rules concerning how, where, and when the information will be shared (Petronio, 2002). Palliative health care specialists are especially concerned with protecting the privacy needs of their patients and their family members at the end of life.

Comforting messages are critical messages at the end of life because they often deal with the physical and emotional suffering that comes with the loss that accompanies death (Keeley, 2009). Individuals are often more aware and careful regarding what they say and how they say it at the end of life than they are in other conversations (Keeley, 2007; see Chapters 2 and 7). Scholarship on politeness strategies and facework messages (e.g., Holtgraves, 2002) suggests that careful attention to what is said and how things are said (especially as it applies to protecting one's own and another's image and identity) helps to cultivate a more open and supportive conversational environment (Burleson & Goldsmith, 1998), creates a greater sense of social support (Sarason, Sarason, & Gurung, 1997), and builds greater acceptance, coping, and trust within relationships (Greenberg, Rice, & Elliott, 1993), all of which benefit individuals and family members in the face of impending death.

Making sense of the death journey, the meaning of life, death, and the afterlife is often an important goal for everyone at the end of life (Kübler-Ross, 1997; Levine, 1984; see Chapter 12). When people are confronted with a terminal illness, they frequently search for meaning by exploring their religious and spiritual belief systems (see Chapter 4). When medical science can no longer offer hope or explanation, spiritual/religious beliefs provide the only consoling explanation available to which people may turn as they face impending death (Keeley, 2009). In addition, sense-making is also achieved through storytelling (Foster, 2002; Keeley & Koenig Kellas, 2005) and with communication with trusted individuals (e.g., a loved one, chaplain, hospice social worker, nurse, hospice volunteer; Keeley & Yingling, 2007; Ragan et al., 2008; see Chapters 2, 5, 7, 8, and 10).

As subsequent chapters inform, to deal successfully with communication at the end of life, people must also have a strong aptitude for empathy, authenticity, compassion, responsiveness, adaptability, mindfulness, and the ability to be truly in the moment (McQuellon & Cowan, 2000). Empathy includes an individual's ability to focus on the emotions of another person, to recognize, appreciate, and comprehend those emotions, and to respond successfully to those emotions (Suchman, Markakis, Beckman, & Frankel, 1997). Authentic communication centers on honest, candid, and heartfelt self-expression and highlights what is important to individuals, revealing what is their real truth (Rosenberg, 2003). Compassionate and responsive communication focuses on kindness, consideration, and immediacy of responses (Keeley & Baldwin, 2012). Adaptability necessitates that individuals be flexible and open to whatever is going on in the moment and to be willing to accommodate communicatively to fit current needs (Keeley & Yingling, 2007; see also Giles & Soliz, 2014). Mindfulness requires attending to both the cues of individuals and to one's own internal cues in order to respond with authenticity, even if it means "abandoning the script" (Wittenberg-Lyles, Goldsmith, & Ragan, 2010, p. 297). By engaging in these other-centered communication behaviors, there is less time and energy wasted on judging, analyzing, complaining, and comparing situations, resulting in more positive outcomes (Rosenberg, 2003). Nonverbal communication is critical to successfully achieving these other-centered communication behaviors because it is often the most revealing (Keeley & Yingling, 2007).

Age is a significant consideration regarding communication at the end of life, both the age of the person who is dying and the age of the family members dealing with the death of the loved one. Acceptance of death, bereavement, and communication may be experienced very differently depending on the age of the person who is dying (Keeley & Yingling, 2007). Death of a child or younger person is often met with anger and denial because of the loss of all that could have been if that young person had lived (see Chapter 9), whereas the death of an individual who had a long and happy life is more readily accepted as a natural part of the life cycle. Children and/or adolescents deal with the death of a family member in different ways depending on their age, cognitive development, and life experiences (Aiken, 2001). Specifically, children under the age of 3 do not understand the finality of death, and, therefore, have difficulty accepting its conclusiveness; children 3 to 6 years of age often understand the concept of death but also believe in magical thinking, and may believe that death can be caused by feelings or thoughts, or may be very curious about the biological aspect of death (Myers, 1986). Children from 7 to 12 years of age have a more accurate view of death in that they understand that death is inevitable, irreversible, and can happen to anybody and at any time; nonetheless, they struggle to talk about death and dying (Aiken, 2001; Myers, 1986). Adolescents (12- to 18-year-olds) clearly know that death is final; they frequently need support but often want to appear independent (Myers, 1986). Furthermore, all children and adolescents are coping with their grief while concurrently carrying out their day-to-day tasks and going through developmental milestones (Oltjenbruns, 2001).

Culture is also an important factor when dealing with communication at the end of life (see Chapter 6). Avoiding talking about or dealing with death is a common part of U.S. culture, at least in part because death as it is generally represented in the U.S. is a taboo topic and is often shrouded in fear, doubt, loss of control, and feelings of awkwardness and discomfort (Giles, Thai, & Preston, 2014). Those from Asian countries are more accepting of death, yet they still believe that it is bad luck to speak about it (Wu, Tang, & Kwok, 2002). Traditional Hispanic culture deals with death according to its own values and religious beliefs, preferring to keep the care of the dying and end-of-life communication within the family, while funerals focus on celebrating the life and new afterlife of the deceased (Moller, 1996). Thus, culture clearly has a strong impact on what people communicate, how they communicate, and when they communicate at the end of life.

CONCLUSIONS

Consequently, the research represented in this volume that communication scholars are conducting offers clear advice and practices for people who are facing the dying process (their own, that of a loved one, or within their palliative health care careers). Communication scholars also contribute explicit communication information and guidance, providing individuals the opportunity to approach the end of life with models to follow. Increasing the information and the communication about death and dying will remove much of the mystery and fear that is often associated with the end-of-life journey. In addition, taking a communication approach allows individuals to look at the pragmatics of the dying process and to offer reassurance to those who want to converse with the dying—but do not know how. It has been our goal that the information gathered in this book helps people to be more successful in their communication at the end of life and that it will stimulate an exciting generation of new theoretical and empirical gains in the very near future (see Epilogue).

One poignant area not touched on in this book is the consequences of a pet dying in cultures (see Gray & Young, 2011) that hold them dear. Although the evidence concerning positive health benefits of having pets is mixed (Amiot & Bastian, 2014), certainly many families—as evident from their holiday card photographs—consider them integral family members. Their loss, therefore, can be psychologically traumatic and the communicative management, and the discourse, of pet bereavement is worthy of serious study as are the emotional repercussions of different kinds of pets' deaths on their owners, both male and female (see Herzog, 2007). The latter can be particularly distressing for persons living alone as well as for younger children and older adults, and there are data to suggest that some people feel the loss of a pet as deeply as they would a close fellow human (Knight & Edwards, 2008). The extent to which empathy and sympathy are genuinely expressed over what period of time—by other pet owners and those more averse to pets—to those enduring the loss is a significant research topic. Certainly there is very little institutional or media support to assist in this grieving process, although a few resource books do exist (e.g., O'Connor, 1994).

These dynamics also raise the intriguing issue as to how pets and animals, in turn, deal with other members of their species dying. There is an intriguing literature, albeit observational and mostly case studies, on how male and female animals deal differentially with the death of their infants, especially with respect to chimpanzees and gorillas (e.g., Anderson, 2011; Cronin, Van Leeuwen, Mulenga, & Bodamer, 2011). Interestingly, Braitman (2014) discusses research on mammals that suggests that they grieve much like humans when a close relationship is ended by death. Indeed, the region of the brain that is activated is similar to the region that activates grief in humans, the prolongation of which can lead to clinical depression.

As mentioned above, this book places communication at the core of our end-of-life experience. It is our hope that this book captures the profound significance of communication as those who are close to death and their networks of family, friends, and both formal and informal caregivers manage the final moments of life.

REFERENCES

Aiken, L. R. (2001). *Dying, death, and bereavement* (4th ed.). Mahwah, NJ: Lawrence Erlbaum.

Amiot, C. E., & Bastian, B. (2014, November 3). Toward a psychology of human–animal relations. *Psychological Bulletin*. Advance online publication. Retrieved from http://dx.doi.org/10.1037/a0038147

Anderson, J. R. (2011). A primatological perspective on death. *American Journal of Primatology, 73,* 410–414.

Baby boomer news & information. (2005, October 19). Retrieved January 22, 2015, from http://www.seniorjournal.com/BabyBoomers.htm

Braitman, L. (2014). *Animal madness: How anxious dogs, compulsive parrots and elephants in recovery help us understand ourselves.* New York, NY: Simon & Schuster.

Burleson, B. R., & Goldsmith, D. J. (1998). How the comforting process works: Alleviating emotional distress through conversationally induced reappraisals. In P. A. Andersen & L. K. Guerrero (Eds.), *Handbook of communication and emotion: Research, theory, applications, and contexts* (pp. 245–280). San Diego, CA: Academic Press.

Caughlin, J. P., Mikucki-Enyart, S. L., Middleton, A. V., Stone, A. M., & Brown, L. E. (2011). Being open without talking about it: A rhetorical/normative approach to understanding topic avoidance in families after a lung cancer diagnosis. *Communication Monographs, 78*(4), 409–436.

Cohen, A., & Nirenberg, A. (2011). Current practices in advance care planning. *Clinical Journal of Oncology Nursing, 15*, 547–553.

Cronin, K. A., Van Leeuwen, E. J. C., Mulenga, I. C., & Bodamer, M. D. (2011). Behavioral response of a chimpanzee mother toward her dead infant. *American Journal of Primatology, 73*, 415–421.

Foster, E. (2002). Lessons we learned: Stories of volunteer-patient communication in hospice. *Journal of Ageing and Identity, 7*, 245–256.

Foster, E. (2007). *Communicating at the end-of-life: Finding magic in the mundane.* Mahwah, NJ: Lawrence Erlbaum.

Giles, H., & Soliz, J. (2014). Communication accommodation theory: A situated framework for interpersonal, family, and intergroup dynamics. In D. Braithewaite & P. Schrodt (Eds.), *Engaging interpersonal theories* (2nd ed., pp. 157–169). Thousand Oaks, CA: Sage.

Giles, H., Thai, C., & Preston, A. (2014). End of life interactions. In J. Nussbaum (Ed.), *The handbook of lifespan communication* (pp. 405–424). New York, NY: Peter Lang.

Goldsmith, J., Ferrell, B., Wittenberg-Lyles, E., & Ragan, S. (2013). Palliative care communication in oncology nursing. *Clinical Journal of Oncology Nursing, 17*, 163–167.

Gray, P. B., & Young, S. M. (2011). Human–pet dynamics in cross-cultural perspective. *Anthrozoös, 24*, 17–30.

Greenberg, L. S., Rice, L. N., & Elliott, R. (1993). *Facilitating emotional change: The moment-by-moment process.* New York, NY: Guilford.

Greenwald, M., & Associates. (2005, September 19). Hartford Financial Services Group "Family Conversations" series, reported in *Senior Journal.* Retrieved from http://www.seniorjournal.com

Herzog, H. A. (2007). Gender differences in human–animal interactions: A review. *Anthrozoös, 20*, 7–21.

Holtgraves, T. (2002). *Language as social action.* Mahwah, NJ: Lawrence Erlbaum.

Hospice care. (n.d.). Retrieved January 22, 2015, from http://efmoody.com/longterm/hospice.html

Keeley, M. P. (2007). "Turning toward death together": Functions of messages during final conversations in close relationships. *Journal of Social and Personal Relationships, 24*, 225–253.

Keeley, M. P. (2009). Comfort and community: Two emergent communication themes of religious faith and spirituality evident during final conversations. In M. Wills (Ed.), *Speaking of spirituality: Perspectives on health from the religious to the numinous* (pp. 227–248). Cresskill, NJ: Hampton Press.

Keeley, M. P. (in press). Final conversations. In T. L. Thompsonn & J. G. Golson (Eds.), *The encyclopedia of health communication.* Thousand Oaks, CA.: Sage.

Keeley, M. P., & Baldwin, P. (2012). Final conversations: Positive communication at the end of life. In M. Pitts & T. J. Socha (Eds.), *Positive communication in health and wellness* (pp. 190–206). New York, NY: Peter Lang.

Keeley, M. P., Generous, M., & Baldwin, P. (2014). Final conversations phase II: Children's final conversation messages with dying family members. *Journal of Family Communication, 14*, 208–229.

Keeley, M. P., & Koenig Kellas, J. (2005). Constructing life and death through final conversations narratives. In L. M. Harter, P. M. Japp, & C. S. Beck (Eds.), *Narratives, health, and healing: Communication theory, research, and practice* (pp. 365–390). Mahwah, NJ: Lawrence Erlbaum.

Keeley, M. P., & Yingling, J. (2007). *Final conversations: Helping the living and the dying talk to one another.* Acton, MA: VanderWyk & Burnham.

Knight, S., & Edwards, V. (2008). In the company of wolves: The physical, social, and psychological benefits of dog ownership. *Journal of Aging and Health, 20,* 437–455.

Kübler-Ross, E. (1969). *On death and dying.* New York, NY: Touchstone.

Kübler-Ross, E. (1997). *Living with death and dying.* New York, NY: Simon & Schuster.

Levine, S. (1984). *Meetings at the edge: Dialogues with the grieving, and the dying, and the healing and the healed.* New York, NY: Doubleday.

Lynn, J., & Harrold, J. (1999). *Handbook for mortals: Guidance for people facing serious illness.* Oxford, UK: Oxford University Press.

McQuellon, R. P., & Cowan, M. A. (2000). Turning toward death together: Conversation in mortal time. *American Journal of Hospice & Palliative Care, 17,* 312–318.

Moller, D. W. (1996). *Confronting death: Values, institutions, and human morality.* New York, NY: Oxford University Press.

Myers, D. (1986). *Child development and its relationship to grief and loss.* New York, NY: Worth.

O'Connor, N. (1994). *Letting go with love: The grieving process.* Tucson, AZ: La Mariposa Press.

Oltjenbruns, K. A. (2001). Developmental context of childhood: Grief and regrief phenomena. In M. S. Stroebe, R. O. Hansson, W. Stroebe, & H. Schut (Eds.), *Handbook of bereavement research: Consequences, coping and care* (pp. 169–197). Washington, DC: American Psychological Association.

Petronio, S. (2002). *Boundaries of privacy: Dialectics of disclosure.* Albany, NY: State University of New York Press.

Ragan, S., Wittenberg-Lyles, E., Goldsmith, J., & Sanchez-Reilly, S. (2008). *Communication as comfort: Multiple voices in palliative care.* New York, NY: Routledge/Taylor & Francis.

Rosenberg, M. (2003). *Nonviolent communication: A language of life.* Encinitas, CA: Puddle Dancer Press.

Sarason, B. R., Sarason, I. G., & Gurung, R. A. R. (1997). Close personal relationships and health outcomes: A key to the role of social support. In S. Duck (Ed.), *Handbook of personal relationships: Theory, research and interventions* (2nd ed., pp. 547–573). New York, NY: Wiley.

Scott, A. M., & Caughlin, J. P. (2014). Enacted goal attention in family conversations about end-of-life health decisions. *Communication Monographs, 81,* 261–284.

Suchman, A. L., Markakis, K., Beckman, H. B., & Frankel, R. (1997). A model of empathic communication in the medical interview. *JAMA, 277,* 678–682.

Wittenberg-Lyles, E., Goldsmith, J., Richardson, B., Hallett, J. S., & Clark, R. (2013). The practical nurse: A case for COMFORT communication training. *American Journal of Hospice and Palliative Care, 30,* 162–166.

Wittenberg-Lyles, E., Goldsmith, J., & Ragan, S. (2010). The comfort initiative: Palliative nursing and the centrality of communication. *Journal of Hospice and Palliative Nursing, 12*(5), 293–297.

Wu, A. M. S., Tang, C. T. S., & Kwok, T. C. Y. (2002). Death anxiety among Chinese elderly people in Hong Kong. *Journal of Aging and Health, 14,* 42–56.

CHAPTER ONE

Health Communication
AND Death Studies

TERESA THOMPSON

As one of the newer areas of study within the field of communication, the topic that has come to be known as health communication has already made important contributions to our understanding of the dying process, to the care accompanying dying, and, to a lesser degree, to grieving and bereavement (see Toller, this volume). All of these issues are addressed separately within the various chapters included within this volume, but I would like to share with you my perspective on them from within the context of the area of health communication in particular. As the Editor of the journal *Health Communication* for 27 years, an editor of the first and second editions of the *Routledge Handbook of Health Communication* (Thompson, Dorsey, Miller, & Parrott, 2003; Thompson, Parrott, & Nussbaum, 2011), and the editor of the recent three-volume, 600-entry *Encyclopedia of Health Communication* (Thompson, 2014a), I am hopeful that I am able to put the study of dying and death issues into the broader context of health communication scholarship for readers. I have also written about dying and death issues, writing my first chapter on the topic in Nussbaum, Thompson, and Robinson's (1988) book *Communication and Aging* during the time that my father died. That event significantly changed my perspective on dying and death issues, of course, and, like most others writing in an area that is personally important to them, I now bring my private standpoint to bear on my work in this area.

Dying and death experiences are something that almost all human beings confront at many times in their lives; initially, most confront the loss of significant others and eventually all of us die. As health care has improved, more and more individuals are aware of the impending terminality of themselves and those around them. As people are living longer, more of us ultimately die of something that is anticipated. The issues relating to communication *with* those who are dying and the communication *of* those who are dying have become increasing relevant both personally and in the literature of health communication as a result. My phrasing of that sentence should not be read to imply that communication with and of those who are dying are separable, of course; the dyadic nature of communication is now self-evident within the field of communication.

Research in the area of health communication has focused more on dying issues than on bereavement/grieving, although my own writing on grief has been done in conjunction with a former graduate student, Cecilia Bosticco, whose youngest daughter died of a rare and aggressive form of cancer during Cecilia's graduate work (Bosticco & Thompson, 2005). Similarly, my work on hope in the dying process came about as a result of the process of helping to care for my sister-in-law as she was dying of ovarian cancer (Thompson, 2011, 2013). All of these experiences have shaped my view on the role of communication in the dying process; I bring them all to bear as I share with you my perspective on the research on dying and death in the health communication literature.

Although historically the field of communication has not been at the heart of death studies, there is much reason to advocate that it should be. From a constructionist perspective, it is evident that interpersonal relationships are co-created through communicative interaction. Relationships do not spring out of nowhere; we create them through our interactions. This is just as true of relationships at end of life as it is of all other relationships, but the relationships at end of life are frequently of even more importance to us than are relationships at many earlier stages. Although a relationship does not end at death, the chance to change the relationship interactionally does. Thus, a focus on communication should be a key component of death studies.

A BRIEF HISTORY OF HEALTH COMMUNICATION

The area that we call health communication includes a focus on provider-patient communication, "everyday" health communication (Cline, 2011; this is the context in which many key health issues are discussed and includes family communication), health information in the media, health education/campaigns, critical/cultural studies of health, especially in developing worlds and among the less privileged, health organizations, and rhetoric and policy dimensions of health. The earliest work falling into this area came out of a sociological tradition and focused on health campaigns; this work began in the 1940s and 1950s (Thompson, 2014b). By the 1960s, physician Barbara Korsch and her colleagues at UCLA (e.g., Korsch, Gozzi, & Francis, 1968) had begun examining provider-patient and provider-parent interaction. This work provided an important foundation for the work that was variously being called "medical communication," "therapeutic communication" (especially that grounded in the Batesonian school of study), and "health communication," and was emphasized by the development of the Health Communication Division of the International Communication Association in the late 1970s. This area of study was encouraged in the early *Communication Year-books*, which included essays by the officers of the division and published the top three papers from the annual convention.

The European journal *Patient Education and Counseling* began publication in 1978 and has consistently focused on issues related to provider-patient interaction; as such, it has steadily published articles focusing on aspects of death studies as they relate to communication. The journal was founded at the first annual conference on Patient Counseling in Amsterdam in 1976 and originally focused exclusively on patient counseling issues before its move toward a broader focus on health communication and promotion. Since those early years, it has also regularly involved scholars from all countries. *Patient Education and Counseling* is now co-sponsored by the European Association of Communication in Healthcare and the American Academy for Communication in Healthcare and publishes three issues a year.

By the mid-1980s, several textbooks had been published on the topic (Kreps & Thornton, 1984; Northouse & Northouse, 1985; Thompson, 1986), and the publisher Lawrence Erlbaum Associates began marketing research to investigate the audience for a journal in the area within the U.S. Finding a positive response, this new journal, *Health Communication*, began accepting articles in the fall of 1987, and the first issue was published in January 1989. The journal now publishes 12 times a year.

Patient Education and Counseling and *Health Communication* were joined over the years by the *Journal of Health Communication, Communication and Medicine*, and the *Journal of Communication in Healthcare*. The *Journal of Health Communication* focuses less on the interpersonal issues that are particularly relevant to death studies and has continued with its primary focus on international social marketing issues relating to health. *Communication and Medicine* is affiliated with COMET (the Conference on Communication, Medicine and Ethics), a primarily European association and currently publishes three issues a year. It has been in publication since 2003. The *Journal of Communication in Healthcare* is published by the American Public Health Association's Health Communication Working Group. It has been published four times a year since 2008. All of these journals were searched during the preparation of this chapter.

AVOIDANCE OF THE TERMINALLY ILL/AVOIDANCE
OF TALK ABOUT TERMINALITY

Among the earliest work on communication and dying issues was Addington and Wegescheide-Harris's (1995) article documenting physician avoidance of the terminally ill. This concern was not a new one in the dying and death literature, particularly from a sociological perspective, but this article was one of the first to discuss the problem in the health communication literature. A classic on the denial of death is Becker's (1973) book by that title. Focusing on ethical concerns, Addington and Wegescheide-Harris (1995) discuss such avoidance within the context of physician-patient interaction, although avoidance of the terminally ill has also been well documented among non-physician health care providers and among non–health care providers. In general, many are reluctant to interact with those they know are terminally ill.

This issue is not discussed as frequently in current literature as it was in the past, however (Thompson, 2014b); it is likely that the increased emphasis both culturally and in health care provision on hospice and palliative treatment may also have increased people's awareness of the problem inherent in such avoidance. However, Bachner and Carmel (2009) did find that caregivers experienced considerable difficulties in communicating with patients about death, and levels of openness in communication were related to caregivers' emotional exhaustion and depression as well as self-efficacy. Similarly, research has found that even in the Netherlands, where euthanasia is legal, there is little discussion among care providers and terminally ill patients about the topic (Borgsteede et al., 2007). This is true despite the pain and suffering experienced by the patient.

None of this avoidance of communication is due to the fact that patients do not desire information about their condition and prognosis, however. Research on cancer patients conducted in Turkey, for instance, indicated that 63% of patients stated that they would like to know all the details about their disease (Durusoy, Karaca, Junushova, & Uslu, 2011). These patients indicated that they generally preferred a sudden, painless death, without any intervention at the last moment, but in a hospital. This is in contrast to research in the U.S., which has determined that most patients want to die at home, but rarely do (Thompson, 2014b). The Turkish study also indicated that the area with the highest reported level of satisfaction was whether patients had complete trust in their doctors, whereas the least satisfaction about the interaction was reported for doctors' explanations during visits. The authors note that the majority of the cancer patients trusted doctors and wanted to learn more about the progress of their cancer, in contrast to the general tendency of their Turkish families to hide the diagnosis.

Also consistent with this research are the findings of Janssen, Engelberg, Wouters, and Curtis (2012), who studied patients with chronic obstructive pulmonary disease (COPD) and determined that advance care planning and conversations about end-of-life care are limited and their quality is often poor. The complexity of such issues and patient desires, however, is demonstrated by findings of research by Buecken et al. (2012) on patients with multiple sclerosis. In this research, 64% of patients indicated a wish for disease progression and death and dying to be addressed by their doctor. A majority (76%) considered it important that progression of their disease be discussed, while 44% regarded addressing death and dying as unimportant. Perhaps denial of impending terminality is relevant here. No tangible disease criteria could be identified to explain the wish for communicating end-of-life issues. Doctors who were later viewed as avoiding critical aspects of the illness were perceived as less empathetic. Thus, while not all patients wanted information about issues of potential terminality, those doctors who did not initiate discussion about the topic were seen less positively.

Additional evidence of the complexity of the approach/avoidance concerns underlying discussion of terminality is provided by research by Piers et al. (2013). Their findings made clear that the majority of participants in their research were willing to talk about dying. In some elderly patients, however, a lack of acceptance of impending terminality made advance care planning (ACP) conversations extremely difficult. Most of the participants desired planning regarding those issues of end-of-life care related to personal experiences and fears, but they were less interested in planning other end-of-life situations. These situations were outside of their "power of imagination" (p. 323). Other factors determining whether patients proceeded to ACP were trust in the family and/or physician and the need for control. Although ACP is considered important by most elderly, there is a risk of "pseudo-participation" (p. 323) in cases of non-acceptance of the nearing death or planning end-of-life situations outside the patient's power of imagination. Such pseudoparticipation may result in end-of-life decisions not reflecting the patient's true wishes.

It is important to note that findings regarding communication at end of life may be disease specific. The studies reported above focused on such disparate health issues as COPD, multiple sclerosis, cancer, and the elderly in general. In a study of women with ductal carcinoma in situ (DCIS), the most common form of breast cancer, De Morgan, Redman, D'Este, and Rogers (2011) discovered misunderstanding and confusion in the women they studied and a desire for more information about their breast disease. About half of the participants worried about their breast disease metastasizing; another half expressed high levels of decisional conflict about it. Several were anxious, and a small percentage was depressed. Worry about dying of the breast disease was significantly associated with not knowing that DCIS could not metastasize, and confusion about whether DCIS could metastasize was significantly associated with dissatisfaction with information.

Focusing on elderly patients dying in nursing homes and their families, Fosse, Ase Schaufel, Ruths, and Malterud (2014) found that both patients and families emphasized the importance of health personnel anticipating illness trajectories and recognizing the information and comfort care/medication needed. Family members frequently became proxy decision makers and reported uncertainty and distress when guidance from health personnel was not available. Families worried about staff shortages and doctor availability. Relatives and health personnel rarely recognized patients' ability to provide consent, and patients' preferences were not always acknowledged. Nursing home patients and their relatives wanted doctors more involved in end-of-life care. They expected doctors to respond to their preferences and provide guidance and symptom relief.

In contrast with a focus in some research on knowledge and competencies, Iedema, Sorensen, Braithwaite, and Turnbull (2004) address how professionals working in an intensive care unit in Australia speak about dying; they provide a focus on the contradictions and complexities that characterize such communication in intensive care. They reflect on the "incommensurabilities" (p. 85) in the talk of the clinicians that they observed, and the effects of this for how they work together and care for very ill patients. They argue that intensive care units are settings where being reflexive about one's work and assumptions is especially difficult because such work involves making decisions and taking responsibility for decisions concerning very sick patients. These decisions and responsibilities make especially relevant the "wicked problems and tragic choices" (p. 85) of end-of-life existence in general and of intensive care in particular. Iedema et al. (2004) demonstrate some of the complex ways in which clinicians' discourse reflects these tensions and responsibilities. They note that these complexities are not likely to be settled with reference to formal knowledge or in-principle conviction.

Other research on patient-provider-family communication at end of life has employed Conversation Analysis and has focused on the Thai context (Pairote, 2013). This research noted that such communication in Thailand is asymmetrical. More specifically, nurses initiate the topic of death by referring to the death of a third person—another patient who has died—with the use of clues and through list-construction. As most Thai people identify with Buddhism, the nurses selected religious support for discussing the topic. Nurses also use Buddhism and list-construction to help their clients confront uncertain futures. However, Pairote (2013) found that the nurses did not bring Buddhism into discussion on its own. They instead combined references to it with other practices such as the use of euphemisms or a focus on care for others.

THEORETICAL FOUNDATIONS

Several studies in the health communication literature examining end-of-life concerns have focused on the application of problematic integration theory to dialysis decisions among the elderly and related issues (Hines, Babrow, Badzek, & Moss, 1997). Problematic integration theory has made important contributions in several areas of the field of communication, but nowhere more so than in health communication. The theory's focus on uncertainty is of obvious relevance to health phenomena. Hines, Babrow et al.'s (1997) application of it to dialysis decisions provided a new and useful perspective for health communication researchers, as it focuses on the communicative processes that are used to untangle the uncertainty that is inherent in health decisions. Hines, Moss, and McKenzie (1997) continued this focus in their follow-up research. These findings help explain the recurrent and continuing tension between hoping for cure versus accepting impending terminality. This theme is continued in Kenny's (2001) application of Burkean principles to acceptance of death, focusing in this case on the family of Karen Ann Quinlan. Kenny's (2005) study on the transvaluation of life in euthanasia further applies this theme. Kenny (2002) also provided an important focus on physician-assisted suicide in his analysis of Carol Loving's book about her son's death, following this up with Kenny's (2007) analysis of medically induced death in the case of Paul Mills. In addition, Rafferty, Cramer, Priddis, and Allen (in press) offer an application of the Theory of Motivated Information Management to marital discussions of end-of-life discussions.

HOSPICE AND PALLIATIVE CARE

Interestingly, one of the first health communication articles on hospice issues focused not on the U.S. or the UK, as one might expect, but on hospice in China. Smith and Smith (1999) wrote about this topic in a special issue of *Health Communication* examining Chinese health communication concerns. This issue came about as a result of David Smith's work at Hong Kong Baptist University. The continent of Asia has continued to be an important area of research on health communication, with Korea perhaps being the leader in this arena.

Although Smith and Smith (1999) published the earliest work on hospice in the health communication literature, much work has followed. Notable among this line of research is Foster's (2007) narrative ethnography of serving as a hospice volunteer. Foster's work eloquently traces her experiences and interviews. Perhaps one of the most important points of her work is the reminder that just being there with a dying individual is sometimes more helpful than talking about death per se. Planalp and Trost (2008) also studied hospice volunteers and identified the communication difficulties that recur in hospice contexts, with particular emphasis on what happens when conditions such as Parkinson's and Alzheimer's affect the communicative process.

With a broader focus on palliative care going beyond an exclusive application to hospice issues, Elaine Wittenberg-Lyles and Joy Goldsmith, frequently coauthoring with their adviser Sandra Ragan and more recently with palliative nursing specialist Betty Ferrell, have been the scholars who have made the most important contributions within the field of health communication to our understanding of the potential role of palliative care in much health provision (see Egbert, this volume, and Galvin, this volume). Their COMFORT curriculum (see Wittenberg-Lyles, Goldsmith, Ferrell, & Ragan, 2013, and Foster and Keeley, this volume) exemplifies the translational nature of such scholarship (Wittenberg-Lyles et al., 2013).

Building on earlier work on palliative care, van Gurp et al. (2012) reviewed 71 articles to identify potential interrelationships between palliative care and telemedicine. Two communication genres in palliative care proved to be dominant: the conversation to connect, which focused on creating and maintaining a professional-patient/family relationship, and the conversation to instill realism, with a focus on telling a clinical truth without diminishing hope. These two themes identify a "logical intertwinement between communicative purposes, the socio-ethical background underlying palliative care practice and elements of form" (p. 504). Van Gurp et al. (2012) conclude that palliative care has an important potential role in telemedicine.

The further import of palliative care is made evident in the work of Barton, Aldridge, Trimble, and Vidovic (2005), who reported an exploratory discourse analysis of a corpus of six end-of-life discussions in a surgical intensive care unit. They identified four phases of end of life. Of particular interest in their findings is Phase 2, in which the presentation of medical information ends with an inferential summary statement that functions to establish the patient's status as terminal. It is this phase that is critical to the functional progression of an end-of-life discussion toward a decision to move from therapeutic to palliative care, since it is in this phase that physicians and families interactionally achieve an agreement that allows a decision to withdraw or withhold further treatment, including life support, which would be futile and would prolong the patient's suffering. Their data indicate how two of the end-of-life discussions in the corpus that did not establish the terminal status of the patient in Phase 2 did not move to decision making.

This focus on phases is consistent with the work of Barton (2007). She argues that "good communication" at end of life is described at only a general level in the literature and that there are few studies of end-of-life discussions drawn from actual talk between providers and families. She presents a discourse analysis of end-of-life discussions from an American intensive care unit and shows how the decision to withdraw life support is positioned in a hybrid ethical frame co-constructed as the final phase of the end-of-life discussion. The final phase of the end-of-life discussion unites the voice of medicine and the voice of the lifeworld, with both physicians and families initiating, developing, and repeating topics that comprise not only the logistics of dying, but also the ethics of the end-of-life decision. Physicians focus their ethical responsibility in terms of medical futility, and families express their accountability in terms of an ethics of consciousness. The shared ethical frame that is co-constructed ultimately focuses on agreement that the "right" decision has been made from both ethical views.

A focus on quality of life is always central to palliative care and is evident in the work of Finlay (2005). Finlay (2005) notes that quality of life is a subjective concept, but there have been some useful attempts to measure the quality of a person's life so that useful comparisons can be made during treatment and as disease progresses. Finlay describes the multifaceted nature of quality of life and the ways that the communication of health care professionals can strongly influence the patient's sense of personal dignity and worth. Central to this as well are the relationships with the family, particularly with children in the family, who may experience great suffering in bereavement. Pressures on patients may make them feel a burden, as if they would be better off dead and particularly as if others would be better off without them. This notion of being a burden is often behind requests for death-accelerating acts such as euthanasia. Finlay (2005) also discusses the deep-seated difference between euthanasia and the termination of futile treatments.

Also relating to quality of life is the work of Sorensen and Iedema (2006), which focuses on the nonmedical status of patients in end-of-life decisions. They argue that taking into account nonmedical factors is not yet customary, especially in decisions to terminate treatment. They contend that the capacity and willingness to withstand continuing treatment are essential to ensure that decisions are in the patient's best interest. They present a qualitative study of intensive care nursing in a large public hospital in Australia and demonstrate the tendency of some care providers to avoid disclosing the medical and nonmedical status to conscious patients; they identify the mistrust and conflict that can result. They instead offer a process of "conferencing"—a consistent, inclusive, ongoing, and dynamic process of communication begun early in the patient's admission—that allows clinicians from different backgrounds to manage their differences, reach consensus on patient-care goals, and prepare the patient and family for the process of dying.

An additional focus on palliative care issues is provided by the work of Considine and Miller (2010), which examined the dialectic tension between following and leading in discussions of spirituality at end of life (see Tullis, this volume). Although some hospice workers chose one end of this dialectic, most shifted between leading and following in different contexts or at different times. Amati and

Hannawa (2014) also focused on dialectic tensions at end of life with an emphasis on physicians. In the work of Considine and Miller (2010), yet other hospice workers handled this tension by moving beyond the dialectic to attend to multiple goals. With a similar focus on multiple goals, although looking at family discussions, Scott (2014) summarized the research on family communication and provider-patient discussions about end of life to determine what leads to "good" conversations (see also Scott & Caughlin, 2014). Her argument is that it is essential to look at what families say when they talk about end-of-life issues, not just whether they do or do not talk about such concerns.

In addition to a focus on the "good conversations" noted in the work of Scott (2014), health communication work has also focused on the notion of a "good death" (see Gubrium, this volume). Such a concern underlies most of the work on issues of terminality and is directly related to palliative care issues. Focusing specifically on the meaning of a good death, Goldsteen et al. (2006) identified five categories of normative expectations in patients' stories: awareness and acceptance, open communication, living one's life until the end, taking care of one's final responsibilities, and dealing adequately with emotions. These data demonstrate that in the search of a good death people show definite differences in their way of referring to as well as in dealing with normative expectations that are part of current cultural paradigms. Goldsteen et al. urge professional caregivers to be responsive to how a patient deals with and relates to normative expectations about a good death and to support patients in their individual process of dying an "appropriate death" (p. 378) for that patient. Not all patients define a good death in the same way.

TALKING ABOUT DEATH/TALKING ABOUT ADVANCE DIRECTIVES

Within the health communication literature, work on final conversations about religion and spirituality stands out as noteworthy (Keeley, 2004; see also Keeley & Yingling, 2007). In fact, all of Keeley's work provides an essential focus on the conversations that we have with significant others as the end of life approaches (see Foster and Keeley, this volume).

Focusing more specifically on conversations about advance directives regarding end-of-life decisions is the work of Clarke, Evans, Shook, and Johanson (2005) and their three-state campaign to encourage the completion of advance directives for elderly citizens. Their results indicated the relevance of participants' sense of future vulnerability and perceptions of the efficacy of advance planning in explaining which seniors requested an advance planning guide. Completion of a directive, however, depended on how the guide was read and how critical care was discussed.

What is surprising is that participants' actual health status correlated with neither seeking information nor completing a directive.

Advance directives were also the focus of the work of Young and Rodriguez's (2006) study of patients in a Veterans Administration center. This examination of the meaning attributed to advance directives by the patients indicated a focus on three themes: quality of life versus quantity of life, benefit of treatment versus cost of treatment, and, most common, control versus lack of control. Their results also demonstrate the value of listening to patients' narratives.

CONCLUSIONS

The most consistent theme that is surely evident in the research noted within this chapter is the avoidance of communication about impending terminality. More research has examined this topic within the provider-patient relationship than in any other context, and this research has repeatedly shown a notable lack of necessary information sending about issues related to potential dying, despite patient desires for such. The reality is not unique to the provider-patient relationship, however. And this is true despite the apparent desire among most patients for information about their prognosis. Families are less likely than patients to desire such openness. In general, especially outside of the U.S., there is a desire among care providers and family members to avoid communication about end of life. Such avoidance makes coping with the process of dying and compliance with end-of-life wishes much more difficult. Patients with desires to communicate about impending terminality may also be disconfirmed, even apart from avoidance issues, if they are implicitly or explicitly told that they are wrong in their beliefs. Most dying patients do know that they are dying even when care providers and family members attempt to keep such information from them. This treatment disconfirms the patients.

There are patients, however, who lack the power of imagination noted above to anticipate impending death or the decisions that need to be made in light of it. The common cultural denial of death (Becker, 1973) interferes with such an ability as well as with the tendencies of families and providers to communicate about death, as referenced earlier. In addition to avoidance of communication about dying from care providers, an important finding in the research in this area is the desire among terminal patients for provider involvement in the illness trajectory. The contradiction between patient desires and provider avoidance tendencies is a striking one.

Out of all the research areas noted above, it is evident that one important topic has been the subject of only one study—a campaign to encourage the preparation of advance care plans. The study by Clarke et al. (2005) reported above made a significant contribution in this area, but it has been the only one in the health communication literature to focus on such. Noting the significance at end of life of advance care planning, it is surprising that there has not been more research and writing on this topic. Most of the work has instead focused on interpersonal communication about advance care planning, and most of it indicates a lack of such planning. This evidence should be interpreted as documentation of the need for much more attention to campaigns on this topic; it appears that the interpersonal channels of communication that have been used to date are not adequately addressing the need. Advance care plans are necessary for three reasons: (1) to ensure that an individual's wishes for end-of-life care are followed as closely as possible; (2) to facilitate decision making for family members rather than leaving them without an indication of the wishes of their loved ones; and (3) to facilitate care provision by physicians, nurses, hospice workers, and so on as a patient approaches the end of life.

Neither campaigns such as that conducted and reported above by Clarke et al. (2005) nor the various studies that have focused on interpersonal channels of communication are sufficient if, however, family members and care providers do not read and follow advance directives. There is much evidence that this lack of attention to advance directives is the case. Research to examine the reasons for lack of such compliance is needed, as is research that helps us understand how to encourage more serious consideration of an individual's advance directives. And, of course, an advance directive is only as helpful as the ability of the writer of such to anticipate possible future situations and to foresee how one would actually feel in the various situations. Both of these are much more complex than is typically assumed. The complexity of all of these topics is further exemplified in another area worthy of more research—those situations characterized by unusual uncertainty about one's disease state. The study mentioned above about women with the most common form of breast cancer not knowing whether the disease could metastasize is a notable example (see also Hines, Babrow et al., 1997, and Hines, Moss, & McKenzie, 1997, on uncertainty).

Also related to the lack of successful communication about end-of-life wishes in provider-patient interactions is the relevance of the topic to everyday interpersonal health communication (Cline, 2011). Although this topic was noted in the early portion of this chapter as of relevance to death studies, too little focus has been apparent in the research on this context. It is likely that this is the context in which the most useful communication about end-of-life wishes occurs, outside of the focus of impending terminality. Scott's (2014) research, cited above, on how families communicate about end-of-life desires is surely a basis for future work, especially in light of her findings about the importance of this communication in terms of consequences within families.

A few of the studies noted above have focused on issues of euthanasia or physician-assisted suicide, but I think that it is fair to say that this ethically important topic has yet to be adequately addressed in the health communication literature. By the time that one has made a decision in favor of euthanasia or physician-assisted suicide, one is well beyond the denial of death or the lack of acceptance of impending death. One is also well beyond the dialectical tension between hope and acceptance that has begun to be uncovered in some research, but has yet to be satisfactorily examined in the writing on the topic.

I am hopeful that this brief review has made evident to the reader the inter-relationships between death studies and health communication. As noted in the beginning of our discussion, communication creates relationships throughout life, including as the end of life approaches. A communicative perspective and incorporation of the work on health communication can help elucidate our understanding of many aspects of the dying process. There is much interesting work that has been conducted in this area, and many areas that remain ripe for investigation.

REFERENCES

Addington, T., & Wegescheide-Harris, J. (1995). Ethics and communication with the terminally ill. *Health Communication, 7,* 267–281.

Amati, R., & Hannawa, A. F. (2014). Relational dialectics theory: Disentangling physician-perceived tensions of end-of-life communication. *Health Communication, 29,* 962–973.

Bachner, Y. G., & Carmel, S. (2009). Open communication between caregivers and terminally ill cancer patients: The role of caregivers' characteristics and situational variables. *Health Communication, 24,* 524–531.

Barton, E. (2007). Situating end-of-life decision making in a hybrid ethical frame. *Communication and Medicine, 4,* 131–140.

Barton, E., Aldridge, M., Trimble, T., & Vidovic, J. (2005). Structure and variation in end-of-life discussions in the surgical intensive care unit. *Communication and Medicine, 2,* 3–20.

Becker, E. (1973). *The denial of death.* New York, NY: Macmillan.

Borgsteede, S. D., Deliens, L., Graafland-Riedstra, C., Francke, A. L., van der Wal, G., & Willems, D. L. (2007). Communication about euthanasia in general practice: Opinions and experiences of patients and their general practitioners. *Patient Education and Counseling, 66,* 156–161.

Bosticco, C., & Thompson, T. L. (2005). The role of narratives in coping during the grieving process. In L. Harter, P. Japp, & C. Beck (Eds.), *Narratives in health and illness* (pp. 391–412). Mahwah, NJ: Lawrence Erlbaum.

Buecken, R., Galushko, M., Golla, H., Strupp, J., Hahn, M., Ernstmann, N. Phaff, H., & Voltz, R. (2012). Patients feeling severely affected by multiple sclerosis: How do patients want to communicate about end-of-life issues? *Patient Education and Counseling, 88,* 318–324.

Clarke, P., Evans, S. H., Shook, D., & Johanson, W. (2005). Information seeking and compliance in planning for critical care: Community-based health outreach to seniors about advance directives. *Health Communication, 18,* 1–22.

Cline, R. (2011). Everyday interpersonal communication and health. In T. Thompson, R. Parrott, & J. F. Nussbaum (Eds.), *Routledge handbook of health communication* (pp. 377–398). New York, NY: Routledge/Taylor & Francis.

Considine, J., & Miller, K. (2010). The dialectics of care: Communicative choices at end of life. *Health Communication, 25*, 165–174.

De Morgan, S., Redman, S., D'Este, C., & Rogers, K. (2011). Knowledge, satisfaction with information, decisional conflict and psychological morbidity amongst women diagnosed with ductal carcinoma in situ (DCIS). *Patient Education and Counseling, 84*, 62–68.

Durusoy, R., Karaca, B., Junushova, B., & Uslu, R. (2011). Cancer patients' satisfaction with doctors and preferences about death in a university hospital in Turkey. *Patient Education and Counseling, 85*, e285–e290.

Finlay, I. G. (2005). Quality of life to the end. *Communication and Medicine, 2*, 91–95.

Fosse, A., Ase Schaufel, M., Ruths, S., & Malterud, K. (2014). End-of-life expectations and experiences among nursing home patients and their relatives—a synthesis of qualitative studies. *Patient Education and Counseling, 97*, 3–9.

Foster, E. (2007). *Communicating at the end of life: Finding magic in the mundane.* Mahwah, NJ: Lawrence Erlbaum.

Goldsteen, M., Houtepen, R., Proot, I. M., Huijer Abu-Saad, H., Spreeuwenberg, C., & Widdershoven, G. (2006). What is a good death? Terminally ill patients dealing with normative expectations around death and dying. *Patient Education and Counseling, 64*, 378–386.

Hines, S. C., Babrow, A. S., Badzek, L., & Moss, A. H. (1997). Communication and problematic integration in end-of-life decisions. Dialysis decisions among the elderly. *Health Communication, 9*, 199–217.

Hines, S. C., Moss, A. H., & McKenzie, J. (1997). Prolonging life or prolonging death: Communication's role in difficult dialysis decisions. *Health Communication, 9*, 369–388.

Iedema, R., Sorensen, R., Braithwaite, J., & Turnbull, E. (2004). Speaking about dying in the intensive care unit, and its implications for multidisciplinary end-of-life care. *Communication and Medicine, 1*, 85–96.

Janssen, D. J. A., Engelberg, R. A., Wouters, E. F. M., & Curtis, J. R. (2012). Advance care planning for patients with COPD: Past, present and future. *Patient Education and Counseling, 86*, 19–24.

Keeley, M. P. (2004). Final conversations: Survivors' memorable messages concerning religious faith and spirituality. *Health Communication, 16*, 87–104.

Keeley, M. P., & Yingling, J. M. (2007). *Final conversations: Helping the living and the dying talk to each other.* Acton, MA: VanderWyk & Burnham.

Kenny, R. W. (2001). Toward a better death: Applying Burkean principles of symbolic action to interpret family adaptation to Karen Ann Quinlan's coma. *Health Communication, 13*, 363–395.

Kenny, R. W. (2002). The death of loving: Maternal identity as moral constraint in a narrative testimonial advocating physician assisted suicide. *Health Communication, 14*, 243–270.

Kenny, R. W. (2005). A cycle of terms implicit in the idea of medicine: Karen Ann Quinlan as a rhetorical icon and the transvaluation of the ethics of euthanasia. *Health Communication, 17*, 17–39.

Kenny, R. W. (2007). An effect of communication on medical decision making: Answerability, and the medically induced death of Paul Mills. *Health Communication, 22*, 69–78.

Korsch, B., Gozzi, E. K., & Francis, V. (1968). Doctor-patient interaction and patient satisfaction. *Pediatrics, 42*, 855–871.

Kreps, G. L., & Thornton, B. C. (1984). *Health communication: Theory and practice.* New York, NY: Longman.

Northouse, P. G., & Northouse, L. L. (1985). *Health communication: Strategies for health professionals.* Upper Saddle River, NJ: Prentice-Hall.

Nussbaum, J. F., Thompson, T. L., & Robinson, J. D. (1988). *Communication and aging.* New York, NY: Harper & Row.

Pairote, W. (2013). Communicative practices in talking about death and dying in the context of Thai cancer care. *Communication and Medicine, 10,* 263–271.

Piers, R. D., van Eechoud, I. J., Van Camp, S., Grypdonck, M., Deveugle, M., Verbeke, N. C., & Van Den Noortgage, N. J. (2013). Advance care planning in terminally ill and frail older persons. *Patient Education and Counseling, 90,* 323–329.

Planalp, S., & Trost, M. R. (2008). Communication issues at end of life. Reports from hospice volunteers. *Health Communication, 23,* 222–233.

Rafferty, K. A., Cramer, E., Priddis, D., & Allen, M. (in press). Talking about end-of-life preferences in marriage: Applying the Theory of Motivated Information Management. *Health Communication.*

Scott, A. M. (2014). Communication about end-of-life decisions. In E. L. Cohen (Ed.), *Communication Yearbook 38* (pp. 242–277). New York, NY: Routledge/Taylor & Francis.

Scott, A. M., & Caughlin, J. P. (2014). Enacted goal attention in family conversations about end-of-life health decisions. *Communication Monographs, 81,* 261–284.

Smith, S. J., & Smith, D. H. (1999). Evaluating Chinese hospice care. *Health Communication, 11,* 223–235.

Sorensen, R., & Iedema, R. (2006). Integrating patients' nonmedical status in end-of-life decision making: Structuring communication through "conferencing." *Communication and Medicine, 3,* 185–196.

Thompson, T. L. (1986). *Communication for health professionals.* New York, NY: Harper & Row.

Thompson, T. L. (2011). Hope and the act of informed dialogue: A delicate balance at end of life. *Journal of Language and Social Psychology, 30,* 1–16.

Thompson, T. L. (2013). Hope vs. openness at end-of-life: A dialectic in narrative. In G. M. Katsaros (Ed.), *The psychology of hope* (pp. 117–139). Hauppauge, NY: Nova.

Thompson, T. L. (Ed.). (2014a). *Encyclopedia of health communication.* Thousand Oaks, CA: Sage.

Thompson, T. L. (2014b). *Oxford bibliography on death and dying.* New York, NY: Oxford University Press.

Thompson, T. L., Dorsey, A., Miller, K. I., & Parrott, R. (Eds.). (2003). *Handbook of health communication.* Mahwah, NJ: Lawrence Erlbaum.

Thompson, T., Parrott, R., & Nussbaum, J. F. (Eds.). (2011). *Routledge handbook of health communication* (2nd ed.). New York, NY: Routledge/Taylor & Francis.

van Gurp, J., Hasselaar, J., van Leeuwen, E., Hoek, P., Vissers, K., & van Selm, M. (2012). Connecting with patients and instilling realism in an era of emerging communication possibilities: A review on palliative care communication heading to telecare practice. *Patient Education and Counseling, 93,* 504–514.

Wittenberg-Lyles, E., Goldsmith, J., Ferrell, B., & Ragan, S. L. (2013). *Communication in palliative nursing.* Oxford, UK: Oxford University Press.

Young, A. J., & Rodriguez, K. L. (2006). The role of narrative in discussing end-of-life care: Eliciting values and goals from text, context, and subtext. *Health Communication, 19,* 49–59.

CHAPTER TWO

Discourse "On OR About'" Dying: Palliative Care

ALLISON WHITNEY

Language inevitably arrives at the limits of expression. For example, in medical and legal discourses, when a precise time or location cannot be isolated, then one must resort to the less specific phrase "on or about." In light of this limited aspect of language, the present chapter admits to addressing discourses merely "on or about" death through palliative care literature. In addition to the endeavor to show the limits of language, the phrase "on or about" was also chosen to emphasize the multiplicity of discourses surrounding end of life and the inability to represent death, and therefore dying, as an immutable, singular, and definitive entity or phenomenon.

We begin with the presupposition that death is not inherently problematic, and that the appropriation of death through the assigning of meaning(s) is epochally contingent. Despite the feeling that our own relationships to death are individualized and extremely personal, our responses to death and dying are "greatly influenced by the beliefs of society which seep into the fabric of institutional power" (Powell, 2011, p. 359). In this way, end-of-life discourses are not mere reflections of individual thoughts and choices, nor are they simply representative of meaning and culture; "they are the very elements that produce meaning and culture surrounding the end of life by becoming routine, naturalized, institutionalized, and accepted" (Candrian, 2013, p. 57).

Through regimes of truth, discursive constructions of the meaning of mortality—and the process of dying—are articulated differently depending on time and space. To pursue this line of thought, I draw on an interpretation of Foucault's (1981) epistemological perspective and his claim "that there is no pre-discursive providence which disposes the world in our favor" (p. 67) to explore existing palliative care literature through an understanding of discourse and the power relations that govern what can be said, thought, and done; "it is in discourse that power and knowledge are joined together" (Foucault, 1978, p. 100). By situating dying within the context of medicalization and the ensuing resistance to the "dehumanization" processes particular to the 20th century, I highlight existing discourse analyses, and critical engagements, of/with palliative care literature to emphasize the interconnections between discourse and practice. The purpose of this chapter, then, is to emphasize the tensions and contradictions within palliative care literature as an *overarching normative discourse* in relation to *expectations* of dying.

REVISITING THE MEDICALIZATION OF DEATH

Any contemporary writing on end of life must be situated within existing research which can often be traced to the original thanatological works, such as Glaser and Strauss (1965, 1968), Berger (1967), Ariès (1981), Illich (1976), Turner (1991), and Elias (1985). These works are heavily cited within contemporary literature and articulate death as a social phenomenon that has shifted from a communal event, bound within symbolic religious meaning, to a private, individual event, situated within scientific medical reductionism. As death became located within the body and reduced to an object, the social aspects of death (regardless of whether or not they are considered contingent), arguably, became irrelevant. This conceptual and practical shift from (pre-modern) communal death toward the (modern) medicalized death is prevalent in contemporary discussions of death and dying. To understand palliative care as discourse within contemporary society, it is important to situate it within this discursive-conceptual shift, as it is discernable in the literature on the management of dying.

The biomedical model is an important aspect of the evolutionary process of palliative care and is imperative in understanding the problematization of end-of-life discourses. Critiques of the biomedical model have been articulated as critiques of medicalization in general, through which various events in life become defined and regulated through the discourse of medicine (Gordon, 1988), and these critiques have been extended to the medicalization of death. Drawing on the work of Foucault (1975), the medicalization of death is a process of redefining natural death as a condition that must be treated. Upon the emergence of the ability to define disease within the body, particular methods for observing and analyzing the body came to be normalized and, as such, became a part of death. As Kaufman (1998) states, "[b]iomedicine has come to provide the fundamental framework for understanding death" (p. 721). Life can be extended through artificial means; it can be reinstated through resuscitation.

With these technological advancements, the ethical and moral dilemmas (see Klugman, this volume) become emphasized, as they are inherent within this process of intervening with the most basic biological processes of life and death. Within this process, dying has shifted from the private sphere to the public sphere, from the home to the hospital, where we are most likely to die. However, while dominant medical and legal discourses are continuously being challenged, they are simultaneously undergoing a process of reification, as subjectivities both constitute and are constituted by discourse and power. In this way, medical discourses not only provide systems of knowledge(s), but also affect the way we experience our own bodies (Lupton, 1997). "Through a process of normalization—through the production of texts, disciplines, practices, which have not preceded this idea of medicine—this particular conception of medicine and the body is legitimated as a discourse" (Whitney & Smith, 2010, p. 70).

RESISTANCE

Despite our participation in the process of normalization, the dominance of bio-medical and institutionalized dying has been resisted. Dying in the hospital has been the topic of much cross-disciplinary research (Ariès 1974, 1981; Wass & Neimeyer, 1995). Ivan Illich is often noted as having a large impact on the attack against the medicalization of dying (Clark, 2002). Death in the hospital has been described as a dehumanizing experience in which the intervention on the body neglects the personhood of the dying "patient." Yet, even before critiques of medicalization were articulated within literature (and academia), there were grassroots responses to institutionalized dying. Alternative conceptualizations of death and dying have emerged over time and can be most distinctly understood through the work of Kübler-Ross (1969) and the growth of the hospice. These "social movement-like phenomena" (Fox, 1981) can be understood as responses to the dehumanizing aspects of the medicalization of death, in relation to technological intervention, as well as the medical space in which it most commonly occurs.

In 1969, Kübler-Ross wrote *On Death and Dying*, a book containing research based on her experience working with terminal patients. Within various disciplines, particularly psychology and sociology, this research is heavily sourced and is known as the Kübler-Ross model or "the five stages of grief." According to Kübler-Ross, there are five steps that occur during the process of dying, her chapters 3 through 5, respectively: (1) denial and isolation; (2) anger and resentment; (3) bargaining and an attempt to postpone; (4) depression and a sense of loss; and (5) acceptance. By bringing awareness to the process of dying, Kübler-Ross could then publicize the "inadequacies in the established institutional care of the dying" (Fox, 1981, p. 51) and speak about death and dying in a positive way. This new philosophy not only challenged societal and medical conceptions of death as negative but also largely impacted contemporary conceptions of hospice and palliative care, and its reverberations can still be felt today.

Similar to the ideologies associated with the work of Kübler-Ross, the hospice movement focuses on the need to reconceptualize end-of-life care philosophically and to effect change in its practice. The first freestanding hospice, designed to treat cancer patients, was opened by Cicely Saunders in the UK in 1967. Saunders's coining of the term "total pain," "a complex of physical, emotional, social, and spiritual elements" (Saunders, 1996, p. 1600), foreshadowed an entire movement that attempts to create a shift in the way we conceptualize care for, and care of, the dying, specifically within an institutionalized medical setting (Clark, 2000; Connor, 2008; Seymour et al., 2005).

Balfour Mount shared these ideas of holistic care for the dying, bringing a "new way of thinking about dying into the very heartland of acute medicine" (Clark, 2002, p. 906). Drawing on the work of Saunders, Mount formed two hospice programs in Canada, one in Winnipeg and one in Montreal (Northcott & Wilson, 2008). In 1973, the term "palliative care" was introduced by Mount to describe this newer approach to caring for the dying, within a Canadian context (Pastrana, Junger, Ostgathe, Elsner, & Radburch, 2008). Similar to the original hospices in the UK, hospices within Canada were introduced to respond to the needs of cancer patients. However, according to the Canadian Hospice Palliative Care Association [CHPCA] (2014), palliative care has branched out from this specificity to a type of care that is, at least in policy, accessible for those with, or at risk of, other life-threatening illness. In 1987, palliative care became a medical specialty in the UK, a discursive formation that largely affected the perceived legitimacy of the movement. There are varying definitions of "palliative care," "palliative medicine," and "hospice care," and the terms are often used interchangeably.

PALLIATIVE CARE AS DISCOURSE

Understanding palliative care as discourse necessitates an engagement with language as an active component of its philosophy and practice. Language is not merely a mechanism for description or expression, but also a condition of thought and action. In this way, the "origins" of palliative care, as discourse(s), have affected contemporary conceptions of dying. As can be seen by the inter-changeability of hospice care and palliative care (and medicine), the definitions of end-of-life care are simultaneously specific and yet, ultimately, dispersed. Pastrana et al. (2008) undertook the task of identifying the key elements of palliative care through definitions used within the specialist literature, using discourse analysis. They emphasize the interconnections between language and actions by highlighting the importance of definitions as "they can serve as an impetus for changing practice, for introducing new programs and for working toward the allocation of more resources for palliative care. Moreover, the understanding of these concepts influences how medicine is practiced" (p. 222). Tishelman (2007) supports this form of semantic exploration, arguing that terminology has implications for the ways care is conceptualized, organized, and provided.

Twycross (2002) and, in turn, Pastrana et al. (2008) preface their deconstructions of the language of palliative care through an engagement with the etymology. Twycross (2002) reduces "palliative" to its derivative in the Latin *pallium*, which is a cloak. In this way, palliative care is conceptualized as a mode of comforting, rather than having a curative function. For Pastrana et al. (2008), it is this definition that relates to the usage of descriptive words such as "comprehensive" and "holistic," in relation to palliative care within the literature. By understanding the origins of the term "palliative care," the authors contextualize the term within medical terminology. Because medicine "utilizes denominations that refer to an object of study" (Pastrana et al., 2008, p. 224), palliative care does not necessarily fit into this world; palliative care refers to a theme, a general protection and comforting of the patient; it instigates a conceptual and practical dilemma because it is simultaneously comprehensive and ambiguous. Clark (2002) theorized this notion earlier on by situating palliative care as a discipline within the realm of postmodernity because it "lacks a specific disease, bodily organ, or life stage to call its own" (p. 906). The seemingly ambiguous nature of the "philosophy" (and by extension, discipline), in its diversity and expectations, seems incompatible with the concrete processes of classification, and orientation, within medical contexts.

Based on a discourse analysis of the specialist literature, the research findings of Pastrana et al. (2008) state that the structural and functional definitions of palliative care vary a great deal. It is generally accepted that this lack of consistent terminology remains and is becoming increasingly confusing (Tishelman, 2007). Some definitions refer to it as a basic concept of care and some as a complementary form of care to specific therapies, both physical and emotional, while others refer to it as a completely new form of care (Pastrana et al., 2008). Despite the lack of explicit definitions of the philosophical tenets of palliative care, it is often referred to as a philosophical concept—perhaps because of its thematic generality. Congruent with an overall sense of the tenets of palliative care, Pastrana et al. (2008) found that the primary principles in the literature were related to justice and autonomy as well as dignity. These concepts are all directly related to the focus on person-centered humane care, which is understandable considering the anti-dehumanization context in which palliative care and hospice movements arose.

These principal tenets correspond to the idea of choice: the empowerment of patients to decide both the place of care and the type of care as well as, in a more general sense, to have access to palliative services. This is congruent with the philosophy on which the CHPCA relies; it is predicated on the idea that when people have more control over the experience of dying—the right to make choices and plan for end-of-life care—they experience a greater sense of meaning (2014). And this, in turn, can be related to notions of "quality of life," which is identified as a central goal of palliative care (Pastrana et al., 2008). Clark (2002) refers to this focus on quality of life goals, arguing that it is a result of the diffuseness of palliative care, as a medical discipline. Randall and Downie (2006) contend that there appears to be no consensus on a definition of "quality of life," and yet there continues to be a plethora of literature on the subject. This lack of definitional consensus appears to be a common theme of concepts that fall under the principles of palliative care, as a discourse. "Quality of life" can also be understood in relation to the remaining lifespan and the varying conceptions regarding the dying trajectory. Some push for the maintenance of a normal life up until the end of life, while others focus on the resolution of existential issues, such as the *meaning of life*. How one's remaining days *ought* to be spent is, obviously, not an agreed-on concept.

The type of disease required for admission to palliative care services is sometimes explicit but, as can be seen by the redefinition of the World Health Organization, which now refers to having association with any potentially life-threatening illness, can be quite open, conceptually. The relationship between palliative care and imminent death is complex, as it can be difficult to establish which patients are dying, and at what stage they are in the death trajectory. Similar to the lack of a concrete definition of palliative care, there is no consensus on what constitutes the terminal care period (El Osta et al., 2008; Pastrana et al., 2008).

Beyond the complexity of the convoluted terminology around the death trajectory, as it relates to specific palliative practices, is the distinction between "other symptoms" and "pain symptoms" within the literature. This dichotomy may be correlated to the separation between mind and body; physical pain is dealt with at a medical level and the pain of the mind is dealt with through other professionals and support workers, including psychologists, psychiatrists, counselors, social workers, and religious leaders. However, at the same time, palliative care is considered, at least conceptually, as a holistic and comprehensive care. A considerably important finding by Pastrana et al. (2008) is that "concepts such as dignity…that have been presented as central concepts of palliative care were less visible in the definitions than symptom control" (p. 226). The significance of the predominance of definitions referring to symptom control and management lies in the relationship between palliative care and biomedicine. The focus on pain and symptom management may be understood in relation to the dominance of the institution of medicine.

COMPETING DISCOURSES

The philosophies of palliative care, in practice, become subsumed by discourses of medicine, particularly because they take place in the spaces where this dominance exists. Palliative and nursing care are consistent with a medical world in which technical expertise is highly valued. The care hierarchy in a palliative care setting indicates that importance is placed on the physical care of patients and the medical response to suffering and death. The medical response to symptom management offers a routinized "certainty" to the "uncertainty" of dying, particularly in comparison with the thematic cloaking or comforting offered by psychological and spiritual counseling (Dahlborg-Lyckhage & Liden, 2009). Based on its corporeality, symptom management is relegated to the medical field as "the emphasis is on the disease symptom, which relates to medical expertise where the dominance of medical discourse is not questioned" (Dahlborg-Lyckhage & Liden, 2009, p. 574). The practice of palliative care can be understood in relation to the technological imperative of the biomedical model previously discussed. The implementation of a holistic philosophy within highly medicalized institutions is perhaps a more complex process than it is given credit for being. The "creeping in of medicalization" (Clark, 2002) may be understood in relation to the nature of the institutions in which palliative care is implemented; they are explicitly structured and bureaucratic.

Dahlborg-Lyckhage and Liden (2009) conducted a study that focused on existing palliative care discourses through an ethnography of a hospital setting. They found that most of the documents and guidelines that outlined palliative care focused on a medical perspective. "The curing discourse grounded on scientific evidence and medical knowledge was highly valued....[I]t was obvious that the work of the other professional categories was not only dependent on the medical knowledge but ruled by it" (p. 579). Based on the structure and organization of the hospital/institution, palliative care was governed by routines and rituals, and as such, the potential to provide individualized whole person (palliative) care was limited. From their perspective, the individualization that is essential to the comprehensive essence of palliative care is counteracted by many old structures and hierarchies; "there is a need for a real power shift from curing to caring.... [M]edical alleviation is important and in line with the aims of palliative care, but there is also an alleviation that is beyond the drugs, samples and examinations" (p. 581).

Randall and Downie (2006) discuss these tensions within palliative care as dissonance between the two traditions of health care, the curative Hippocratic tradition, and the Asklepian tradition of comfort and relief of suffering. They portray the tension between palliative care and curative care as a contradiction, arguing that "symptom alleviation, rather than improved quality of life, is the primary goal for such care" (Tishelman, 2007, p. 5).

TENSIONS AND CONTRADICTIONS

It becomes increasingly obvious that there are competing discourses within palliative care and, in turn, palliative medicine. They are difficult to disentangle, as there are discursive relationships between them. There are increasingly more critiques of the medicalization of palliative care: that pain management and relief have become directly related to the "healing" function that doctors must fulfill. Others contend that the focus on symptom management is a more feasible and realistic goal (McNamara, 2004), "one that is more compatible with the wider goals of medicine and which might help to address problems about futility and overtreatment" (Clark, 2002, p. 906). This area also offers measurable outcomes. In references to hospices, Zimmerman and Wennberg (2008) explain that there are technological interventions that have been designed with the sole purpose of palliation; they argue that this could be seen as an indication that the ideals of hospice are being incorporated into conventional clinical care. Again, the focus is on the physical symptoms, rather than the "total pain" that is understood to be an essential characteristic of palliative care. This practical and discursive change emphasizes how palliative care is subsumed under the master discourses of medical institutions. However, this is to be expected in relation to the evolution of palliative medicine as a discipline. Clark (2002) articulates this clearly:

> The new specialty is delicately poised. For some, integration with the wider system is essential for success and the only realistic way to address unrelieved suffering,...[F]or others, it marks the entry into a risky phase of a new development where early ideals might be compromised. (p. 907)

The concern as to whether or not palliative care philosophies, in their entirety, can be implemented in practice within the existing institutions is further explained through the complexities of issues such as spirituality (see Tullis, this volume). Walter (2002) questions to what extent it is even possible to incorporate spiritual care within such a context, with particular emphasis on the ensuing "responsibility" that falls on nurses to provide such care. He explains that there has been a shift away from a religious definition of spirituality, to a more individualized and personal quest for meaning in life and death. The focus on spirituality, in this sense, can then be understood as a reaction against the dehumanizing aspects of the institution of medicine, as well as a shift away from strictly institutionalized religious connotations of spirituality. However, Walter (2002) problematizes the notion of moving away from a universal sense of spirituality in terms of its practicality. To what extent can people who also have their own potentially radically individual conceptions of spirituality, without adhering to a strictly phenomenological approach, address individual differences of spirituality within an institution? He states that we might "be well advised to drop the assumption that any health care professional can offer spiritual care to any patient, and to attend more carefully to the differences between and among patients and staff" (p. 138). The heterogeneity of existential issues may be problematic within homogenizing and highly structured institutions.

The varying discourses of palliative care largely affect the implementation of practices based on the philosophy of comprehensive care. This can be understood through our systems of health care: the settings, structure, and organization. The focus on "quality of life," which is conceptually disjointed, enables medical discourses to dominate palliative care practices and focus on physical symptoms, as a form of palliation. The existential issues, which are posed as central tenets of palliative care within the ideological realm, become problematic in practice based on the proponents of individualization, and the complexity of non-physical symptoms being alleviated in a structure that is not designed, physically or ideologically, to address them.

BINARY DISCOURSE

Crucial elements in understanding palliative care as an active discourse are the conceptual dichotomies that have arisen within it, particularly a "good death," which relies on the foundations of palliative care philosophies. The "good death" (see also Robinson, this volume) is often defined in opposition to a "bad death"; this can be understood as a response to the narratives of the dehumanization of death within hospitals, with technological intervention exceeding its necessity. Kauffman (1998) refers to this as a *cultural conversation* in which a "good death" or "death with dignity" is conceptualized in relation to the simultaneity of "personal control in dying" and "a lack of autonomy brought about by the use of advanced technology medicine in the hospital setting" (p. 715). Despite the varying approaches and mechanisms for operationalizing a "good death," the concept is inextricably tied to philosophies of palliative care (Canadian Institute for Health Information, 2007; Gott, Small, Barnes, Payne, & Seamark, 2008).

During a "good death," individuals die without pain, they have choice as to the space they will occupy during the dying process, they are aware of their death (and have acknowledged it explicitly), and have dealt with existential issues—the "meaning" of life. This particular conception of a "good death" is obviously only applicable in specific death trajectories; defining imminent death (and thus the beginning of palliative care treatment) is difficult. Because many older adults have multiple chronic conditions and potential co-morbid conditions, for example, their ultimate prognosis is affected (Gott et al., 2008). This, in turn, affects the interactions between medical doctors and individuals regarding terminal illness; the opportunity to discuss mortality outside of cancer is limited. The awareness of death, in itself, is a contentious issue as described in the work of Gott et al. (2008), where some participants did not acknowledge the imminence of their death, and therefore, arguably, this allowed them to enjoy their present.

The acceptance of death, or even the awareness of imminent dying, also becomes problematic in relation to health care policy. Eligibility for medical coverage is predicated on this notion of death awareness and acceptance.

> For example, patients electing hospice care under the Medical Hospice Benefit [in the U.S.] often do not qualify for Medicare coverage for services related to treatment of their terminal illness, including palliative chemotherapy. Conversely, patients tend not to receive hospice care until the last 4 to 6 weeks of life, although it has been shown that suffering that could be mitigated by palliative care may occur many months before life's end. (Zimmerman & Wennberg, 2008, p. 256)

DEATH, DENIAL, AND THE "GOOD DEATH"

"Death denial" does not fit into the cultural script or discourse of a "good death," which overtly affects lived experiences. Zimmermann (2007) goes into great detail regarding denial in death and its relationship to palliative care. Based on a discourse analysis of clinical literature, she notes that denial is often described as an impediment to discussion and acceptance of death and thus planning of death, dying outside of the hospital, and withdrawing from futile treatment. Individuals who resist this ordering of death become labeled as being in "denial." She suggests "the very conceptualization of denial as an obstacle to these components of care has been integral to building and sustaining the 'way we die'" (p. 296). This notion of "denial" can also be understood through the individual, psychological process that is deemed as essential to a "good death."

Drawing on the work of Kübler-Ross (1969), and the ensuing discourses surrounding the psychological journey of the dying, specific processes of dying are *normalized*. It is understood that palliative caregivers must support this journey, and inherent in this process is an open acknowledgment of imminent death. However, following Gott et al. (2009), "ageing scripts offer little opportunity for personal growth amongst the frail, ill and oldest old, with such opportunities available to those who manage to age 'successfully and healthily'" (p. 1115). And, perhaps, those who are able but do not partake in this normalized, psychological journey are understood as resisting the natural phenomena of aging and dying. Discourses of palliative care and the "good death" are predicated on notions of autonomy and choice. However, Gott et al. (2008) concluded that these concepts of autonomy and individuality appeared "alien" to most older adults who may rely on traditional discourses, preferring to place trust in the institution of medicine and prefer to have them or family make decisions for them.

Perhaps, then, discourses of a "good death" become a mechanism of defining the right way to die without acknowledging the heterogeneity of the dying process. These discourses affect practices that in turn normalize an expectation of dying, which may not be appropriate for all, specifically that of the aging population (with and without cancer). The very conceptualization of the *denial* of death is discursively and practically understood as an obstacle to the successful implementation of palliative care. "The personal struggle with mortality has become an important instrument in the public problem of managing the dying process" (Zimmerman, 2007, p. 296). Openness to and awareness of death are foundational to the rest of palliative care. But, as can be seen through the work of Zimmerman (2007) and Gott et al. (2008), the homogenized discursive conception of the "good death" may not be appropriate for everyone, and yet, those who resist are deemed as resisting the correct way to die.

Discourses of palliative care have had profound effects on determining the "good death" in opposition to a "bad death"; this discursive dichotomy is very real in its consequences for a heterogeneous society. This dominant discursive dichotomy, and its potential implications in the management and experience of dying, defines and overshadows individuality. As per Vahabzadeh (2003):

> Hegemony penetrates the field of everyday experiences and appropriates them as its "Grass roots" conceptual constituents. As hegemony becomes more global, hegemonic experiences gradually become universal and add up to the smooth hegemonic operations ordaining a new modality of life.... Once experiential hegemony (i.e. Hegemony appropriating doxic knowledges into its epistemic universe), becomes prevalent, hegemony derives consent from the subject's hegemonic (or hegemonized) experiences, that is, those experiences manifest themselves, in every locus of action, as conceivable, viable, and desirable under the current hegemony. (p. 68)

By (re)thinking discourses of palliative care in relation to hegemony, and as part of shifting historical paradigms, we can then understand the connection to the management and ordering of death. It is often said that we are a death-denying society, that we do not speak of death; that it has been silenced (Ariès, 1974; Armstrong, 1987; Zimmerman, 2007). However, it may be that we have replaced this silence with an idea of truth through palliative discourses and the construction of the "right way to die," which in turn leads to the management of death, and therefore, *experience of dying*, in a very specific way. Zimmermann (2012) suggests that "the discourse on acceptance of dying represents a productive power, which disciplines patients through apparent psychological and spiritual gratification, and encourages participation in a certain way to die" (p. 217). Perhaps understanding cultural attitudes toward death should not be thought of in terms of denial but rather as strategies of ordering death: "culturally and historically specific social frameworks for handling, regulating, giving meaning to, and experiencing death" (Bayatrizi, 2008, p. 5). The social *problem* of death—as it has been pursued in this chapter—which has been constructed by discourses of medicine, and then palliative care, creates the need to order it in a specific way. In this way, normative discourses are created that shape, and are shaped by, expectations of dying in a particular way. "It implies the existence of a historical and conceptual tension between two regimes of ordering death, one striving to give meaning to death as a symbolically powerful and ritually ordered event and the other attempting to subject death to various modes of discursive ordering" (Bayatrizi, 2008, p. 12). While palliative care philosophies can be understood as symbolically powerful mechanisms for creating meaning in death, the essence is predicated on individualism, which may be paradoxical to a structured management of death.

CONCLUSIONS

The multiplicity of discourses related to dying become apparent in the tensions within palliative care literature, in both research and practice. Originally articulated as an alternative to medicalized and institutionalized dying, the proliferation of palliative care, as both philosophy and practice, has become embedded within the institutions (physically and discursively) it criticized. The holistic, person-centered (existential) goals of palliative care become contentious in relation to bureaucratic, institutional structures, and the focus on physical symptom alleviation is oft considered a more feasible goal in relation to increasing technological innovation. However, the goal for individualized dying, and what it means to have a "good death," discursively, is still presented within the literature (as goals of palliative care practices); the right to die with dignity, a very personal and subjective conception, becomes a universal discourse—there becomes a right way to die. In this sense, this discourse of the "good death," and the ensuing practices, can be explored in relation to hegemonic experience; thus, the management of dying, and the proposed *paradox of the universalization of individual dying*, can be problematized more abstractly.

The discursive practices of palliative care can be understood as ways of thinking and acting, particular to our epoch (opposed to a fundamental, immutable, relationship to dying and death); the "good death" becomes interconnected with the conception of dying as a continuation or telos of disease, and, therefore, limits the conception of death as an ontological component of living. When thinking of palliative care and end-of-life practices as discourses, further theoretical engagements with existing research (from an interdisciplinary perspective) are required to provoke critical and reflexive research practices, in light of the shifts in social theory and philosophy. Rethinking the foundations of our conceptions of dying as individuals, as they relate to larger social and cultural understandings and discourse, is a starting point to incite further contemplation of death in a new way, and to show beyond doubt that even the critique of the current literature is inevitably informed by the existing dominant discourses. Future research must be cautious about the reification of universal ways of being toward death and end-of-life care, and at the same time, adamantly and consistently acknowledge that authentic life is linked to the singularity of dying as an event that defies normative institutions—a singularity that makes us who we are as individual human beings.

REFERENCES

Ariès, P. (1974). *Western attitudes toward death: From the Middle Ages to the present* (P. M. Ranum, Trans.). Baltimore, MD: The John Hopkins University Press.

Ariès, P. (1981). *The hour of our death*. New York, NY: Oxford University Press.

Armstrong, D. (1987). Silence and truth in death and dying. *Social Science and Medicine, 24*, 651–657.

Bayatrizi, Z. (2008). *Life sentences: The modern ordering of mortality*. Toronto, Ontario, Canada: University of Toronto Press.

Berger, P. (1967). *The sacred canopy: Elements of a sociological theory of religion*. New York, NY: Doubleday.

Canadian Hospice Palliative Care Association. (2014). Caregivers' frequently asked questions. Retrieved from http://www.chpca.net/family-caregivers/faqs.aspx

Canadian Institute for Health Information. (2007). *Health care use at the end of life in western Canada*. Ottawa, Ontario, Canada.

Candrian, C. (2013). Taming death and the consequences of discourse. *Human Relations, 67*, 53–69.

Cherny, N. I. (2006). Definition of palliative care. In R. Catane, N. I. Cherny, M. Kloke, S. Tanneberger, & D. Schrijivers (Eds.), *European Society for Medical Oncology handbook of advanced cancer care* (pp. 11–16). London, UK: Taylor & Francis.

Clark, D. (2000). Palliative care history: A ritual process. *European Journal of Palliative Care, 7*, 50–55.

Clark, D. (2002). Between hope and acceptance: The medicalization of dying. *British Medical Journal, 324*, 905–907.

Connor, S. (2008). Development of hospice and palliative care in the United States. *Omega, 56*, 89–99.

Dahlborg-Lyckhage, E., & Liden, E. (2009). Competing discourses in palliative care. *Supportive Care in Cancer, 18*, 573–582.

Elias, N. (1985). *The loneliness of dying*. Oxford, UK: Blackwell.

El Osta, B., Palmer, L., Paraskevopoulos, T., Pei, B., Roberts, L., Poulter, V.,…Bruera, E. (2008). Interval between first palliative care consult and death in patients diagnosed with advanced cancer at a comprehensive cancer center. *Journal of Palliative Medicine, 11*, 51–58.

Foucault, M. (1975). *The birth of the clinic: An archaeology of medical perception* (S. Smith, Trans.). New York, NY: Vintage Books.

Foucault, M. (1978). *The history of sexuality: An introduction* (Vol. 1, R. Hurley, Trans.). New York, NY: Vintage Books.

Foucault, M. (1981). The order of discourse. In R. Young (Ed.), *Untying the text: A post-structural anthology* (pp. 48–78). Boston, MA: Routledge & Kegan Paul.

Foucault, M. (2000). Truth and juridical forms. In C. Gordon (Ed.), *Power: Essential works of Michel Foucault 1954–1984* (3rd ed., pp. 1–89). New York, NY: Pantheon.

Fox, R. (1981). The sting of death in American society. *The Social Service Review, 55,* 42–59.

Glaser, B., & Strauss, A. (1965). *Awareness of dying.* Chicago, IL: Aldine.

Glaser, B., & Strauss, A. (1968). *Time of dying.* Chicago, IL: Aldine.

Gordon, D. R. (1988). Tenacious assumptions in Western medicine. In M. Lock & D. R. Gordon (Eds.), *Biomedicine examined* (pp. 19–58). Boston, MA: Kluwer.

Gott, M., Small, N., Barnes, S., Payne, S., & Seamark, D. (2008). Older people's views of a good death in heart failure: Implications for palliative care provision. *Social Science and Medicine, 67,* 1113–1121.

Illich, I. (1976). *Limits to medicine.* London, UK: Marion Boyers.

Ireton, S. M. (2007). *An ontological study of death: From Hegel to Heidegger.* Pittsburgh, PA: Duquesne University Press.

Kaufman, S. (1998). Intensive care, old age, and the problem of death in America. *Gerontologist, 38,* 715–725.

Kübler-Ross, E. (1969). *On death and dying.* New York, NY: Macmillan.

Longino, C. (1998). The limits of scientific medicine. *Journal of Health and Social Policy, 9,* 101–116.

Lupton, D. (1997). Foucault and the medicalization critique. In A. Peterson & R. Bunton (Eds.), *Foucault, health and medicine.* London, UK: Routledge.

MacKinlay, E. (2012). *Palliative care, ageing and spirituality: A guide for older people, carers and families.* London, UK: Jessica Kingsley.

McNamara, B. (2004). Good enough death: Autonomy and choice in Australian palliative care. *Social Science and Medicine, 58,* 929–938.

Northcott, H., & Wilson, D. (2008). *Dying and death in Canada.* Peterborough, Ontario, Canada: Broadview Press.

O'Connor, M., & Payne, S. (2006). Discourse analysis: Examining the potential for research in palliative care. *Palliative Medicine, 20,* 829–834.

Pastrana, T., Junger, S., Ostgathe, C., Elsner, F., & Radburch, L. (2008). A matter of definition: Key elements identified in a discourse analysis of definitions of palliative care. *Palliative Medicine, 22,* 222–232.

Pernick, M. (1988). Back from the grave: Recurring controversies over defining and diagnosing death in history. In R. Zaner (Ed.), *Death: Beyond whole-brain criteria* (pp. 15–67). Dordrecht, the Netherlands: Kluwer Academic.

Powell, J. (2011). Foucault, discourses of death, and institutional power. *Illness, Crisis, and Loss, 19,* 351–361.

Randall, F., & Downie, R. (2006). *The philosophy of palliative care: Critique and reconstruction.* Oxford, UK: Oxford University Press.

Saunders, C. (1996). Into the valley of the shadow of death. *British Medical Journal, 313,* 21–28.

Seymour, J., Witherspoon, R., Gott, M., Ross, H., Payne, S., & Owen, T. (2005). *End-of-life care: Promoting comfort, choice and well-being for older people.* Bristol, UK: Polity Press.

Tishelman, C. (2007). Advances in contemporary palliative and supportive care. *Contemporary Nurse, 27,* 3–6.

Turner, B. (1991). *Religion and social theory.* London, UK: Sage.

Twycross, R. (2002). Palliative care: An international necessity. *Journal of Pain and Palliative Care Pharmacotherapy, 16,* 61–79.

Vahabzadeh, P. (2003). *Articulated experiences: Toward a radical phenomenology of contemporary social movements.* Albany, NY: State University of New York Press.

Walter, T. (2002). Spirituality in palliative care: Opportunity or burden? *Palliative Medicine, 16*, 133–139.

Wass, H., & Neimeyer, R. (1995). *Dying: Facing the facts* (3rd ed.). Washington, DC: Taylor & Francis.

Whitney, A., & Smith, A. (2010). Exploring death and dying through discourse. *The Arbutus Review, 1*, 68–80. Retrieved from http://journals.uvic.ca/index.php/ arbutus/article/view/3264

Zimmerman, C. (2007). Death denial: Obstacle or instrument for palliative care? *Sociology of Health and Wellness, 29*, 297–314.

Zimmermann, C. (2012). Acceptance of dying: A discourse analysis of palliative care literature. *Social Science and Medicine, 75*, 217–224.

Zimmerman, C., & Wennberg, R. (2008). Integrating palliative care: A postmodern perspective. *American Journal of Hospice and Palliative Medicine, 23*, 255–258.

CHAPTER THREE

Benchmarking THE End OF Life IN Long-Term Care

JABER F. GUBRIUM

Oddly enough, the first sentence of Stephen King's (1989) thriller *The Dark Half* is especially pertinent to the subject matter of this chapter. Not because the end of life is thrilling, but because what King says about life at the beginning of the book is to the point. Making a distinction, King writes: "People's lives—their real lives, as opposed to their simple physical existences—begin at different times" (p. 3). If asked, King would probably agree that, likewise, the end of life concludes at different times. This would suggest that an individual can have many lives, each or all of which can begin and end at different times. This chapter addresses the communicative contours of the distinction in long-term care, part of a larger concern about the narrative organization of aging and dying (see Kenyon, Bohlmeijer, & Randall, 2011).

The distinction between life and living is commonplace in the corpus of empirical material drawn upon for this chapter. It was often mentioned, for example, in interviews with Helen, an 86-year-old nursing home resident who lamented, "I'll go on living, but my life is over."[1] As Helen spoke about life, I came to know what many of us informally recognize, that *the life* is as experientially real—more real perhaps if we are to believe King—than concrete bearings, such as the bodies that undergird it. The life is not reducible to its materiality, even though it significantly relates to that. Nor is end-of-life communication limited to the later years, as some star athletes assert at the end of their careers. Here, I will focus on old age and suffering, especially as the end of life is constructed in nursing facilities.

Pseudonyms such as Helen's have been assigned to individuals and places throughout the chapter.

It has been said that end-of-life communication ultimately transpires in places such as nursing homes, hospitals, and hospices. Sheldon Tobin and Morton Lieberman (1976) observed decades ago that more and more the nursing facility is "the last home for the aged." Since then, another venue has emerged for managing the end of life, one that was there all along but not recognized as a site of long-term care, and that is the family home. Previously taken to be the place one left at the end of life to play out what remained of living, the family home has become part of a long-term care system.[2] It increasingly structures dying and death in institutional terms, because its moral sensibilities and technical resources borrow heavily from institutional practices (see Gubrium & Holstein, 1999). The lines of demarcation between Tobin and Lieberman's last home for the aged and the family home left behind have been blurred if not eliminated. The key question is, *How* and with *what* communicative resources do those *who* are concerned construct the end of life in this landscape?

THE HOWS, WHATS, AND WHOS

The question has three parts, dealing, respectively, with the *hows*, the *whats*, and the *whos* of the matter. These direct us to the operating components of assertions such as "my life is over," which work together to shape the meaning of the entity taken to be separate and distinct from living.

The *How* Component

The *hows* refer to the communicative mechanisms used to construct everyday understanding. For example, in a much referenced article titled "The Social Construction of Unreality: A Case Study of a Family's Attribution of Competence to a Severely Retarded Child," Melvin Pollner and Lynn McDonald-Wikler (1985) describe six mechanisms by which the five-and-a-half-year-old child's family communicatively sustains the normality of their retarded child. One is the mechanism of "putting words in Mary's [the child] mouth," which might be likened to visible ventriloquizing. While Mary's verbalization is limited to "gurgling," when Mary does gurgle in interaction with family members, they methodically speak for her following each gurgled utterance, thus constructing her turn-by-turn as normal.

On one occasion, when Mary is wearing a newly purchased robe and is asked whether she wants to see herself in a mirror, the following exchange is reported to have taken place. The exchange is "excerpted from a tape [recording] Mary's family made at home."

Father: [*Addressing Mary*] Want to see it in the mirror?
Mary: [*Gurgling*]
Father: She doesn't like it.
Mother: You don't like the robe? It fits you.
Mary: [*Gurgling*]
Mother: What did you say about Daddy?
Mary: Mmmmmm [*gurgle*]
Father: She thinks it's too cheap. (p. 249)

We can quickly see that the meaning of the gurgle is not obvious in its own right, but is interactionally made meaningful, in this case in collaboration with the parents. Pollner and McDonald-Wikler (1985) note that the point is not whether Mary or the family is delusional, a question they set aside for the purpose of their study, but rather that Mary's everyday competence requires communicative work. According to the authors, putting words into Mary's mouth is an operating mechanism of that work.

I will make a similar point for end-of-life communication, which is that the end of life is not self-evident, but rather is communicatively constructed through a mechanism I have called "benchmarking" (Gubrium, Rittman, Williams, Young, & Boylstein, 2003).[3] Benchmarking is the ordinary process of applying a useful standard, or benchmark, for designating and communicating where one is in life, such as explaining that compared with such-and-such (the benchmark), one's life is over or not over, as the case might be. Julius Roth (1963) coined the term. He discovered that he was using a version of the mechanism to construct the progress he was making in recovering from tuberculosis in a "TB" sanatorium. While he and other patients had access to medical reckonings of recovery, both patients and professional practitioners also used various patients' progress in treatment to benchmark their own or their patients' recovery. We can imagine that Roth—like 86-year-old Helen—upon seeing the rapid recovery of another patient similar to himself in the light of his own lack of progress, might have concluded, "I'll live for a while longer maybe, but my life is over."

This is something we do all the time in assessing ourselves and it is, indeed, quite ordinary in that regard. But understood as a distinct communicative mechanism among other possible everyday mechanisms of meaning-making, benchmarking becomes a useful analytic tool for discerning the variety of ways those in dire circumstances construct the end(s) of life. Kathy Charmaz's (1991) book *Good Days, Bad Days*, for instance, provides an intriguing view of how those with chronic illnesses use their ailments' daily vicissitudes as benchmarks for the shape and borders of their lives as a whole. On good days, life seems to be endless; on bad days, the end is near—along with their respective moral horizons such as one's sentiments about life, the resulting choices, and related courses of action.

The *What* Component

If benchmarking (the verb) is an important mechanism by which the end of life is constructed, the benchmarks (the noun) used are the *whats* of the matter. This turns us from process to substance. In this regard, we can ask, What communicative resources do those concerned apply to benchmark the end of life? This will take us to the specific empirical material I have collected in studying how benchmarking constructs the end of life in long-term care. But before turning to that, let us consider the general issue concerning where answers to questions about the end of life are derived. Where, in other words, do those concerned obtain the benchmarks they use to construct the end of life?

One source of benchmarks is personal life history. We might figure that from time immemorial, the end of life has been constructed, in part, based on how one views other parts of the life. As I will illustrate later in long-term care, it was not uncommon in a study of recovery benchmarking among stroke survivors to assess their current level of functioning in terms of their views of previous levels of functioning (Gubrium et al., 2003). For example, when asked about the quality of his life now, a survivor who described his past as very active and who now felt himself inactive was likely to make the same distinction that 86-year-old Helen did, such as saying that he will go on living, but that the life he once knew is over.

A second source of benchmarks is others' experience. Others are the communicative resource Roth (1963) used to evaluate his own progress in recovery from tuberculosis. This, too, we might figure has been a source of benchmarks for the end of life since time immemorial. For example, when the question of why she felt the way she did about life came up in interviews with Helen, she would sometimes explain that "going on living" was not the same as "having a life." As if to instruct me in the matter, she would sometimes add, "Just look around you, Jay," directing my attention to other residents to make her point. I should note that Helen was not just mincing words, but was literally designating the basis of a distinction. Occasionally, she would extend her personal assessment to nursing homes in general, whose residents' lives by the fact of being residents were over (see Gubrium & Holstein, 1999, for a discussion of the nursing home as a discursive anchor).

A third source of benchmarks has not always been available and makes the end of life today different in this regard from what it was in the past. I am referring to today's booming cultural rationalization of suffering and dying (Gubrium & Holstein, 2000). What I mean by rationalization is that designated terms of reference, categories, formal accounts, and related systems of meaning are now widely available for discerning the end of life, if not the end of living. One no longer need look to his or her past or to others for benchmarks. Brochures, books, and videos are an ever-present part of the public information side of the death and dying industry, distributed by nursing homes, hospices, funeral homes, and grief counselors. Virtually every bookstore and supermarket checkout point has a plethora of such resources readily available to customers.

Perhaps the most familiar and most widely used resource is the five-stage model of dying presented by Elisabeth Kübler-Ross (1969) in her book *On Death and Dying*. The model depicts the experiential course of the dying person's view of life. Since the 1960s, the model has been applied to all manner of end-of-life experiences, from those of dying persons themselves to those who are witness to a death or who care for the dying, the latter of whom may be regarded as the so-called second victims of the end of life. The home caregivers of long-standing disease sufferers are depicted as experiencing the end of lives parallel to that of sufferers cared for, with an equivalent five stages of adjustment in their case to the dying and death of their loved ones. In the long-term home care of Alzheimer's disease sufferers, the progressive dementia of those cared for presents caregivers with incremental benchmarks for their own adjustment to the "brain failure" of care receivers. An equally popular resource is the signs-and-symptoms model found both in medically oriented popular texts and in scientific literature.[4] This model combines personal and medical categories for designating the end of life as well as the end of living. I will return to both later in illustrating communicative usage in institutional context.

The *Who* Component

In today's world, we all are exposed to models of life experience. Benchmarking the course of life seems to be everyone's business. We not only benchmark stages of experience for ourselves, but others do it for us, both professionals and laypersons. It is everyone's language game, so to speak. Personal experience is constructed through time by way of the actions and sentiments of friends, significant others, and family members, from the liked to the disliked, from the intimate to the estranged. All of them, in turn, respond to messages and images from networks of others with institutional bearings.

Consider Helen again in this regard. I once asked her to talk about her future. "You mean the future me?" Helen asked. Following a moment of thought, in a small way she brought a form of benchmarking-by-others with institutional bearings into the picture. A simple statement about "what to think about...life after cancer" derived meaning from constructions of others both close to her and far removed from living in her nursing home.

> You know, Jay, I've just been thinking that maybe in the future it'll [*her cancer*] disappear, just like Harriet said it did for her and I can have a life again. [*Harriet is Helen's sister-in-law, who, according to Helen, is now in remission from her own cancer and frequently recounts her remission as a possible model for Helen's cancer.*] Wouldn't that be wonderful? To have a life

again? Like Harriet said she learned about in those [*support*] groups she goes to. Wouldn't it, Jay? I'm so glad about that—that Harriet told me what to think about that, you know, life after cancer.

Not only the *whats* but many of the *whos* in today's world are institutionally informed. It appears that no one any longer is on his or her proverbial own in communicating matters of experience (see Gubrium & Holstein, 2000). Endless others, in and about countless going concerns such as Harriet's support groups and their institutional sponsors, make it their business (some literally) to benchmark the end of life. The line of demarcation between self and others, while hardly ever clearly drawn, is now more difficult to discern than ever. As Helen and Harriet's exchanges over the matter indicate, benchmarking the end of life is a *collaborative* accomplishment mediated by countless models of experience, with influences extending well beyond the immediate environments of those whose living and end of life are in question.

THE INSTITUTIONAL CONTEXT OF BENCHMARKING

Let us consider the way institutions shape the *whats* and *whos* of benchmarking for the end of life. What anthropologists call "apt illustration" is a well-established way of describing the lived detail of general mechanisms of action. The importance of exploring benchmarking's institutional bearings in situ stems from the overwhelming influence of institutions on the construction of experience, in our case for constructing the end of life. As I will show, traced ethnographically, the three sources of benchmarks discussed in the previous section—life history, social comparisons, and familiar models of experience—have remarkably complex institutional bearings, especially when the varied *whats* and *whos* of the matter are taken into account. The complexity stems from the broad communicative contingencies of ostensibly personal experience.

Life History in Institutional Context

To illustrate the use of personal life history to benchmark the end of life, I draw on narrative material dealing with constructions of the quality of life gathered in a series of interviews with nursing home residents. Some of the material was published in the book *Speaking of Life: Horizons of Meaning for Nursing Home Residents* (Gubrium, 1993), but the overall corpus is much larger. The corpus includes not only interview transcripts, but also field notes consisting of paraphrased ethnographic interviews, accounts of emotional expression, and observational records of real-time events, such as family visits and patient-care staffings. Evident in the subtitle of the book, the focus of the study was on how the residents themselves spoke of, and in particular how they assessed, the quality of life now that they resided in a nursing home. The study was not so much concerned with residents' evaluations of the quality of the nursing home or its care as it was with the quality of lives as figured in their present circumstances. In the following illustration, note how life history benchmarks the end of life in relation to the in situ perspectives of contrasting *whos* in the matter.

Alec Ranelli was an 84-year-old man who had been in skilled care at Holly Plaza for three years when I met him. He suffered from severe diabetes and the continuing pain of a double leg amputation. Alec, who had been a heavy smoker, now also suffered from chronic obstructive pulmonary disease and, according to the staff, exhibited early signs of dementia. As with other residents in this study, he was interviewed several times over the course of a year, and was interacted with casually at various locations on the premises, including convivial chats with him and others in and out of their rooms. I came to know Alec and family members well, especially his 82-year-old wife, Sara, and his adult, middle-aged children, Mark, Nina, and Kitty, who were regular visitors.

It did not take much prompting in interviews for Alec to speak about his life, both before and after becoming a Plaza resident. He was naturally chatty, as several of the other residents were, not hesitating to reminisce at length about what they referred to as "the old days," more recent times, and their present and future lives in the facility. Said by the staff to be enduringly "active and busy," Alec was a big man and reported to have lived with adventure in his veins. One of the daughters described him as the Ernest Hemingway of the family. As a younger man, Alec had been a lumberjack and later continued to work in other capacities in the lumber industry.

The following is an interview extract, one of many similar exchanges that illustrate the use of life history to benchmark what Alec's life once was compared with what it is now living at the Plaza. The bold contrast of then-and-now not only designated a life ending, but also was emotionally palpable.

Alec: You know how it is when you're that age [*his 20s*], you're as active as all get-out. Look at me now; you wouldn't know it, would ya, Jay? I'm a big guy. Shit, buddy, I was a really a big lunk then; I got around like none of the other guys [*at work*]. What a life! I was looked up to, too. No messin' around with Alec. No sir! [*He elaborates, detailing his life at the time, pausing here and there, marveling and then sighing, as if to convey what he once was in relation to what he'd become.*] Hey, what a difference, huh? I'll bet you can't believe it, can you, Jay? [*Pause*] Can you believe that this ole dying body once upon a time coulda had a life? Can ya, buddy?

Jay: That's amazing, Alec. Tell me about it.

Alec: Aw, come on. What's to tell? You heard me a hundred times by now.
            [*Laughs*] I'm like a broken record, right buddy? Well, hells' bells, they
            take good care of you here; don't ya know. But this ain't no life. I'm
            dead meat, man. I sit here [*laughing*] and I shit here. Right here, right?
            [*Points to his bottom and we both laugh*] Sit and shit. You wouldn't find
            me doin' that before I got here. Don't get me wrong, the gals [*nursing
            aides*] are really good...they better be or else! Big talk, huh? Can't wipe
            my own ass. [*Sighs*]

Jay: Well, life...

Alec: Well, life nothin', period. [*His voice breaking*] That's it. That's gone. It's
            over. Goodbye and farewell.

But this was not the whole story when others' benchmarking was taken into
account. What interviews with Alec told could contrast mightily with what interviews or passing chats with others such as family or staff members suggested.
Stories and life histories have multiple versions. What Alec benchmarked in this
account was benchmarked differently by family members, for example. Set side by
side with other constructions, both past and present, the end of Alec's life becomes
communicatively complex, beset by the perspectival contingencies of the construction process.

As I had become what Alec's wife and three adult children called a "trusted
friend," they often took me into their confidence in private chats that often started
with the question "How's Alec doing, Jay?" In these chats, what Alec clearly and
sometimes emotionally demarcated in interviews could be a source of considerable
contrast. Put simply, the *whats* of benchmarking could run up against *whos* of
validation. If Alec emphatically and consistently communicated in interviews with
me that his life was over, interactions with family members often challenged what
was otherwise forcefully designated.

For example, in the Plaza's lobby one evening, far from Alec's room, something
I had said about Alec's feelings about life prompted Sara and the children to set me
straight, so to speak, before I saw them off. As the following reconstruction from
field notes indicates, family members used aspects of the same life history I had
heard Alec recollect recounted in an equally emphatic, but distinctly different, way.
Dismissing Alec's insistence that his life was over, they used life history to benchmark life continuity. Virtually teaching me the social psychology of benchmarking
to start, Alec's wife Sara described the perspectival side of a personal construction,
suggesting that usage is linked with one's circumstances.

Sara: [*Facing me*] I'd take some of what he [*Alec*] says with a grain of salt. You
            know what he's like, Jay. [*Explains*] At the same time, I know you know
            what it's like for him. Like it would be for you, too, right? [*Whimpering*

	as she elaborates] Living in a place like this does that to you. I could cry when he tells me like that, that his life is over…So many of them here are just, I hate to say it, just vegetables, but not my Alec. No way, José.
Mark:	Come on, Ma, don't get yourself all riled up. He's [*Alec*] being dramatic. You know Pa. Always puttin' on a show. [*Sarcastically*] His life is over, my foot! Give him a drink and you'll see whose life is over. Good thing he can't drink anymore. That's why his life is over.
Sara:	[*Annoyed*] That's not true and you know it! Don't talk about your father like that. I know exactly what he means and he's right, goddamn it!
Kitty:	You guys, geez. Stop beating yourself up, Ma. Now you're going to make me cry.
Nina:	[*Gathering the family*] See ya later, Jay. Thanks for looking out for him.

The competing truths of the preceding accounts are not uncommon in the empirical material, which differential positions in institutional life can pattern in vivid contrasts. While I will not exemplify it here, staff members' own varied positions in nursing facilities add to the complexity in distinctive ways. Their varied professional training and job descriptions mediate the construction of residents' life endings in their own right. Professional staffings are especially eye opening in this regard, where models of experience are brought forth and applied in complex ways to the construction of residents' past, present, and future experience, in particular constructions of the end of life (see Gubrium, 1997/1975, for illustrations of the influence of different institutional "worlds" on the construction of individuals and events).

Life history is also used in distinctive ways by residents with contrasting preinstitutional backgrounds. If the preceding extract from one of Alec's interviews reflected a popular construction of life in nursing homes, it was not the only way the personal past was used to figure life in the circumstances. Equally compelling usages could be presented by residents to benchmark new lives as well as life continuity in the nursing home. Extracts from interviews with two other nursing home residents serve to make the point.

The first extracts are from interviews with Martha Gilbert, a 76-year-old widow suffering from congestive heart failure and emphysema. She had lived at Oakmont Nursing Home for five years when first interviewed. Lifelong illness, hard work, and poverty were the continuing themes of her recollections. She emphasized that hers was a difficult and unhappy life from the start, far worse than her life at Oakmont. She pointed out that she had been "on my own practically since I've been eleven years old." Dividing her responses into thens and nows, she repeatedly marked the distinction between her older life and her life now. Her two sons' reluctance to maintain contact with her had been especially distressing. She wanted them to be part of her life. But, as she explained, when she began to construct a new life without them, it became easier. They are not a part of her life at Oakmont, which is another life—a different life—one yet to end that she had reluctantly grown to like.

> It's [*Oakmont*] part of my life now. It's home. I know I can't depend on my sons. I haven't seen my son from South Carolina in ten years. Not much of a son, huh? He's not one to visit. And Jimmy, my youngest one, he drives those big convoys and he's on the road [*much of the time*].

> They [*her sons*], neither one, was ever too homey anyway, I guess. So here I am. It's hard, but after you accept the things you know you can't have, things begin to run a little bit smoother.

> But when you look back, I've never had a family life. I always had to work. It was bad, real bad.

> Well, after the rough life that I've lived all my life and then you come along and live in here and you don't have your problems, I mean that's easy. If I didn't have such a hard time breathing sometimes, I think I'd be on Easy Street.

The second extracts are from interviews with Peter Rinehart, a 77-year-old widower, paralyzed from the waist down, the result of a roof fall. He had spent much of his life on the road selling Oster products, taking his wife along with him, a house trailer hitched to the back of their van. Theirs was a life together on the road, as he put it, living here and there along the way. He now suffers from severe chronic back pain, cannot sit upright, and is completely incontinent. As far as living is concerned, he figures he is in good health. If talk about his life is sprinkled with references to time before and time after the fall, this is not used to benchmark a new life, but rather a change only in venue and lifestyle. In his view, life has continued into the three-and-a-half years he has resided at the Bayside Nursing Home and will move along there into the foreseeable future.

In what follows, at first Peter compares himself with others, one of the *whats* more directly illustrated in the next section. He moves on to describe a life that hasn't ended, but rather that has had distinct "points" along a continuum, such as the point at which he was no longer able to sit upright.

> I see people that are worse off than I am. I feel sorry for them, but I'm not looking back with remorse. It's something I can't help. It happened [*his fall*] and I have to live with it. Life's been happy and pretty good to me otherwise. I made a good living. You take the good with the bad.

> [*Asked whether he feels living at Bayside is "part of your life or separate from it"*] I think it's part of my life. I've seen people that weren't as well off as I am and some of them were very far from where I am. They're very despondent. Can't face it. Well I don't have that feeling. I can adjust very easily. I think part of that is the fact that we traveled so much.

Yeah, it's part of my life all right. What would I do if this place weren't here? I'd be in another place like it, probably not as good as this place. I've adapted myself for quite a while here. I did adapt all right.

So that's life for me. Easy come, easy go. Barring a change, Jay, I'll be just like I am. Hopefully, I'll get to the point where I can sit up.

Social Comparison in Institutional Context

Countless social comparisons can serve as benchmarks for where one is in life in residential care, especially for whether a life has ended. This is particularly glaring in an institutional context, as there are so many sources of comparison immediately available for benchmarking. I often heard such comparisons in fieldwork conducted in the early 1980s in support groups for the home caregivers of Alzheimer's disease sufferers. The institutional bearings of the Alzheimer's disease movement were looming in importance at the time (see Gubrium, 1986a). The movement's aim, in part, was to construct the failing mind in old age as a disease, rather than just a normal part of aging. As a disease, it justified professional intervention and institutional management, not just continued family living.

Part of that study dealt with how family members benchmarked the difference between normal forgetfulness in loved ones cared for at home, otherwise called "benign senescent forgetfulness" or BSF, on the one hand, and Alzheimer's disease (AD) or senile dementia, on the other. The difference centered on whether those affected continued with lives only compromised by BSF or were now the "empty shells" of what they once were and whose lives had ended for all practical purposes. It was a significant divide to cross and could be heartbreaking, because the new understanding framed the experience in question as leading to the end of life, if not living. To figure that someone loved and intimately cared for had become "the mere shell of a former self," was to conclude that that person's life was over, the moral consequences of which were deep and often frightening.

According to a growing number of caregiver guidebooks, widely available informational brochures, and the seemingly endless messages communicated and caregiver newsletters distributed in local chapters of the Alzheimer's Association, being an empty shell was no life at all for either the AD sufferer or the caregiver. The received wisdom was that, in time, nursing home placement was the only reasonable course of action for an empty shell. It would not only "realistically" recognize the end of life for the disease sufferer who was "no longer there" and required institutional management, but also did not cause the caregiver to be the disease's second victim. For family caregivers, recognizing that "it's time" (for nursing home placement) avoided the risk of their own lives ending.

End-of-life communication in the support groups for family caregivers interlarded the family home and institutional placement. Participants not only were ensconced in home care but also had varied degrees of knowledge about AD and spoke poignantly about what it would mean for themselves (respite) and their loved ones (life as empty shells) to live in a nursing home. As will be evident in the following illustration reconstructed from field notes of the proceedings of one of the support groups studied, discerning the end of life was anything but straightforward. Comparisons of home care experiences could be as contentious and emotional as they were earlier in Alec's interview and during his family's departure one evening following a nursing home visit. Benchmarking navigated its way between what participants had learned about AD from professionals, were persuaded to think, or had read on their own, on the one hand, and what they believed they knew and deeply felt from the personal experience of caring for a loved one at home, on the other. In such circumstances, the end of life not only was benchmarked comparatively but also was dyadic. The moral contours of one life ending (the AD sufferer's life) were profoundly linked with the moral contours of another life ending (the home caregiver's life).

Participants in the illustration are the caregiving spouses of AD sufferers. They are well acquainted with each other, are generally friendly and supportive, and speak openly about their circumstances and the decisions they either have made or are being confronted with concerning continued home care. Here again, the benchmarking presented is not just a set of anecdotal details, but a lived microcosm of the institutional complexity of social comparison. At one point in the proceedings, as participants compare each other's home care experience, attention turns to the mental status of caregiver Rita's husband, George. One of the other participants asks Rita how she feels about George's "very demented" behavior of late. Earlier in the meeting, Rita had described her husband's increasingly troublesome "wandering," his growing incontinence, and his inability to communicate properly, which had generated lengthy discussion. The following extract begins as the conversation returns to George's home care. Rita is admittedly puzzled and states,

> I just don't know what to think or feel. It's like he's not even there anymore, and it distresses me something awful. He doesn't know me. He thinks I'm a strange woman in the house. He shouts and tries to slap me away from him. It's not like him at all. Most of the time he makes sounds but they sound more like an animal than a person. Do you think he has a mind left? I just wish I could get in there into his head and see what's going on. Sometimes I get so upset that I just pound on him and yell at him to come out to me. Am I being stupid? I feel that if I don't do something quick to get at him he'll be taken from me altogether.

Another participant, Cora, responds immediately. As if to say that the continuation of life and not just living depends on maintaining the semblance of a life in your "heart of hearts," Cora explains that the end of life is as much others' moral obligation as it is an individual decision.

> We all have gone through it. I know the feeling, like, you just know in your heart of hearts that he's in there and that if *you* let go, that's it. So you keep on trying and trying and trying. You've got to keep the faith, that's it's him and just work at him, 'cause if you don't…well, I'm afraid we've lost them. That's Alzheimer's. It's up to the ones who care because they [*AD sufferers*] can't do it for themselves.

Other participants question the wisdom of "keeping the faith" that life has not ended for sufferers like George. While support group participants can be supportive, they also are not mere puppets of received wisdom, professional or otherwise. The received wisdom in question is the familiar refrain that once a sufferer has become the proverbial empty shell, it is reasonable to conclude that life is over for the sufferer and to seek institutional care. There was as much contested in the groups studied as there was agreement on this matter. If this institutional wisdom was a continual communicative resource, it also was continuously open to differential usage. One of the participants, Jack, whose wife, Louise, suffered from AD at home, soon asked Cora whether she would not feel foolish to realize that all her faith and effort were for naught because, as he claimed about Louise, "She's like the living dead," adding:

> That's why I'm looking for a nursing home for her. I loved her dearly but she's just not Louise anymore. No matter how hard I try, I can't get myself to believe that she's there anymore. I know how that can keep you going, but there comes a point where all the evidence points the other way. Even at those times—which is not very often—when she's momentarily lucid, I just know that's not her speaking to me but some knee-jerk reaction. You just can't let that sort of thing get your hopes up because then you won't be able to make the kind of decision that's best for everyone all around.

At this point, Cora interjects, challenging Jack by raising questions that could be metaphysical if they were not so ordinary. The *whos* and the *whats* of the matter rise in comparative tension and institutional bearings to become an existential dilemma.

> Well, I know what you've gone through and I admire your courage, Jack. But you can't be too sure. How do you *really* know that what Louise says at times is not one of those few times she's been able to really reach out to you? You don't really know for sure, do you? You don't really know if those little plaques and tangles are in there, do you? I hate to make it hard on you, Jack, but I face the same thing day in and day out with Richard [*her husband*]. Can I ever finally close him out of my life and say, "Well, it's done. It's over. He's gone." How do I know that the poor man isn't hidden somewhere, behind all that confusion, trying to reach out and say, "I love you, Cora"? [*Weeps*]

The Everyday Accountability of Institutional Models

If it was not explicit in the preceding extracts, support groups participants, including Rita, Cora, and Jack, knew of and referred to a popular five-stage model framing the end-of-life experience of AD caregivers. It was an adaption of the Kübler-Ross (1969) five-stage model of dying, with the last stage referring to the caregiver giving up on home care and seeking nursing home placement. Whereas there were different views of the model's applicability, it was, nonetheless, a part of home care benchmarking culture. Participants in support groups were continuously accountable for why they did or did not follow the model in benchmarking the end of life for themselves. Being communicatively accountable meant that, regardless of personal preferences, when the issue of the model's applicability in particular cases was raised, participants were expected to account for the reasons their own or the sufferers' experience did or did not conform to the model's designated benchmarks. In everyday accountability, the model presented itself to caregivers as a pathway to alternative futures—one foreclosing "any life I have left of my own" with continued home care, and one "returning to my life" following institutionalization.

Another popular model for benchmarking the end of life is a resource that cuts across the health care landscape in general. This is the typical signs-and-symptoms model present in what Lester King (1982) calls "medical thinking," and adapted to the end of life. Signs refer to what professionals look for in arriving at diagnoses, while symptoms are what patients or sufferers report or complain of. The hospice movement especially has taken this approach in describing the stages of the end of life, providing widely available lists of the usual signs and symptoms of dying for both professional and lay consumption (see Szabo, 2010, chapters 18 and 25).

If this model also was not referenced in so many words in Rita, Cora, and Jack's preceding exchange, everyday lay communication about the "signs" (medical thinking's "symptoms") of the end of life were legion in the AD support groups. Indeed, inasmuch as everyone is somewhat familiar with medical thinking, the model has a lurking presence in all groups. Time and again, for example, support groups' participants both discussed and argued about whether the AD sufferers they cared for showed signs of the end of life, some comparing professional opinion with their own sensibilities. When Jack described Louise's actions as "not her speaking to me," he implicitly referenced an absence of signs of a former life in his still living wife. According to Jack, Louise was now completely incommunicative and just living. In contrast, what Cora sensed in her interactions with her husband, Richard, was a life that was no longer able to reach out to her and say, "I love you, Cora." In their respective accounts, the same *whats* were light-years away from each other in meaning.

Like other *whats* of benchmarking, if such models and lists are clear-cut combinations of physical and behavioral indicators, they are, nonetheless, continually subject to the practical vicissitudes of everyday reckoning. Lack of communicativeness, for example, appears to be one of the most frequently listed benchmarks of the end of life, ostensibly evident in observable conditions such as losing interest in others, focusing inward, and feeling less need to talk. Some lists are divided into conditions that sequentially benchmark the so-called pre-active and those that benchmark the later active phase of the end of life. But, if the signs-and-symptoms model and its lists are widely known, accepted, and applied, the general pattern is that they are working *whats*, variably accountable in practice.

CONCLUSION

Across the landscape of long-term care, there is empirical warrant for concluding that life can end at different times, with time itself losing its linear bearings. As the first sentence of King's *The Dark Half* (1980) suggests, like the start of life, life's conclusion has variable and variegated endings. The illustrations presented above are just the tip of the larger world of life endings. The end of life is as changeable as the communicated spaces that populate that world, from chance encounters and ordinary chitchat to the venues of going concerns such as support groups, nursing homes, and hospices. Both in time and in space, there are more life endings in practice than physical living and dying can possibly indicate.

What *The Dark Half* does not broach is that, in today's world, the shape of life communicatively navigates discernible networks of concern. The start and the end of life are hardly a matter of individual reckoning. Inasmuch as we have always lived in relationships, it would be difficult to imagine that ever being truly the case. In a world of going concerns, it now is especially hard to imagine. Whether or not one is physically alive or dead, countless others, perspectives, models, and institutions refer to and serve to construct the shape of life. More and more, in discernible settings and at regularized intervals, those considering the end of life are encouraged to speak of, and reflect upon, their own dying and that of others. The end of life does not just happen. It is communicatively and institutionally assembled into being, locally contingent, and, as the case might be, similarly challenged and undone.

This provides two directions for future research. Centered on the *hows*, one direction is to explore other communicative mechanisms for constructing the end of life. In their work, Pollner and McDonald-Wikler (1985) identified six communicative mechanisms, one of which was described earlier. An additional mechanism, the one under consideration in this chapter in relation to the end of life, is benchmarking. It is entirely possible that each of the mechanisms identified by Pollner and McDonald-Wikler for everyday communication with a severely retarded child would apply to the communicative construction of the end of life, extending the *hows* of end-of-life communication well beyond benchmarking.

A second direction for future research centers on the *whats* and *whos* of communication at the end of life when specific institutional contexts are taken into account. In a growing world of going concerns, resources such as personal history, others' experience, and local cultures are likely to vary in pertinence from one institution to another. Comparing the institutional usage of particular resources should provide promising findings on the specific institutional *whats* and *whos* of communicative practice on this front. One hypothesis to consider, for example, is whether constructions of the end of life in home care differ significantly and, if so, in what ways from constructions in a hospice. While I suggested earlier that cultural resources for constructing the end of life resonate across the broad spectrum of long-term care, its specific patterning should be subjected to systematic comparative analysis.

NOTES

1. In an edited book dedicated to the exploration of a narrative gerontology (Kenyon et al., 2011), Mark Freeman (2011) refers to this as "narrative foreclosure," noting that the phenomenon is not restricted to later life. Compare, for example, Cassandra Phoenix's (2011) chapter in the same book, which addresses the phenomenon as it is expressed among athletes and bodybuilders. Also see Carol Rambo Ronai's (1992) article on the aging table dancer.
2. This chapter includes the home as a venue of family care for increasingly frail elderly. It is in regard to the associated increasing burdens of home care for family members that Tobin and Lieberman (1976) argued that institutionalization and the nursing home were becoming the "last home for the aged." The growing legion and professionalization of home health workers complicate this, especially as care takes place in the households of families who can afford this form of care, in which case the nursing home may not be a last home for the aged. See Eileen Boris and Jennifer Klein's (2012) book *Caring for America* for a history of this long-hidden facet of long-term care.
3. See Gubrium and Holstein (2009) for a discussion of communicative mechanisms and Gubrium (2011) for consideration of the eventfulness of life constructions.
4. See chapter 3 of Lester King's (1982) book *Medical Thinking* for a presentation of this resource.

REFERENCES

Boris, E., & Klein, J. (2012). *Caring for America: Home health workers in the shadow of the welfare state.* New York, NY: Oxford University Press.

Charmaz, K. (1991). *Good days, bad days: The self in chronic illness and time.* New Brunswick, NJ: Rutgers University Press.

Freeman, M. (2011). Narrative foreclosure in later life: Possibilities and limits. In G. Kenyon, E. Bohlmeijer, & W. L. Randall (Eds.), *Storying later life* (pp. 3–19). New York, NY: Oxford University Press.

Gubrium, J. F. (1986a). *Oldtimers and Alzheimer's: The descriptive organization of senility.* Greenwich, CT: JAI Press.

Gubrium, J. F. (1986b). The social preservation of mind. *Symbolic Interaction, 9,* 37–51.

Gubrium, J. F. (1993). *Speaking of life: Horizons of meaning for nursing home residents.* Hawthorne, NY: Aldine de Gruyter.

Gubrium, J. F. (1997/1975). *Living and dying at Murray Manor.* Charlottesville: University of Virginia Press.

Gubrium, J. F. (2011). Narrative events and biographical construction in old age. In G. Kenyon, E. Bohlmeijer, & W. L. Randall (Eds.), *Storying later life* (pp. 39–50). New York, NY: Oxford University Press.

Gubrium, J. F., & Holstein, J. A. (1999). The nursing home as a discursive anchor for the ageing body. *Ageing and Society, 19,* 519–538.

Gubrium, J. F., & Holstein, J. A. (2000). The self in a world of going concerns. *Symbolic Interaction, 23,* 95–115.

Gubrium, J. F., & Holstein, J. A. (2009). *Analyzing narrative reality.* Thousand Oaks, CA: Sage.

Gubrium, J. F., Rittman, M. R., Williams, C., Young, M. E., & Boylstein, E. A. (2003). Benchmarking as everyday functional assessment in stroke recovery. *Journal of Gerontology, 58B,* S203–S211.

Kenyon, G., Bohlmeijer, E., & Randall, W. L. (Eds.). (2011). *Storying later life.* New York, NY: Oxford University Press.

King, L. (1982). *Medical thinking.* Princeton, NJ: Princeton University Press.

King, S. (1980). *The dark half.* New York, NY: Penguin Books.

Kübler-Ross, E. (1969). *On death and dying.* New York, NY: Macmillan.

Phoenix, C. (2011). Young bodies, old bodies, and stories of the athletic self. In G. Kenyon, E. Bohlmeijer, & W. L. Randall (Eds.), *Storying later life* (pp. 111–125). New York, NY: Oxford University Press.

Pollner, M., & McDonald-Wikler, L. (1985). The social construction of unreality: A case study of a family's attribution of competence to a severely retarded child. *Family Process, 24,* 241–254.

Rambo Ronai, C. (1992). Managing aging in young adulthood: The "aging" table dancer. *Journal of Aging Studies, 6,* 307–317.

Roth, J. (1963). *Timetables.* Indianapolis, IN: Bobs-Merrill.

Szabo, J. (2010). *Death and dying: An annotated bibliography of the thanatological literature.* Lanham, MD: Rowman & Littlefield.

Tobin, S. S., & Lieberman, M. A. (1976). *Last home for the aged.* San Francisco, CA: Jossey-Bass.

CHAPTER FOUR

End-OF-Life Communication AND Spirituality

JILLIAN A. TULLIS

I don't believe in God. I think once I'm dead, it's over.... I don't believe my energy goes anywhere or anything like that. (Barbara, 65, hospice patient dying of breast cancer)

I can't wait to walk down streets paved with gold. And be in the presence of my Lord and Savior. (Carl, 72, hospice patient dying of heart disease)

Life is finite, and the permanence of death makes taking the time to listen and share essential throughout life, but especially at the end of life (Kübler-Ross, 1969). While dying is a normal part of life, many people struggle with this reality and frequently fail to communicate about their beliefs and wishes. Coming to terms with death for a dying person, her loved ones, and her health care providers is inherently a spiritual process (Puchalski, 2006). Dying raises myriad existential and spiritual questions: Why do we suffer? What's the meaning of life? Was I a good person? Have I done everything I was here to do? What is going to happen to my soul? Why do we die?

While the importance of spirituality at the end of life is more readily acknowledged than at any other time in a life, spiritual needs are not always recognized or met. Often, spirituality goes unnoticed because it is not well understood. As the quotes that introduce this chapter reveal, what constitutes spirituality at the end of life ranges from atheism to devoutly religious. In the West, especially in the U.S., we are encouraged to keep our spiritual and religious beliefs private. Therefore, some people may grapple with spiritual questions through internal dialogue.

Others may choose to ignore, or fail to address, pressing spiritual questions and experience spiritual suffering or spiritual pain. Whatever the case, there is little public discourse about spirituality. Without a shared language, it is difficult to recognize others' spiritual needs or communicate about them at the end of life.

The state of medical care is another reason spirituality and spiritual care remain on the fringes. The health care literature widely documents the benefits of spiritual care, and the relationship between a person's spiritual well-being and health (Balducci, 2008; McClain, Rosenfeld, & Breitbart, 2003; Puchalski, 2002, 2006; Schenck & Roscoe, 2008; Wills, 2007, 2009). When individuals' spiritual needs are met, they will feel a sense of peace and comfort that helps minimize pain and suffering. Thanks to advances in medical technology, life expectancy has increased, and people are living longer with serious illnesses (Puchalski, 2006). Yet despite these advances, people eventually die, and medicine has few answers to this mystery of life. As a result, many clinicians and their patients are at a loss when the limits of technology are reached and death is imminent. Spirituality and addressing spiritual questions at the end of life provide a path to comfort and healing when curing what ails the body is not possible.

Communication scholars are just now beginning to understand how people communicate about spirituality and spirituality's value to health and well-being. Parrot (2004) wrote that communication scholars had "collective amnesia" about the role of spirituality and religion in health communication. She argued that "[i]ndividual predisposition to think, feel, or act based on belief in a spiritual power greater than humans affecting the course of human nature and the role of humans within that realm has far-reaching health effects" (Parrott, 2004, p. 1). A keyword search of the journal *Health Communication* indicates that, in a decade, 100 articles have been published that include some focus on spirituality and health communication, with two articles focusing on spirituality and the end of life or dying (e.g., Considine & Miller, 2010; Keeley, 2004).

There is growing interest in spirituality, how it is communicated and assessed, and how spiritual care is delivered (Ferrell & Thrane, 2011). In 2012, the John Templeton Foundation sponsored several HealthCare Chaplaincy grants to understand how chaplains assess spiritual needs ("Caring for the Human Spirit," n.d.). Physician Christina Puchalski has published widely about the need for spiritual care in health care settings, but especially at the end of life (Puchalski, 2002, 2006; see also Tullis, 2010). Communication scholars Keeley and Yingling (2007) wrote about the final conversations dying individuals had with family members and loved ones, dedicating a chapter to spiritual messages. And in 2009, the first edited text about health communication and spirituality was published, which included a chapter about communicating at the end of life (Wills, 2009). Taken together, these texts illustrate that communication about spirituality at the end of life is important for understanding not just what types of messages dying people share, but how spirituality influences attitudes about health, guides decisions about health care, and shapes beliefs about not just life, but the meaning of death and what happens after death.

In this chapter, I explore spiritualty and communication at the end of life. To accomplish this, I elaborate on the existing research and describe some of the challenges and opportunities to enhance our understanding of this topic. Throughout the chapter, I draw upon my personal and professional experiences conducting research about communication at the end of life and spiritualty in settings such as hospices, cancer centers, and hospitals. Before we go further, it is important to define spirituality, since how this concept is understood and applied directly influences what constitutes spiritual messages and spiritual care.

DEFINING SPIRITUALITY

My maternal grandmother, Evelyn, was an artist, a jewelry maker, and a teacher. She could knit, make baskets, and sew—a true craftswoman. When she was diagnosed with inflammatory breast cancer, a rare and incurable form of cancer, we knew she would not live long. Despite the unlikelihood that any treatment would eradicate my grandmother's disease, she decided to undergo experimental treatment at the cancer center in the community where she lived with my mother, her youngest daughter. Four months before Grandma Evelyn died, I traveled home to California from Florida where I was in my first year of my doctoral program. I knew the treatments were wearing on my grandmother. She was tired and sick from the treatments, and still the disease was progressing. The damage to my grandmother's body was visible, but she seemed generally upbeat. My mother, however, was more vocal about how my grandmother was coping and how she was feeling being a caregiver. During one particularly emotional conversation, my mother told me she was concerned about my grandmother's soul. "I'm worried, since she's not a Christian, that we won't see each other again." I tried to console my mother, but I really had no idea how. My mother's beliefs and my grandmother's beliefs were not in line, and they were not likely to be reconciled to my mother's satisfaction before my grandmother's death. So, during my brief visit, the three of us tried to spend time together. We spent time eating, going on drives through the rolling foothills of Northern California, and visiting my grandmother's favorite casino. I had a few articles of clothing that needed alteration so I asked my grandmother if she would fix them for me, and she happily agreed. I stood perfectly still as my grandmother carefully pinned the blouse she would take in for me. "This is when I feel most alive," she said as she placed the final pin, "when I'm creating something" (see Gubrium, this volume). This was the last time I would see my grandmother, and that conversation is still one of the most memorable to me.

I learned after the death of a mentor that it is important to give dying people a chance to live fully until they die, not to deprive them of the opportunity to do the things that make them feel most alive as long as they are capable. My grandmother was most certainly dying the day that she pinned and sewed my blouse, but she was also still living, and she was reveling in the moment. I later shared this story with my mother, hoping it would offer her some peace because perhaps recognizing that although my grandmother was not religious, she was certainly spiritual. And during the last few months of her life, my grandmother's life still had meaning and purpose—my grandmother lived a spiritual life.

Kirkwood (1994) was one of the first communication scholars to attempt to define spirituality and establish criteria for the study of communication about spirituality. He argued that without a clear definition, scholars run the risk of creating and reinforcing a spirit/matter dualism. His concern was that experiences that involve Spirit are immaterial, or mystical, and nearly impossible to convey in language. Kirkwood believed that communication scholars were well suited to study communication about spirituality, which includes music, language, imagery, rituals, traditions, and practices. Spiritual consequences of communication, or the results of spiritual messages and practices, could also be the focus of study and investigation. While Kirkwood does not specifically focus on end-of-life communication, his explications are relevant for communication at the end of life.

Although not a focus of Kirkwood's (1994) project, many scholars draw clear distinctions between spirituality and religion, associating spirituality with a search for meaning, whereas organized structures and practices constitute religion and religiosity (Egbert, Mickley, & Coeling, 2004; Hall, 1997; Hermsen & ten Have, 2004; Keeley, 2004). Wills (2007) contends that spirituality is a private matter, whereas people enact religion collectively and in public settings. More often than not, the concepts frequently inform each other rather than subsisting apart. In other words, according to Hermsen and ten Have (2004), "Religion usually expresses spirituality, but spirituality does not necessarily relate to religion" (pp. 354–355). The distinctions between spirituality and religion acknowledge that while not everyone embraces a religion, all people are spiritual and can benefit from spiritual care. It is important to note, however, that scholarly distinctions between spirituality and religion may reflect contemporary American discourse, and not necessarily mirror cultural or social practices that take place in health care settings. Therefore, communication scholars and practitioners may need to define spirituality or inquire about an individual's understanding of the term rather than assuming academic definitions are commonly held.

Embracing the distinction between spirituality and religion, Wills (2007, 2009) offered a version of spirituality relevant to health and health outcomes, one which focuses on connection, action, and hope. These concepts exist on a continuum to exemplify the strength of an individual's alignment. The continua look something like this:

Active ←-------------→ Passive
Hopeful ←----------→ Hopeless
Connection←--------→ Separation

Spirituality, Wills argues, is an active process involving a sense of hope essential for well-being, and connecting to others and/or something greater than ourselves. These components are universal across faith traditions and, therefore, offer a more comprehensive analysis of spirituality in the context of health than does Kirkwood's (1994) definition alone, yet their usefulness at the end of life is worth considering. Learning that we are dying can lead some people to feel depressed or physically or emotionally isolated. Therefore, disease progression and the dying process itself may limit an individual's ability to actively participate in spiritual practices, maintain hope, or feel a sense of connection to others. Wills's (2007, 2009) framework ultimately encourages loved ones and lay and professional caregivers to meet dying people where they are. For example, if a dying person cannot attend church, referring her to a chaplain, calling on clergy, or bringing religious symbols or imagery to her may help. Hope for a cure may no longer be possible, but hope for peace, comfort, and freedom from suffering can help. Finally, connecting with others through presence, silence, and touch may meet a person's spiritual needs when action, hope, and connection are limited or absent.

Defining spirituality is a necessary first step in recognizing, researching, or effectively communicating at the end of life. Whatever definition we might adopt, it is wise to select a definition that is broad and inclusive. It will be important for some groups to explicitly include a person's essence, soul, or spirit in a definition of spirituality, since many spiritual questions or issues involve the state of a person's soul. By focusing first on what gives a person's life meaning or purpose, we can then consider the types of communication behaviors in which they may engage and the level of commitment they bring to enact their spiritual beliefs.

SPIRITUALITY AND COMMUNICATION: THE END OF LIFE AND THE ROLE OF THE CHAPLAIN

Some people say that we begin dying as soon as we are born, but most of us do not spend our lives thinking about this fact until death is imminent. Once someone is hospitalized with a life-threatening injury or illness, or diagnosed with a terminal illness, spiritual questions become more salient. The importance of spirituality at the end of life may seem like a 21st-century trend, but, according to Fife (2011), "a new view of dying began to emerge [in the 1950s and 1960s] that took into account things such as meaning and dignity" (p. 102). Dr. Cicely Saunders, founder of the St. Christopher's Hospice in London, recognized the universality of dying people's spiritual needs, believing that the best type of care combined medical treatment (for pain and symptom control) with pastoral care (Bradshaw, 1996). Saunders's model of care is the foundation of how hospice is practiced today in the U.S. What began as a grassroots movement in communities dissatisfied with care at the end of life, having people die in hospitals, alone and in pain (Egan & Labyak, 2006), hospice now provides care to more than 1 million patients and families across more than 3,500 hospice organizations (*Hospice Facts & Statistics*, 2010).

According to Bradshaw (1996), Saunders believed "quite clear[ly] that the work of caring for the incurable and dying called for a Christian foundation" (p. 411). Yet, hospice encourages people from all belief systems, not just Christianity, to serve and receive care from hospice. Hospice, therefore, has emerged as one system of health care that integrates spiritual care (Puchalski, 2006). According to Ferrell and Thrane (2011) "[t]here is a growing attention to spirituality as an aspect of health care, due in large part to hospice as a model of whole-person care" (p. 7).

The hospice philosophy of care (see Egbert, this volume) is concerned with helping terminally ill patients and families experience a *good death*—a death free of physical and spiritual pain (Leming, 2003). The patient and her family members (as designated by the patient) make up the unit of care, and, together, they directly influence the types of support needed during the dying process for a good death. Hospices use interdisciplinary teams to care for the whole person. While all members of the team can inquire about spiritual needs and offer spiritual care, it is the responsibility of a board-certified chaplain to complete a spiritual assessment or spiritual history. These assessments begin at the time of admission and continue throughout the dying process until death; the goals for assessment include, for example, identifying spiritual and religious beliefs and patterns, the presence of spiritual pain, and struggles to find meaning (Fife, 2011). Chaplains do not seek to convert patients or family members to any particular belief system or religion. In fact, despite whatever formal theological or seminary education they have, chaplains learn during clinical pastoral education the principles of providing spiritual care to all people regardless of their beliefs. In hospice in particular, a chaplain's process involves coming alongside patients, meeting them where they are, determining their spiritual needs, and then providing appropriate interventions. These interventions include such things as facilitating life review, guided meditation and religious rituals such as prayer, offering communion, or anointing with oils. To put it more simply, if you invite a chaplain to go with you on a road trip, she or he will not try to force you to listen to country if you are a fan of hip-hop. She or he will also let you control the volume. At best, she or he may explore the boundaries of your musical knowledge by introducing you to Tupac, Yo Yo Ma, or Sia, but not much more.

Meeting individuals' spiritual needs is challenging. Diagnosing and treating physical pain are relatively easy when compared with other types of pain people experience at the end of life (Callanan & Kelley, 1992; Puchalski, 2006). Despite the difficulties lay and professional caregivers experience while trying to determine a person's spiritual beliefs and struggles, Kaut (2002) states that "the evidence of spirituality is likely to be expressed in observable attitudes, beliefs, and behaviors" (p. 226). This is an important realization for communication students and scholars because it means that communication behaviors about spirituality at the end of life are accessible. However, some patients may not know, easily identify, or understand their spiritual needs because they have never been asked. Yet others may easily articulate them to their hospice care team. Chaplains hold expertise in a variety of techniques, including question asking and listening skills, to facilitate patients and families in identifying spiritual needs.

Not only do chaplains help dying people explore spiritual questions, they are also frequently skillful communicators who can help make sense of sometimes complicated medical issues, and for this reason they are frequently responsible for coordinating and facilitating family meetings. These meetings bring together members of a patient's health care team, a patient (if possible), and her caregivers or family for a focused discussion about decision making, such as continuing or withdrawing treatment. Chaplains can serve as translators of health information, and may work to ensure that patients' and families' spiritual values are acknowledged and incorporated into a plan of care.

I witnessed a family meeting in 2013 at a small community hospital. Betty, a patient in her 80s, underwent a routine surgery and never woke up. The medical team suspected she had a stroke while under anesthesia and was now surviving with the assistance of a breathing tube. After almost 72 hours of observations and neurological testing, it was the medical team's opinion that the patient was not likely to recover, and life support should be withdrawn. The patient's husband, William, however, continued to ask for more testing. When the chaplain inquired about the case, nurses caring for the patient believed the physician who performed the surgery continued encouraging William to ask for more tests even though Betty was not improving. The chaplain called a family meeting with all four of the physicians who were caring for Betty, two of her nurses, William, and his family. During the family meeting, the members of the care team gave their medical assessment, and the chaplain inquired about Betty's wishes.

"What would Betty want?" the chaplain asked. William paused. He was finally beginning to connect the dots and was devastated. He and Betty had been together for more than 60 years. "How long can she stay like that?" William asked. "I want her to stay here [alive] for as long as possible." William put his hands over his face and began crying. After just a few moments, William raised his head, "But I know she wouldn't want to be like that...hooked up to machines." During the family meeting, William came to the conclusion that keeping Betty connected to life support was not consistent with her spirituality or quality of life. He agreed to have the breathing tube removed and allow her to die naturally. Following the family meeting, the chaplain gathered the family and members of the care team in Betty's room for prayer. The intervention of the chaplain created an opportunity for this important discussion during a family meeting. Betty died the next day.

The chaplain was instrumental in Betty's and William's care because she focused on the goals for both the physical and spiritual care needs of the patient. Although there are times when people are hospitalized with the knowledge they are dying, spirituality and end-of-life communication in a hospital setting, as this scenario reveals, frequently involve decisions about discontinuing treatment that will lead to death. With more and more palliative care (pain and symptom management for the chronically and terminally ill) teams emerging in acute care settings such as hospitals, there is more and more emphasis on caring for the whole person with acute and chronic conditions (for more on communication and palliative care, see Ragan, Wittenberg-Lyles, Goldsmith, & Reilly, 2008).

Chaplains, however, are frequently underutilized despite their abilities to facilitate communication and care for dying people's spiritual needs. In many cases, a lack of education about what chaplains do and reluctance to raise spiritual issues keep health care providers from referring their patients (Ferrell & Thrane, 2011). Chaplains are often wrongly understood as only serving people who are highly religious and Christian. In other instances, chaplains are only called upon when a patient is perceived as experiencing religious, rather than spiritual, issues (Tullis, 2009). How patients and caregivers define spirituality, whether or not they foreground religion, also influences spiritual care. For example, during a yearlong study with a hospice, Tullis (2009) observed that hospice team members' definitions of spirituality frequently focused on the conception of a supreme being and patients' relationships with God. This significantly limited the scope of what constitutes spirituality and thus spiritual pain. The spiritual issues people described when narrating their lives, including topics such as giving up a child for adoption, drug use, addiction, and sexual abuse, did not involve God or a supreme being.

Questions about God may arise when talking with people who are dying, but chaplains are aware that spiritual issues often involve material, emotional, or philosophical concerns, not theological ones. Chaplains then are concerned with the caring for, and honoring of, a person's essence and those aspects of a person's sense of self that ensure dignity. This should be a concern for all of us who may find ourselves communicating with a person facing the end of life. Ferrell and Thrane (2011) observe:

Spiritual care can involve a compassionate presence, a caring touch, a prayer if requested, or participating in a religious ceremony. Spiritual care can be a sharing of the self. Spiritual healing can result from being fully present for the patient, connecting with the patient on a level of deep respect for him or her as a human being. Spiritual care can also take place without direct intervention. (p. 11)

Communicating with a person at the end of life, then, is spiritual care. How people communicate about spirituality at the end of life may not involve God or concerns about heaven or hell. Sometimes spirituality includes what we perceive are the mundane aspects of life, and there is indeed magic in the mundane (Foster, 2006).

STRATEGIES FOR FOSTERING SPIRITUAL COMMUNICATION

Communicating about spirituality at the end of life might be easy for chaplains and others who have a lot of experience spending time with the dying, but many people experience anxiety at the mere prospect of communicating with someone who is terminally ill (Servaty & Hayslip, 1996). They may also feel unprepared to communicate (Ellis, 1995; Miller & Knapp, 1986). Most do not know what to say and avoid conversations with the dying for fear of saying the wrong thing. Miller and Knapp (1986) outlined three strategies used by caregivers when communicating with the dying: avoidance, confrontation, and reacting.

In the first strategy, avoidance, people would evade talking about dying or death by trying to bolster a dying person's spirits. Being upbeat, talking about current events, and recounting memories from the past are all examples of avoidance strategies. The second, confrontation strategy, involves offering platitudes, such as "It's all part of God's plan," or definitive statements such as "Everyone must die," or more demonstrative displays, such as openly crying in front of a dying family member or friend. Finally, the reacting strategy involves being more reflexive than the other two approaches, and includes such practices as asking open-ended questions and mirroring emotions. The latter is ideal for communicating about spirituality at the end of life.

In addition to outlining these strategies, Miller and Knapp (1986) interviewed professional caregivers, specifically chaplains and hospice volunteers, about their experiences communicating with terminally ill people. Through retrospective self-reports, these caregivers offered examples of what Miller and Knapp (1986) called *wrong behaviors*, as well as advice for effective communication with the dying. Poor timing, offering false hope, platitudes, and withholding feelings were some of the examples of wrong behavior. Advice included such suggestions as listening more and talking less, showing emotional commitment, and not worrying about saying the wrong thing.

Miller and Knapp (1986) and others (Foster, 2006; Keeley, 2004; Keeley & Yingling, 2007; Toller, 2005; Zhang & Siminoff, 2003) draw attention to the need to move past our fears of saying the wrong thing. I would argue the same is true for communicating about spirituality. Not only does avoiding such conversations harm people who are dying, but it also hurts the people who love them. Zhang and Siminoff (2003) found that people who fail to talk about cancer reported higher levels of stress, while those family members (about 15%) who spoke openly about illness reported less tension. The health benefits of candidly communicating may sound appealing, but the question remains: How do we get over our trepidation?

I encourage my students and health professionals to be open, to practice flexibility, to look for a wide range of cues about needs, and never to assume that there is one right way to communicate about spirituality at the end of life. However, I also do have some specific suggestions for promoting conversations about these powerful and sometimes emotional topics:

1. *Just ask.*

A good open-ended question can promote conversation: What is most important to you today? Which is more important to you, quality of life or quantity of life, and why? Would you want to be on life support? Why or why not? What do you believe is the meaning of life? What do you think happens after we die? How do you want to die and who would you want to be there? These are all good questions for initiating conversations about spirituality. Communicators who are interested in initiating conversations about spiritual beliefs should consider a few things, however, before delving into the subject of spirituality. First, consider your motives and goals for starting the conversation. If you're responsible for assessing and providing spiritual care, some of the direct questions may be appropriate. In other instances, it might be helpful to preface questions by indicating your own interest or questions about spiritual topics. Second, consider the relationship you have with the person you're communicating with. Several of the questions above are suitable for family members and loved ones, but perhaps not strangers. Third, be mindful of the context or setting. In the midst of a crisis or emergency may not be the best time to pursue a philosophical discussion about spiritual beliefs.

2. *Use others as examples.*

Talking about dying raises concerns about our own mortality and talking about spirituality is, for some people, too intimate or taboo; therefore, another effective strategy is to talk about someone else's choices, personal values, or beliefs or focus on a story that is featured in the media. For example, physician and ethicist Ezekiel Emanuel (2014) wrote an essay for *The Atlantic* explaining why he would like to die at age 75. Nationally known cases about the right-to-die movement involving Terri Schiavo[1] or Death With Dignity laws in states such as Oregon can serve as catalysts for conversations about attitudes, values, and wishes for care at the end of life as well. Through these discussions we can not only sort out our own beliefs, but also gain a better understanding of our loved ones' and friends' spirituality.

3. *Understand your own spiritual beliefs.*
I often tell my students that providing spiritual care is not about changing someone's mind or having our minds changed. If you do not know where you stand, it is much easier to have your own weak foundation shifted when faced with beliefs that are different from your own. The next suggestion can help.

4. *Attend a death-related event.*
This is a perfect time to attend a death-related event. All around the globe people are offering death programming, such as Death Café, Death Salon, or Death Over Dinner.[2] Or host one of these events yourself. You will have an opportunity to hear about other people's beliefs while communicating about your own.

5. *Practice.*
Practice having these conversations when there is no pressure, when there is no health crisis looming. The more we talk about the end of life and spirituality in our day-to-day lives, the easier it is to communicate about these issues when death is imminent.

6. *Don't shush.*
Consider, for example, a 90-year-old grandmother who says, "Look around the house and tell me what you want. Put your name on it." "Oh, Grandma!" The granddaughter replies. "We don't need to do that now. You're going to live a long time." Or the 86-year-old father who wants to tell his son that he does not want life-prolonging measures and what kind of funeral he would like, but his son changes the subject. In both of these instances, the grandmother and father are in good health, but of advanced age and by definition at the end of their lives. It might be important for this grandmother to see her granddaughter enjoy the well-worn mixing bowls that have been in the family for decades. Perhaps having an advance directive and funeral plan in place may provide peace for the father and, eventually, the son. But, in both instances, their loved ones have shushed them, shutting down the conversation, which is of no help to anyone. Feeling uncomfortable for a few minutes will pass, and the knowledge we can gain is significant.

7. *When in doubt, ask. Then listen.*
Too often, we think we have to know what people want and need or we wrongly assume that what we want is universal. The Golden Rule just does not always apply. Dying people and the dying experience can vary greatly, making it impossible to anticipate everyone's spiritual needs all the time. So just ask. Let a person who is facing the end of life teach you about his spirituality and how he would like to communicate. Then listen. During one of my hospice training sessions, one of facilitators would say, "God gave you one mouth and two ears for a reason." Listening may be our greatest, yet most undervalued and underused, communication skill for communicating about spirituality at the end of life.

THE FUTURE OF SPIRITUALITY AT THE END OF LIFE

Researchers and scholars can contribute a great deal to the ongoing discourse in important ways. There are at least four contexts in which more research into spirituality at the end of life would benefit our understanding of the topic. First, interpersonal and family communication scholars should consider research at the dyad and family levels. Such research would provide us with a better understanding of how attitudes, values, and beliefs about spirituality develop. Longitudinal research about how dyads and in families would be helpful to understanding how spiritual beliefs evolve through the life course. Second, understanding how health care professionals are trained could prove a particularly fruitful area of study. Given what we know about how medical professionals are trained to communicate about the end of life (from diagnosis of a serious illness to death), it makes sense to consider the type of training, if any, health care professionals receive to prepare them to address spiritual issues at this time in life. Communication scholars would be well suited not merely to study communication but also to develop communication-centered training programs. Third, in addition to the work sponsored by the John Templeton Foundation referenced earlier, more research is necessary to understand and quantify communication about spirituality at the end of life in such settings as cancer centers and hospitals where individuals and their families may first learn of a terminal diagnosis, and settings where the end of life is more obvious, such as nursing homes and hospices. Not only would these studies help determine which elements of spirituality are generalizable, but such research could also lead to empirically based assessment tools and interventions. Moreover, the difference in communication across acute and long-term care settings may provide new insight into spiritual care at different stages of disease progression and life stages. Descriptive studies that identify who initiates talk about spirituality, and the content of those conversations, can lead to the development of research questions and hypotheses that can help scholars develop better interventions that can be initiated sooner. Fourth, while the origins of spiritual beliefs are likely to begin in the home, it is worth considering the public messages in religious institutions and the media which may enable or constrain communication about spirituality. More specifically, I can envision studies focusing on outlining a macro-level, or big picture, view of spirituality, asking individuals from a range of demographics to articulate their beliefs before and during a health crisis. Such research could also help improve our definitions of spirituality, making them more person centered while increasing our understanding of how spirituality evolves as the end of life approaches. Another research question could focus on the link between spirituality and a *good death*, one free of physical and spiritual pain.

Research in these areas will lend itself to the development of a theory of communication about spirituality at the end of life. The great challenges facing theory development are the vast differences among people and across cultures. Yet, scholars and health professionals clearly believe in the importance of spirituality at the end of life and that it is worth pursuing empirical study further. Therefore, more research about the presence or absence of spirituality at the end of life, its influence on the dying experience, and the effectiveness of interventions are necessary before we can develop any theories that explain this phenomenon.

Although not universal or used consistently, tools for use by clinicians and chaplains do exist to capture and identify spiritual needs. Forms such as advance directives and living wills, and designating a health care power of attorney exist to help ensure that individuals' health care wishes are honored, but there are no such tools designed for individuals that would help guarantee their spiritual needs are honored. A Spiritual Care Statement would allow an individual to articulate her most closely held beliefs in writing. Like advance directives, a Spiritual Care Statement could be included as part of a person's advance care plan and shared with loved ones and other care providers. And like an advance directive, a Spiritual Care Statement could be updated as desires for spiritual care shift and used to facilitate dialogue about spiritual beliefs before a crisis arises or referenced to help make decisions about spiritual care when a person is unable to communicate.

CONCLUSION

Life in its passing is a sacred thing, never to be repeated.

(Author unknown)

Serious illness, aging, dying, and death raise existential and spiritual questions and concerns. Yet "[d]ying people are not listened to—their wishes, their dreams, their fears go unheeded. They want to share those with us" (Puchalski, 2002, p. 289). Perhaps I am unusual, but I have dedicated a portion of my life to seeking out people who are dying. What I have come to learn as a researcher and hospice volunteer is that these issues do not go away if we avoid them. In fact, they can increase our loved one's suffering as well as our own (Kaut, 2002; Puchalski, 2006). Communication may not be the panacea because the challenges at the end of life are vast, involving many people, many institutions, and many structures that will take time to change. Yet, in response, I have suggested potential areas of research and provided several strategies for encouraging communication about spirituality and overcoming some of the unease we may experience when faced with the end of another's life.

Taking the time to be present at the end of a person's life is profound and sacred, some say it is a gift, and recognizing this sacredness is essential for effective communication about spirituality at the end of life. Effective communication does not require a perfectly phrased message, delivered at the "right" time. Appropriate and effective communication is about showing up and asking about what is most important today. And, at times, the best communication does not involve words at all. Whether the messages are verbal or nonverbal, we can capture the wisdom or the insights dying people have to offer only if we take Kübler-Ross's (1969) advice to sit and listen.

NOTES

1. Terri Schiavo collapsed at the age of 26. As a result, her brain was deprived of oxygen, which left her in a persistent vegetative state. For the next 15 years, her husband and parents fought over whether to withdraw her life support. The case drew protests outside of the hospice where Schiavo resided as well as national media attention. A Florida state court eventually sided with Schiavo's husband and ordered her feeding tube removed; she died shortly thereafter (Haberman, 2014).
2. Death Café (http://deathcafe.com) is a movement that started in Europe and consists of informal gatherings held to talk about death. Death Salon (www.deathsalon.org) is best described as a conference, focusing on a range of death-related topics. Death Over Dinner (www.death overdinner.org) is designed for participants to discuss death while having a meal. Some of these sessions conclude with completing legal documents, such as advance directives.

REFERENCES

Balducci, L. (2008). And a time to die. *Journal of Medicine and the Person, 6*, 99–103.

Bradshaw, A. (1996). The spiritual dimension of hospice: The secularization of an ideal. *Social Science Medicine, 43*, 409–419.

Callanan, M., & Kelley, P. (1992). *Final gifts: Understanding the special awareness, needs, and communications of the dying.* New York, NY: Bantam Books.

Caring for the human spirit. (n.d.). Retrieved September 26, 2014, from http://www.healthcarechaplaincy.org/templeton-research.html

Considine, J., & Miller, K. (2010). The dialectics of care: Communicative choices at the end of life. *Health Communication, 25*(2), 165–174.

Egan, K. A., & Labyak, M. J. (2006). Hospice palliative care: A model for quality end-of-life care. In B. R. F. N. Coyle (Ed.), *Oxford textbook of palliative nursing* (2nd ed., pp. 1–57). New York, NY: Oxford University Press.

Egbert, N., Mickley, J., & Coeling, H. (2004). A review and application of social scientific measures of religiosity and spirituality: Assessing a missing component in health communication research. *Health Communication, 16*, 7–27.

Ellis, C. (1995). Speaking of dying: An ethnographic short story. *Symbolic Interaction, 18*, 73–82.

Emanuel, E. J. (2014, September). Why I hope to die at 75. *The Atlantic.* Retrieved from http://www.theatlantic.com/features/archive/2014/09/why-i-hope-to-die-at-75/379329/

Ferrell, B., & Thrane, S. (2011). Spirituality, religion, and end-of-life care In K. J. Doka & A. S. Tucci (Eds.), *Spirituality and end-of-life care* (pp. 7–15). Washington, DC: Hospice Foundation of America.

Fife, R. B. (2011). Spiritual care: An organizational perspective. In K. J. Doka & A. S. Tucci (Eds.), *Spirituality and end-of-life care* (pp. 101–113). Washington, DC: Hospice Foundation of America.

Foster, E. (2006). *Communicating at the end of life: Finding magic in the mundane.* Mahwah, NJ: Lawrence Erlbaum.

Haberman, C. (2014, April 21). From private ordeal to national fight: The case of Terri Schiavo. *The New York Times.* Retrieved from http://www.nytimes.com/2014/04/21/us/from-private-ordeal-to-national-fight-the-case-of-terri-schiavo.html?_r=0

Hall, S. E. (1997). Spiritual diversity: A challenge for hospice chaplains. *American Journal of Hospice and Palliative Care, 14,* 221–223.

Hermsen, M. A., & ten Have, H. A. M. J. (2004). Pastoral care, spirituality, and religion in palliative care journals. *American Journal of Hospice and Palliative Medicine, 21,* 353–356.

Hospice facts & statistics. (2010). Washington, DC: Hospice Association of America. Retrieved from http://www.nahc.org/assets/1/7/HospiceStats10.pdf

Kaut, K. P. (2002). Religion, spirituality, and existentialism near the end of life. *American Behavioral Scientist, 46,* 220–234.

Keeley, M. P. (2004). Final conversations: Survivors' memorable messages concerning religious faith and spirituality. *Health Communication, 16*(1), 87–104.

Keeley, M. P., & Yingling, J. M. (2007). *Final conversations: Helping the living and the dying talk to each other.* Acton, MA: VanderWyk & Burnham.

Kirkwood, W. G. (1994). Studying communication about spirituality and the spiritual consequences of communication. *Journal of Communication & Religion, 17*(1), 13–26.

Kübler-Ross, E. (1969). *On death and dying.* New York, NY: Macmillan.

Leming, M. R. (2003). The history of the hospice approach. In C. D. Bryan (Ed.), *Handbook of death and dying* (Vol. 2, pp. 485–494). Thousand Oaks, CA: Sage.

McClain, C. S., Rosenfeld, B., & Breitbart, W. (2003). Effect of spiritual well-being on end-of-life despair in terminally ill cancer patients. *The Lancet, 361,* 1603–1607.

Miller, V. D., & Knapp, M. L. (1986). The Post-Nuntio dilemma: Approaches to communicating with the dying. In M. L. McLaughlin (Ed.), *Communication Yearbook 9.* Thousand Oaks, CA: Sage.

Parrott, R. (2004). "Collective amnesia": The absence of religious faith and spirituality in health communication research and practice. *Health Communication, 16*(1), 1–5.

Puchalski, C. M. (2002). Spirituality and end-of-life care: A time for listening and caring. *Journal of Palliative Medicine, 5*(2), 289–294.

Puchalski, C. M. (2006). *A time for listening and caring.* New York, NY: Oxford University Press.

Ragan, S. L., Wittenberg-Lyles, E. M., Goldsmith, J., & Reilly, S. S. (2008). *Communication as comfort: Multiple voices in palliative care.* New York, NY: Routledge.

Schenck, D. P., & Roscoe, L. A. (2008). In search of a good death. *Journal of Medical Humanities, 30,* 61–72.

Servaty, H. L., & Hayslip, B. (1996). Death education and communication apprehension regarding dying persons. *Omega: Journal of Death and Dying, 34,* 139–148.

Toller, P. W. (2005). Negotiation of dialectical contradictions by parents who have experienced the death of a child. *Journal of Applied Communication Research, 33,* 36–66.

Tullis, J. A. (2009). *Communicating spirituality, dying and a "good death" at the end-of-life: The role of hospice interdisciplinary team members* (Unpublished doctoral dissertation). University of South Florida, Tampa, FL.

Tullis, J. A. (2010). Bring about benefit, forestall harm: What communication studies say about spirituality and cancer care. *Asian Pacific Journal of Cancer Prevention, 11* (Suppl. 1), 67–73.

Wills, M. (2007). Connection, action, and hope: An invitation to reclaim the "spiritual" in health care. *Journal of Religion and Health, 46*, 423–436.

Wills, M. (2009). *Communicating spirituality in health care.* Cresskill, NJ: Hampton Press.

Zhang, A. Y., & Siminoff, L. A. (2003). Silence and cancer: Why do families and patients fail to communicate? *Health Communication, 15*, 415–430.

CHAPTER FIVE

Mass Media Depictions OF THE Dying Process

JAMES D. ROBINSON

Perhaps the single most powerful example of the role the media plays in public perceptions of the end-of-life experience (EOL) occurred in 2014 when Brittany Maynard documented her decision to end her life after being diagnosed with cancer. She was diagnosed with stage IV glioblastoma (GBM)—a type of brain cancer that spreads quickly, is extremely difficult to treat, and is relatively uncommon among younger adults. In the U.S., approximately 12,000 people are diagnosed with GBM annually and the median age of those who die of GBM is 71. At the time of her diagnosis and at the time of her death, Maynard was only 29 years old. Maynard moved to Oregon with her husband so that she could legally end her life under Oregon's Death With Dignity Act, but not before she documented her EOL experience in a series of YouTube videos. These videos have been watched by tens of millions of viewers. Many social critics and pundits have credited Brittany with bringing the right-to-die movement back to the forefront of the public's consciousness. While the ultimate impact of Maynard's documentary efforts are not known, a growing body of research examining media portrayals of the EOL experience has emerged. This chapter reviews that literature and discusses the implications of such portrayals on audience attitudes toward death and dying.

MEDIA PORTRAYALS

Death is a widely employed vehicle in storytelling (Walter, Littlewood, & Pickering, 1995) and nowhere is that prevalence more obvious than in the case of popular films. Schultz and Huet (2000/2001) estimate that between World War I and the end of the 20th century, more than 500 movies with the word "dead" or "deaths" in the title were released in the U.S. alone. In their analysis of 65 Academy Award–nominated and high-grossing American films, they identified 857 death-related scenes in the films—or about 7.5 death-related scenes per movie and further they suggested depictions of death and dying are often sensational and unrealistic. Similarly, children's films also employ death as an integral component of the plot and the depictions of death were often characterized as being unrealistic (Cox, Garrett, & Graham, 2005; Schultz & Huet, 2000/2001). So unrealistic, that Cox et al. (2005) note 26% of the characters that died in 10 Disney films were brought back to life or reanimated before the end of the film. The potential impact of these films should not be discounted simply because they are not a definitive picture or profile of how death is portrayed in children's films. Nonetheless, these films are extremely popular and viewed by millions of children repeatedly. Previous research suggests that children's understanding of death depends on their personal experience (actual life experience), what they have been told about death (symbolic life experience which can be gained through interpersonal interaction or vicariously through the mass media), and their level of physical and mental development. In fact, this research has shown that children do not understand that death is irreversible, permanent, and inevitable until they are about 10 years of age (Brent, Speece, Lin, Dong, & Yang, 1996; Grollman, 1990; Speece & Brent, 1984). Media portrayals that suggest death is reversible are certainly not helping children understand the EOL experience in a realistic or useful way.

Similarly, research suggests children's grief responses to death are also often unrealistic (Cox et al., 2005; Schultz & Huet, 2000/2001). Moore and Mae (1987) analyzed 49 books nominated for children's book awards that contained an identifiable central character and their grief responses to the death of another character. They identified 60 deaths in the 49 books and 88% of deaths were coded as a prominent event. Mature adults were most likely to die (43%), children were the second most likely age cohort to die (25%), and older adults were least likely to die (15%). In 83% of the cases, the death was caused by illness, accident, or murder and 60% of the books included some type of cultural expression of mourning (22 funerals, 18 burials, 4 family gatherings after a funeral, 5 mentions of cremation, and 4 actual viewings). Female characters were more likely to grieve (83%) than their male counterparts (53%) and the authors concluded that death is used for dramatic effect and is often unaccompanied by emotional reactions that children may experience. Finally, the authors suggest that factual accounts (e.g., biographies) may be better sources of information for helping children come to grips with death than fictional works.

Television news stories also frequently contain messages about death and dying. McArthur, Magaña, Peek-Asa, and Kraus (2001) examined local news programs and identified 195 traumatic death and injury stories across nine local news channels in Los Angeles. The stories aired during a three-month period and each news segment was coded using the *International Classification of Diseases.* McArthur et al. (2001) found that the most common causes of death reported in local news stories included homicides/assaults ending in death, automobile deaths, suicides, and accidental poisonings (see Tables 1 and 2). After comparing the number of accidental deaths appearing on the local news with the number of actual accidental deaths that occurred in Los Angeles during that same three-month period, they found that some types of accidents were more likely to appear as news items than others. For example, they found that every incidence of death resulting from an air disaster, fire, environmental accident (e.g., mudslide), and legal intervention ending in death (e.g., euthanasia) made the news. Further, 97.7% of all homicides and 64% of all motor vehicle deaths made the local news. While all of these deaths are tragic, homicides represent only 0.06% and automobile accidents represent only 1.33% of all deaths in the U.S. (Centers for Disease Control and Prevention [CDC], 2011). Such portrayals could certainly contribute to inaccurate impressions about causes of death.

Table 1: Death Portrayals on Los Angeles Local Television News.

Cause of Death	Actual Deaths, #	Local News Depictions, %
Motor vehicle accidents	216	63.9
Air transport accidents	3	100
Accidental poisonings	129	3.9
Falls ending in death	56	12.5
Fire deaths	14	100
Natural or environmental deaths	1	100
Submersion or drowning	26	26.9
Other types of accidents ending in death	31	6.5
Suicides & self-inflicted deaths	188	5.9
Homicides & assaults ending in death	307	97.7
Legal interventions ending in death	2	100

Note: Railway, watercraft, and non-traffic motor vehicle deaths were excluded because the numbers were too small for statistical analyses.

Table 2: Leading Causes of Death in the U.S.

Cause of Death (Rank)	Deaths Annually, #	Total Deaths, %
Heart disease (1)	596,577	23.71
Cancer (2)	576,691	22.92
Chronic lower respiratory diseases (3)	142,943	5.68
Strokes & cerebrovascular diseases (4)	128,932	5.12
Accidents (5)	126,438	5.02
Alzheimer's (6)	84,974	3.37
Diabetes (7)	73,831	2.93
Influenza & pneumonia (8)	53,826	2.13
Kidney disease (9)	45,591	1.81
Suicide (10)	39,518	1.57
Automobile accidents	33,561	1.33
Firearm deaths	31,672	1.25
Alcohol deaths	25,692	1.02
Drug overdoses	17,000	0.07
Homicides	16,259	0.06

The emphasis on accidental causes of death also occurs in fictional TV programming. Schiapa, Gregg, and Hewes (2004) identified the causes of death on 10 episodes of the very popular HBO TV series *Six Feet Under*. While the CDC (2011) estimates that nearly 47% of all deaths are actually caused by cancer and heart disease, on *Six Feet Under* 90% (9 of 10) of the deaths were caused by an accident or homicide. In addition, the causes of the accidental deaths were often quite unusual (e.g., a man is chopped to death in an industrial mixer accident and a newly divorced woman is decapitated after standing up through the sunroof of her limousine) and occurred to characters who were relatively young. The median age for deaths on *Six Feet Under* was 41; in the U.S., 70% of all individuals who die are 65 years of age and older (U.S. Census Bureau, 2012). See Table 3 for a complete list of death causes and ages of deceased characters on *Six Feet Under*.

Table 3: Deaths as Depicted in Ten Episodes of the HBO Program *Six Feet Under*.

Gender/Age	
Male (50)	Killed in a car accident when his hearse is hit by a city bus
Male (38)	Dies after diving into a swimming pool and hitting his head
Male (56)	Accidently chopped to pieces by an industrial dough mixer

Gender/Age	
Male (6)	Accidentally shoots himself playing with his mother's gun
Male (23)	Beaten to death for being gay
Male (20)	Is shot to death by a rival gang member
Female (43)	Electrocuted when cat knocks a curling iron into the bath
Female (79)	Dies in her sleep of unspecified causes
Female (41)	Has her head crushed by a cherry picker after standing up in a limousine
Female (61)	Dies after being struck in the head by a golf ball at a country club

Of course, the Schiapa et al. (2004) investigation was not a small sample content analysis of the program *Six Feet Under*. Rather, it was an experiment examining the impact of media portrayals on student attitudes toward death. The investigators asked student participants to watch episodes of the program during a five-week period and found that students reported higher levels on a fear of death measure and on the death avoidance scale after viewing the program. In addition, their levels of neutral acceptance and approach acceptance of death were lower than their unexposed student counterparts. This is an important finding, because it demonstrates that in the media even relatively low levels of exposure influenced student attitudes toward death. Further, the research corroborated the work by Niemeyer, Dingemans, and Epting (1977), who found that exposure to a short film (32 minutes) describing Nazi atrocities during World War II also produced increased levels of death anxiety. These studies by Niemeyer et al. (1977) and Schiapa et al. (2004) suggest that concern about unrealistic portrayals of death is warranted.

Of course, death is also a common story element in newspaper and magazine articles. For example, Williamson, Skiner, and Hocken (2011) found 18,482 death-oriented articles that appeared in the 10 most widely read daily newspapers in the UK during a 12-month period. Williamson et al. (2011) then compared portrayals of death with actual epidemiological data and found some illnesses were overrepresented (e.g., flu/pneumonia, breast cancer, dementia, prostate cancer, and heart failure), other illnesses were underrepresented (e.g., chronic obstructive pulmonary disease, cerebrovascular accident, and respiratory cancer), and still others appeared in news stories at a rate that is close to epidemiological expectations (e.g., ischemic heart disease and bowel cancer). Similarly, Fishman, ten Have, and Casarett (2010) examined eight widely read newspapers and five national magazines for stories about cancer. Of the 436 articles they identified, 35.1% focused on breast cancer, 14.9% focused on prostate cancer, and 20.0% discussed cancer in general. They also noted that 32.1% of the articles focused on surviving or being cured of cancer, and only 7.6% focused on individuals dying of cancer. When a specific person was identified as being a cancer patient, 78.7% survived and 21.3% died of cancer or cancer complications. For all types of cancer, the five-year survival rate is about 43% for men and 56% for women but obviously varies dramatically by type and stage of cancer at diagnosis.

Clarke and van Amerom (2008) examined media portrayals of cancer and heart disease in the 20 highest circulating English-language mass market magazines available in Canada in 2001. All 40 of the articles they analyzed focused on medical determinants of heart disease and cancer (e.g., caused by a faulty cell or organ) and all of the articles were written with the assumption that treatment and social support were available to everyone. Generally, the articles suggested that cancer and heart disease are largely preventable by avoiding unhealthy behaviors (e.g., smoking) and engaging in healthy behavior (e.g., exercise) and ignored the role social determinants play (e.g., income, education level, ethnicity, early life experiences, employment and working conditions, food accessibility and quality, housing, social services, social exclusion, or unemployment and employment security) in health. These findings are consistent with earlier research focusing on death and dying, which found that a medical perspective dominated these articles about end-of-life issues and that the social determinants identified above were largely ignored (Commers, Visser, & DeLeeuw, 2000; Westwood & Westwood, 1999).

These findings suggest that portrayals of life-threatening illnesses do not always reflect reality and that the chances of survival are often exaggerated or overly optimistic. In addition, the media tend to focus on the role that genetics and medical science play in the process and largely ignore the social determinants of health. Such portrayals, again, do not help people accurately assess their health risks or the relative effectiveness of various treatment options. In addition, the portrayals appear to vary somewhat by the racial profile of the target audience. For example, Fishman et al. (2012) compared media portrayals of end-of-life care in African American and mainstream media outlets. They examined eight newspapers and national magazines targeted at African American readers and compared them with 12 widely read newspapers and national magazines not targeted at African Americans. Their analysis yielded a total of 660 stories focusing on cancer and about 40% of those stories appeared in the African American sources. They found that reportage of adverse effects of cancer treatment was more common within African American media than in mainstream media, and that discussion of aggressive cancer treatments failing was less common in the African American media. Similarly, the stories appearing in the African American media were less likely to mention death and less likely to discuss EOL cancer care. Of course, since only seven of the 660 articles contained any discussion of EOL cancer care, differences in articles designed for different racial audiences may not indicate a meaningful difference, but they certainly point to the fact that EOL cancer care is not a common topic in either print forum.

The lack of realism that occurs in discussions of cancer survivability is also apparent in other media depictions and discussions. For example, Casarett, Fishman, MacMoran, Pickard, and Asch (2005) identified 67 characters depicted as being in a coma on daytime serial programs. These programs aired between January 1995 and May 2005 and Cassarett et al. (2005) noted that the typical "soap opera" coma lasted a median of 13 days (IQR = 7–25 days). Perhaps most important, 89% of the patients recovered fully from their coma and 86% (*n* = 47) exhibited no signs of reduced function after being in the coma and did not need therapy of any kind. Comparisons with actual patients suffering comas suggest that nontraumatic coma patients were far less likely to die on daytime serials than they were in reality, and that they were far more likely to recover fully than their real counterparts. The authors suggest that such portrayals produce unrealistic expectations for recovery and consequently may contribute to disagreements about treatment options and end-of-life decisions. Given the low actual incidence of coma, direct experience with coma patients is extremely low and increases the likelihood that such portrayals may influence audience members' attitudes and EOL decisions.

Brussel, Van Landeghem, and Cohen (2014) examined a variety of newspapers and magazines for portrayals of EOL decisions. They analyzed mainstream newspapers (3) and magazines (3), medical newspapers (2), a religious newspaper, and one magazine aimed at an older adult audience published in the Dutch-speaking part of Belgium. Within 929 articles there were 1,602 references to end-of-life decisions, and 49.3% of those references were to euthanasia. An additional 30.6% referred to palliative care decisions, and 13.7% referred to nonvoluntary euthanasia. Nonvoluntary euthanasia refers here to the administration of drugs that will decrease the time until death without explicit instruction from the patient to do so. Finally, references to physician-assisted suicide were identified in 6.4% of the articles.

In 22.2% of the articles, a specific illness was not identified and the reason for euthanasia cited was simply a "terminal illness." The most commonly identified specific illnesses discussed within the context of an end-of-life decision were Alzheimer's/dementia (15%), cancer (12.4%), and psychological diseases (11.9%). The least commonly mentioned diseases observed included heart disease (0.9%), multiple sclerosis (0.9%), neuromuscular diseases—excluding MS (2.0%), and coma (6.4%). Diseases described as nonterminal conditions represented 12.7% of the references, and disability represented 7.6%. It certainly appears that illnesses of the mind and illnesses that developed late in life are more likely to be discussed in terms of assisted suicide than chronic conditions that began earlier in life and those that do not affect the cognitive abilities of the patient. Why illnesses of the mind and illnesses that occur among older adults are a more suitable topic for articles on euthanasia is an extremely interesting question and one that needs a great deal of further investigation. At the risk of being accused of deconstructing the articles and findings, such a finding could be described as an indication of a negative relationship between the value of life and age. Again, more analysis of this issue is sorely needed.

Similarly, Daoust and Racine (2014) selected 940 articles published in high-circulation Canadian and American newspapers that contained the term "brain dead" or "brain death." Brain death is a commonly used criterion for determining when life actually ends and it is an important decision marker because the organs of a patient who has been declared brain dead can often be used to supply organs for individuals in need. Daoust and Racine (2014) found that only 3.3% of the headlines contained the term "brain death" or its variants and only 3.1% of the articles made any effort to define what the term "brain death" actually means. In 21.9% of the articles, the patient identified in the article was kept on an unspecified life support system and 10.7% of the articles mentioned that the patient was taken off life support.

Racine, Amaram, Seidler, Karczewska, and Illes (2008) identified 1,141 articles published in four newspapers that focused on the Schiavo case. They found that 56% of the articles were published during 2005 (the year that Schiavo was removed from life support), and only two articles were published before 2000. Keep in mind that Schiavo was diagnosed as being in a persistent vegetative state in 1990. Within the newspaper articles, Schiavo's neurologic condition/diagnosis was most commonly referred to as a "persistent vegetative state," "brain damage," "vegetative state," "severe brain damage," and "coma." The most common description of Shaivo's behavioral abilities was that "she responds" or "she reacts," which is inconsistent with a diagnosis of persistent vegetative state. In addition, articles suggested Schaivo "smiles" and "laughs," which were actually reflexive behaviors but were often used to connote meaningful and/or purposive behavior. In fact, 21% of the articles suggested that Schiavo might improve, and an additional 7% indicated she might recover. Conversely, 13% of the articles suggested that her condition would not improve, and 13% indicated that she would not recover. Schiavo ultimately died on March 31, 2005. During the autopsy, it was determined that her brain weighed only about half as much as expected for a woman of her age and body size at the time of her death and is a clear indication that she would not have improved or recovered. Again, such media attention can lead to misunderstandings about the likelihood of recovery and do little to help if terms such as "brain death" are defined in only 3.1% of the articles (Daoust & Racine, 2014).

The CDC (2011) reported that in 2010 more than 2.5 million people died in the U.S. and about 70% of those deaths occurred among individuals 65 years of age and older and 80% of all deaths occurred within a hospital or other such health care facility. The public's attitudes about nursing homes are generally less than favorable, with only 25% of Americans surveyed rating nursing home operators highly in being honest and/or ethical and only 33% believing nursing homes are doing a good job (Jones, 2010; Kaiser Family Foundation, 2001, 2005, 2007). In fact, in a recent survey of opinion leaders within the long-term health care industry, more than 50% reported that the quality of care in the average nursing home was no better than fair or poor. Perceptions of nursing homes can come from direct experience, but in two recent surveys 25% of the adults indicated they gained their knowledge about nursing homes from what they heard or saw in the mass media (Kaiser Family Foundation, 2001, 2005). In addition, 60% of all adults report being exposed to one or more media accounts of nursing homes annually (Kaiser Family Foundation, 2001) and 80% report that they have learned about nursing homes from the media at some point. This suggests media portrayals of nursing homes are sources of information that figure in the belief structure of the public.

Research on media portrayals of nursing homes is often traced back to Smith's (1981) examination of portrayals in the *New York Times*. Analyzing stories from 1956 to 1978, Smith concluded that the increase in story frequency was attributable to criminal activities occurring within the facilities. More recently, Ulsperger (2002) examined stories focusing on nursing home reform in six U.S. newspapers and found that between 1987 and 1992 the stories focused on resident-specific issues such as patient abuse and restraint use. Ulsperger (2002) also noted that between 1995 and 1999 there was a change in article focus. During that time, the articles tended to focus on institutional issues (e.g., billing and staffing). Most recently, Miller, Tyler, Rozanova, and Mor (2012) examined portrayals of nursing homes in the *New York Times*, *Washington Post*, *Chicago Tribune*, and *Los Angeles Times*. Specifically, they analyzed 1,704 stories that appeared between 1999 and 2008 and found that the number of stories focused on nursing homes varied dramatically. For example, 45.7% of the articles appeared in 1999, 2000, and 2005. Nearly 90% were news stories (89.8%) and focused on government (42.3%) or industry (39.2%) issues. Only 13.3% focused on residents and/or their families and only 5.3% addressed community issues. The tone of most articles was negative (45.1%) or neutral (37.0%) and the most commonly addressed issues were quality of care (57.0%), economic or financing concerns (33.4%), and negligence or fraud in the industry (28.1%). Given the small number of positively valenced (9.6%) or mixed valence stories (8.3%), it is no wonder Miller et al. conclude that such negative portrayals contribute to the public's negative view of nursing homes and the people who live and work in them. They further contend that media reports such as these put nursing homes at a competitive disadvantage in the marketplace and may negatively affect health delivery reform. These findings are consistent with the research by Frick, Rehm, and Eichhammer (2002), who concluded that many of the claims in newspapers were exaggerated.

While what constitutes a good death can vary from culture to culture (see Gubrium, this volume), the archetypal bad death is that of an individual dying alone. This reduction in ability to control the environment and the inability to participate in the construction or the reconstruction of a life history means dying is little more than the end of the line. In this model of dying, the individual has no last chance to give life coherence and meaning to self or to others. These individuals are not dying in their own chosen way; instead, they are simply being buffeted by environmental and biological forces and under the local control of health care providers.

The term "revivalist death" (Walter, 1994) is used in cases in which the terminally ill individual has chosen the way to deal with his or her own death. Good or revivalist deaths are often described as confessional and those experiencing them describe their lives as having a heroic life trajectory. In these confessionals, life is dissected into heroic activities and discussions of those life events, and the terminally ill person is described as fighting valiantly with his or her illness. The individual must come to grips with and face impending death and ultimately accept death. During this process, those terminally ill individuals may reconcile themselves with loved ones or even rewrite their life story. In short, in a good death the dying person takes charge and constructs her identity and defines how her life should be viewed by others. Conversely, in a bad death, the individual has no control or decision-making capacity, no opportunity to recap his life and goes through the process alone.

Based on the notion of bad death portrayals, Seale (2004) examined newspaper accounts of people who died alone. The sample contained 90 articles appearing between October 1 and 7, 1999, in national and local newspapers published in English. Specifically, the newspapers were published in the following countries: U.S. (n = 48), UK (n = 29), Canada (n = 7), Ireland (n = 3), New Zealand (n = 1), and Thailand (n = 1). Within these 90 stories, 38 identified a specific individual who died alone. Four of the stories referred to multiple individuals who died alone, and 12 stories reported about individuals who nearly died alone but were somehow saved. Five stories focused on issues and problems surrounding people who die alone—without specific references to individuals who actually died alone. Twelve stories contained references to fears about dying alone as a noncentral component of the story, five stories contained concerns about palliative care professionals stating people should not have to die alone, and two stories were about animals/pets that died alone.

The largest category of individuals dying alone was identified as elderly (n = 14). Five additional stories were about drug abusers dying alone, and four were about people dying alone in distant places while traveling. Finally, three of the stories were about children who died alone and either explicitly or implicitly suggested parental neglect. In most stories, the cause of death was not identified, but in the cases in which cause of death was known they occurred in the following frequencies: murder (n = 4), drug overdose (n = 4), suicide (n = 3), accident (n = 2), heat wave (n = 2), trapped in a hot car (n = 2), heart attack (n = 2), natural causes (n = 1), alcohol poisoning (n = 1), carbon monoxide poisoning (n = 1), house fire (n = 1), and hypothermia (n = 1). Again, we see that the most deaths are caused by accidents and caused by unusual or sensational circumstances. While these stories are not consistent with what we might describe as a typical death, clearly the goal of the newspaper or other media outlet is not necessarily to reflect normative distributions of events in their editorial policies. For the newspaper reader, however, these depictions of the EOL experience for older adults are disturbing, particularly accurate, and may contribute to misperceptions and negative attitudes toward aging and death.

Seale (2004) suggests as much—pointing out that most of the deaths were attributable to human agency and not illness. This is consistent with the event bias so prevalent in the media—that is to say, newspapers tend to report events because they are new and therefore news and less inclined to report chronic problems—until there is an event that precipitates such reportage. Those individuals who died alone were often described as reclusive eccentrics. The elderly in particular were characterized as being self-neglecting—unable or unwilling to take care of themselves (Seale, 2004). Further, individuals dying alone were also described as suffering from mental illness or alcohol dependence or were unable to form adequate relationships with other people. Finally, those deaths that occurred in health care institutions were often described as the result of negligence and, by implication, a failure of society.

In one of the few studies examining EOL portrayals in films, Ristovski-Slijepcevic (2013) describes the good deaths of four mothers diagnosed and ultimately dying of cancer. In these four very popular and successful films (*Sunshine*, 1973, *Terms of Endearment*, 1983, *Stepmom*, 1998, and *My Life Without Me*, 2003), she describes these women as good mothers dying a good death. Their EOL experience occurs throughout most or all of the film, and this allows them to explain themselves and their lives as well as communicate love and concern for their families. In addition, these mothers are not passively at the mercy of their health care provider because they are depicted as competent human beings and completely capable of making EOL decisions right up to the end (see Pecchioni and White, this volume). While these portrayals are certainly not as negative as those identified by Seale (2004), they come close to ignoring the disabilities associated with the illness. With the notable exception of my mother, few people handle their lives with that kind of grace and dignity in times of good health—let alone while being ravaged by cancer.

CONCLUSIONS

As can be noted from the foregoing, only a small body of research has focused on EOL portrayals in the media. Generally, the research suggests that the media tend to focus on relatively rare and novel illnesses more so than on illnesses that actually present a higher risk to audience members. In addition, newscasts are more likely to employ sensational and alarming messages than reassuring or neutral descriptions of illness. The literature also suggests that death is a common story element in popular films, newspaper stories, magazine articles, daytime serial TV programming, local news, prime-time fictional programming, children's films, and books and it suggests portrayals of death are often unrealistic. While 70% of all deaths in the U.S. occur among adults 65 years of age and older, younger adult characters are far more common and far more likely to die than their older counterparts. In addition, this research suggests that portrayals of death are unrealistic and most often caused by accidents. In the media, few deaths occur in hospitals or nursing homes or after a prolonged illness, and the grief responses to character deaths are also characterized as being unrealistic. Similarly, patients are far more likely to live in news stories and in fictional stories than epidemiological tables would suggest, and news stories often exaggerate the availability of treatments and treatment options and overemphasize the effectiveness of medical treatments. These same news stories also intimate that social support is generally available to everyone and that many illnesses can be avoided by avoiding unhealthy behaviors such as smoking. Yet these same stories often completely ignore the role that social determinants, such as poverty, play in health. Stories about nursing homes are generally negative and often focus on issues such as staffing, costs, patient care/neglect, and fraud. Given that so many people report learning about nursing home care from the mass media, it is no wonder that public attitudes toward nursing homes are less than positive—an attitude that holds true within the nursing home industry.

This research suggests that relatively low levels of exposure to media portrayals of death can affect audience attitudes toward death and dying (Niemeyer, Dingemans, & Epting, 1977; Schiapa et al., 2004) and that emotional responses to media portrayals can motivate health information–seeking behavior. Myrick, Willoughby, Noar, and Brown (2013) suggest that 93% of the 401 college students surveyed recognized that Apple CEO Steve Jobs died of pancreatic cancer and 66.6% of those students reported searching out information about his death. Not surprisingly, 97% used the Internet to find such information and 50% reported using social media to learn more about Job's death and/or pancreatic cancer. The authors suggest that it was not identification with the CEO Jobs that motivated their interest but rather their emotional response to his death. This of course suggests that research examining the impact of EOL portrayals on audience attitudes toward death and dying is sorely needed, as is research on palliative or EOL care—which goes largely unexamined within the literature.

REFERENCES

Brent, S. B., Speece, M. W., Lin, C., Dong, Q., & Yang, C. (1996). The development of the concept of death among Chinese and U.S. children 3–17 years of age: From binary to "fuzzy" concepts? *Omega: Journal of Death and Dying, 33*, 67–83.

Brussel, L., Van Landeghem, P., & Cohen, J. (2014). Media coverage of medical decision making at the end of life: A Belgian case study. *Death Studies, 38*, 125–135.

Casarett, D., Fishman, J., MacMoran, H., Pickard, A., & Asch, D. (2005). Epidemiology and prognosis of coma in daytime television dramas. *British Medical Journal, 331*, 1537–1539.

Centers for Disease Control and Prevention. (2011). Deaths and mortality. Retrieved from http://www.cdc.gov/nchs/fastats/deaths.htm

Clarke, J., & van Amerom, G. (2008). Mass print media depictions of cancer and heart disease: Community versus individualistic perspectives? *Health and Social Care in the Community, 16*, 96–103.

Commers, M., Visser, G., & DeLeeuw, E. (2000). Representations of preconditions for and determinants of health in the Dutch press. *Health Promotion International, 15*, 321–332.

Cox, M., Garrett, E., & Graham, J. (2005). Death in Disney films: Implications for children's understanding of death. *Omega: Journal of Death and Dying, 50*, 267–280.

Daoust, A., & Racine, E. (2014). Depictions of "brain death" in the media: Medical and ethical implications. *Journal of Medical Ethics, 40*, 253–259.

Fishman, J., ten Have, T., & Casarett, D. (2010). Cancer and the media: How does the news report on treatment and outcomes? *Archives of Internal Medicine, 170*, 515–518.

Fishman, J., ten Have, T., & Casarett, D. (2012). Is public communication about end-of-life care helping to inform all? Cancer news coverage in African American versus mainstream media. *Cancer, 118*, 2157–2162.

Frick, U., Rehm, J., & Eichhammer, P. (2002). Risk perception, somatization, and self-report of complaints related to electromagnetic fields: A randomized survey study. *International Journal of Hygiene and Environmental Health, 205*, 353–360.

Grollman, E. A. (1990). *Talking about death: A dialogue between parent and child* (3rd ed.). Boston, MA: Beacon Press.

Jones, J. M. (2010). *Nurses top honesty and ethics list for 11th year.* Princeton, NJ: Gallup. Retrieved from http://www. gallup.com/poll/145043/Nurses-Top-Honesty-Ethics-List-ll-Year.aspx

Kaiser Family Foundation. (2001). *National survey on nursing homes.* Retrieved from http://www.pbs.org/newshour/health/ nursing homes/highlightsandchartpack.pdf

Kaiser Family Foundation. (2005). *May /June 2005 health poll report survey.* Retrieved from http://www.kff.org/kaiserpolls/upload/ May-June-2005-Kaiser-Health-Poll-Report-Toplines.pdf

Kaiser Family Foundation. (2007). Update on the public's views of nursing homes and long-term care services. Retrieved from http://www.kff.org/kaiserpolls/upload/77 1 9.pdf

Maynard, B. (2014). The Brittany Maynard Fund. Retrieved from https://www.youtube.com/watch?v=yPfe3rCcUeQ&feature=iv&src_vid=1lHXH0Zb2QI&annotation_id=annotation_1855568639

McArthur, D., Magaña, D., Peek-Asa, C., & Kraus, J. (2001). Local television news coverage of traumatic deaths and injuries. *Western Journal of Medicine, 175*, 380–384.

Miller, E., Tyler, D., Rozanova, J., & Mor, V. (2012). National newspaper portrayal of U.S. nursing homes: Periodic treatment of topic and tone. *The Milbank Quarterly, 90*, 725–761.

Moore, T., & Mae, R. (1987). Who dies and who cries: Death and bereavement in children's literature. *Journal of Communication, 37*, 52–64.

Myrick, J., Willoughby, J., Noar, S., & Brown, J. (2013). Reactions of young adults to the death of Apple CEO Steve Jobs: Implications for cancer communication. *Communication Research Reports, 30*, 115–126.

Niemeyer, R. A., Dingemans, P. M., & Epting, F. R. (1977). Convergent validity, situational stability and meaningfulness of the Threat Index. *Omega: Journal of Death and Dying, 8*, 251–265.

PLOS Medicine Editors. (2008). False hopes, unwarranted fears: The trouble with medical news stories. *PLOS Medicine, 5*, 681–683.

Racine, E., Amaram, R., Seidler, M., Karczewska, M., & Illes, J. (2008). Media coverage of the persistent vegetative state and end-of-life decision-making. *Neurology, 71*, 1027–1032.

Rainie, L., Fox, S., & Madden, M. (2002). *One year later: September 11 and the Internet.* Washington, DC: Pew Internet and American Life Project.

Rainie, L., & Kalsnes, B. (2001). *The commons of the tragedy.* Washington, DC: Pew Internet and American Life Project.

Ristovski-Slijepcevic, S. (2013). The dying mother. *Feminist Media Studies, 13*, 629–642.

Schiapa, E., Gregg, P., & Hewes, D. (2004). Can a television series change attitudes about death? A study of college students and *Six feet under. Death Studies, 28*, 459–474.

Schultz, N. W., & Huet, L. M. (2000/2001). Sensational! Violent! Popular! Death in American movies. *Omega: Journal of Death and Dying, 42*, 137–149.

Seale, C. (2004). Media constructions of dying alone: A form of "bad death." *Social Science and Medicine, 58*, 967–974.

Sedney, M. A. (1999). Children's grief narratives in popular films. *Omega: Journal of Death and Dying, 39*, 315–325.

Sedney, M. A. (2002). Maintaining connections in children's grief narratives in popular film. *American Journal of Orthopsychiatry, 72*, 279–288.

Smith, D. B. (1981). *Long-term care in transition: The regulation of nursing homes.* Washington, DC: Beard Books.

Speece, M. W., & Brent, S. B. (1984). Children's understanding of death: A review of three components of a death concept. *Child Development, 55*, 1671–1686.

Ulsperger, J. S. (2002). Geezers, greed, grief, and grammar: Frame transformation in the nursing home reform movement. *Sociological Spectrum, 22*, 285–406.

U.S. Census Bureau. (2012). The 2012 statistical abstract. Retrieved from http://www.census.gov/compendia/statab/cats/births_deaths_marriages_divorces/deaths.html

Walter, T. (1994). *The revival of death.* London, UK: Routledge.

Walter, T., Littlewood, J., & Pickering, M. (1995). Death in news: The public invigilation of private emotion. *Sociology, 29*, 579–596.

Westwood B., & Westwood G. (1999). Assessment of newspaper reporting of public health and the medical model: A methodological case study. *Health Promotion International, 14*, 53–64.

Williamson, J., Skiner, C., & Hocken, D. (2011). Death and illness as depicted in the media. *The International Journal of Clinical Practice, 65*, 547–555.

CHAPTER SIX

End-OF-Life Communication IN Cross-Cultural Patient Care

MARCIA K. CARTERET

While the end-of-life experience is universal, the way human beings negotiate meaning about the experience of dying is not. The thoughts, emotions, and interpersonal interactions at the end of life are very much influenced by culture. In any given set of circumstances in which people come from different cultural backgrounds, false assumptions based on one set of values will quickly lead to failed communication. This is especially true of communication at the end of life because we cannot assume shared meaning about anything as uncertain as the experience of death. When crossing cultural boundaries especially, communication is only effective when it is highly intentional (Bennett, 2013). With close attention and earnest intention, communication becomes the very thing that can bring people through a time of great uncertainty.

COMMUNICATION BETWEEN HEALTH CARE PROFESSIONALS, PATIENTS, AND FAMILIES

Coming to terms with death is a lifelong process for most human beings. Even though health care professionals deal with the uncertainty of death and dying as part of their work—sometimes daily—as human beings, they have their own unresolved fears and questions about death, and in any case, it never becomes easy to talk about death with their patients. It is never comfortable to give bad news, to shock and devastate with a telling of a terminal diagnosis or a death by trauma. The challenge of talking about the end of life is especially difficult when a patient's cultural norms differ significantly from a medical culture driven by core American values emphasizing individual autonomy and rights. While health care providers cannot be expected to know the specific mourning ceremonies and traditions of each family's culture, there is arguably an ethics of awareness that applies to understanding fundamental differences between culturally diverse groups in the U.S. It is essential, for example, that health care professionals, doctors especially, grasp basic cultural differences in how families prepare for and respond to death and dying.

Much has been written about the continued need for enhanced cultural competency in health care providers—pediatric and family practice physicians, hospice nurses, social workers, psychiatrists, and many more. The term "cultural competency," although it is commonly used in health care fields, is less accurate than the term "cultural responsiveness." No human being can be deemed competent or incompetent in culture, but certainly health care providers can learn enhanced communication skills and increase their own effectiveness with patients and families during cross-cultural encounters in hospitals, clinics, hospices, and long-term care settings. Awareness of the medical culture too is important during every interaction, though it is often overlooked. The culture of Western medicine in the U.S. is a professional culture with a very specific style of communication. In all cross-cultural interactions, the inability to use intentional communication skills can lead to fragmented care and a poor death for the patient. There are numerous studies that support this conclusion (Bednarz, Schim, & Doorenbos, 2010; Betancourt, Green, Carillo, & Park, 2005; Campinha-Bacote, 2011; Huff & Kline, 2008).

Examining Cultural Identities

Fundamental to understanding a person from a different culture is awareness of the values and beliefs that shape our own cultural identities. It is difficult to make meaningful comparisons if we do not have a clear baseline from which to work. Americans often struggle to describe their national culture because superficial concepts such as the melting pot and the fruit bowl have been perpetuated for so long. Many Americans still say, "There is no American culture because we are a melting pot of other cultures." The melting pot metaphor actually encourages assimilation by promoting the idea that people who come to live in this country should want to become fully Americanized. More recently, efforts toward cultural sensitivity have countered this assimilation-based metaphor by suggesting a common identity model for all Americans that supports cultural diversity. Shweder, Minow, and Markus (2002) note that Americans are different, but also similar.

People who say this kind of thing will often invoke the fruit bowl as an even better metaphor for American culture.

In health care situations, this common identity model leads some people to minimize important cultural differences. Treating all patients the same is an ideal based on the Golden Rule, and it sounds good, but in cross-cultural health care encounters the Golden Rule can lead to serious miscommunication in high-stakes situations. When dealing with terminal diagnoses or death from trauma, avoiding the important impact of cultural differences could be extremely problematic. Returning to the concept of intentional communication at the end of life—communication based on paying close attention with earnest intention—health care professionals must first examine their own beliefs about death and look for the cultural variances that are most important to their patients. Making assumptions based on our own feelings and expectations makes it easier to believe we have all the answers, but only intentional communication really serves the process of understanding another person's experience. By asking questions and actively listening, we demonstrate true empathy and support for those struggling with the end of life. Just giving the same answers that work for us—professionally or personally—is not really communicating.

Three Key Cultural Differences in End-of-Life Treatment

The challenges for physicians and other providers who care for people at the end of life will surely increase as the U.S. society becomes more diverse. No one can possibly be expected to demonstrate in-depth knowledge about every patient's culture, and that is why individual patients and families should always be viewed as the true source of knowledge about their cultural norms and expectations. What health care professionals often need the most help with is recognizing which cultural differences are most important to ask patients and families about. The next section discusses three key areas worth special attention with families from other cultures: family-focused decision-making, communication of "bad news," and advance directives.

Collectivist cultures expect family-focused decision making. Individualistic cultures stress self-reliance, decision making based on individual needs, and the right to a private life. Collectivist cultures, by comparison, stress loyalty to one's immediate and extended family. The term "familism" is often used to describe the dominant social pattern in which decision-making processes emphasize the family first, and the concept of having a "private life" may not even exist.

In stark contrast to the values of collectivist cultures, medical ethics in the U.S. health care system during the past 30 years have shifted to promote more patient autonomy. Since 1990, an individual's right to make health care choices has been protected under the Patient Self-Determination Act (PSDA, 1990).

Covered under this act are the fundamental rights of the individual to facilitate his or her own health care decisions, accept or refuse medical treatment, and make an advance health care directive. Ultimately, the purpose of the acts is to assure open communication with health care providers so that controls over life and death health care choices rests firmly in the hands of the patient. Many collectivist cultures, however, deemphasize autonomy, perceiving it as isolating rather than empowering. These non-Western cultures believe that communities and families, not individuals alone, are affected by life-threatening illnesses and accompanying medical decisions (Searight & Gafford, 2005). One study (Lind, Lorem, Nortvedt, & Hevrøy, 2012), exploring how relatives of terminally ill patients perceived their involvement in end-of-life decision making, revealed that some relatives saw their role as crucial in safeguarding the patient's values and interests. However, actual inclusion in decision making varied from active participation in the process to acceptance of the physician's decision or merely receiving information.

The families that did not participate in the doctor-patient dialogue also experienced limited communication with nurses and were allowed less time with the patient than desired. Hence, they were unsure how much and what kind of information the patient had received, especially regarding end-of-life decisions and treatment termination. This was a difficult matter for these families. They felt that important issues between the patient and themselves remained unresolved. For instance, they were uncertain whether the patient actually knew that he or she was going to die. Feeling unable to raise the subject themselves, they had diminished ability to give support at a crucial moment in the patient's life. One husband believed that his wife knew all that she wanted to know, but he himself did not know what she knew. Another spouse had asked the doctors what her husband knew, because he did not show her any sign that he was informed, and the family never heard that anyone had informed him (Lind, Lorem, Nortvedt, & Hevrøy, 2012).

In the U.S. and other countries with patient autonomy legislation, there needs to be enough flexibility in the health care system to accommodate communication patterns that look different from family to family. The assumptions and values behind the Patient Self-Determination Act of 1990 are not shared by all persons in the U.S., including many families of European American heritage who might be expected to endorse "mainstream" values. The imminent death of any one important person disrupts the lives of many who must face enormous transitions together—emotional, logistical, and financial. Family-based decision making is not just a cultural norm for some families. It may be essential.

Cultural expectations for communicating "bad news." Culturally sensitive communication at the end of life is impossible without acknowledging that families from different cultural backgrounds have different expectations about the communication of "bad news." This is especially true in the case of life-threatening diagnoses and/or illnesses that carry extreme stigma—cancer and AIDS being examples (Liamputtong, 2013). Patients and families that value group decision making may actually place the greatest value on the right *not to know* the truth. In fact, truth telling may be considered extremely inappropriate for physicians and others who are expected to withhold potentially distressing information from patients. Families will expect to choose how much truth will be revealed, to whom, and when. This can create both a legal and ethical dilemma for health care professionals. It is important to explain to every patient and family that the U.S. health care system follows certain laws to protect the patient's right to open communication. Families are extremely important, and their needs are considered too, but health care conversations should begin by exploring patient preferences. How much does a patient want to know about his or her medical condition? Do patients prefer that someone else make decisions for them? If yes, who? Patients can provide important insight into the decision-making dynamics within their unique family. Only after asking a patient about preferred communication of his or her medical diagnosis (and documenting the conversation) should families be included in the dialogue. However, unless a patient expresses the desire to exclude the family from communication with the medical team, the family should be included at every stage in the process.

Cultural resistance to advance directives. An advance directive is a written statement of a person's wishes regarding medical treatment, often including a living will, made to ensure those wishes are carried out should the person be unable to communicate them to a doctor. In a report to Congress by the U.S. Department of Health and Human Services in 2008, only 18% to 36% of Americans have completed an advance directive.

> Individuals with serious medical conditions, a group for whom advance directives are particularly relevant, have completed advance directives at only a slightly higher rate than the general population. Fewer than half of severely or terminally ill patients had an advance directive in their medical record, and among individuals with chronic illnesses, only one in three completed an advance directive. In addition, studies suggest that two-thirds of physicians whose patients had advance directives were unaware of the existence of those documents. (Wenger, Shugarman, & Wilkinson, 2008)

Patients from minority backgrounds, including immigrants and refugees from a broad range of cultures, are often least inclined to complete advance directives. Cultural differences often make it difficult to understand the concept of planning for death simply because doing so is at odds with their spiritual beliefs. In some cultures, for example, planning for death may be understood to actually invite death. Physicians should offer information about why written advance directives can be important for dying patients and their loved ones. Cultural resistance may prove too strong for some people to act on their physician's suggestion, but at least they are made aware of this important option. Many people need help navigating our complex system of care. Offering information about community resources such as low-cost legal services is often helpful. Ideally, discussion about advance directive planning should be performed well before a health crisis. It should be an ongoing discussion as patients become responsible for growing families, grow older, or see their health status declining; perspectives on advance directives do change as people's lives change. Incorporating an advance directive discussion with patients during routine physicals on a yearly basis is advisable (Coolen, 2012). .

EXPLORING THE ROLE OF RELIGION WITH PATIENTS AND FAMILIES AT THE END OF LIFE

For many people, placing death within a religious perspective is the only way to find meaning at the end of life. In many regions of the world, religion and culture often blend into each other—it is impossible to say where one begins and the other ends. The degree of acculturation into mainstream U.S. culture is sometimes a strong indicator of how strictly immigrant and refugee families will follow religious traditions for death, mourning, and post-death arrangements. Across all sociocultural groups, including mainstream Americans, it is not uncommon for religiosity to become more pronounced in some people at the end of life, though others may suddenly choose to break with religious traditions entirely—which often creates chaos within families. Also, mixing cultural and religious beliefs about death and dying can become very complex because of marriages between faiths. Health care professionals in all roles—from family physicians to hospice nurses—must find their own way to broach the subject of religion with patients at the end of life. It is a good idea to learn at least the basics about the world's major religions. These religious practices function as systems of meaning to help solve problems of uncertainty, powerlessness, and scarcity at the end of human life.

Monotheistic Religions

The events of 9/11 changed many people's view of Islam and created many unfortunate stereotypes about the people who follow this religion. There are, however, many similarities between Christianity and Islam. Both believe death is a transition to a more glorious place. Both Muslims and Christians believe in the afterlife and view time on earth as preparation for eternal life. Followers of both faiths believe in the sovereignty of a God (Allah). In moments when they seek reassurance from a higher power, they invoke phrases such as "Allah giveth and Allah taketh away." Both faiths rely on a single scripture, founder, and sacred place of origin.

Muslims and Christians alike use readings from their holy book, the Koran or Bible, to recognize the departure of a loved one from this life.

Judaism is the other major monotheistic religion. Jewish mourners recite "The Lord has given and the Lord has taken, blessed be the name of the Lord" before a funeral begins. Jews also believe in the sovereignty of one God. Jews focus on their purpose during earthly life, which is to fulfill one's duties to God and one's fellow humans. Succeeding at this brings reward; failing at it brings punishment.

The traditions around death and dying differ greatly across all three major monotheistic religions (as well as within different branches of each faith, i.e., Jehovah's Witnesses and Mormonism in Christianity). These end-of-life traditions are often hard for outsiders to understand. Notable differences occur with preparation of the deceased person's body, the permissibility of organ donation, and the choosing of cremation versus burial.

Buddhism and Hinduism

Hinduism, the world's third largest religion, is also the world's oldest religion, with sacred writings dating as far back as 1500 to 1400 B.C. Hinduism is a conglomeration of religious, philosophical, and cultural ideas and practices that originated in India. Its followers represent many different sects. Hinduism has neither a specific instance of origin nor a specific founder. Buddhism, however, does have a single founder, but the Buddha is not prayed to in the same sense as God or Allah. Buddhism is often described as a set of philosophies for living. The Buddha is not revered as a god, but rather followed by the faithful as being "the great one" who achieved an exemplary life. There are marked differences between Buddhism and Hinduism, but there are also similarities. Followers of both traditions focus on the impermanence of life, but death is not seen as final in either faith; it is merely the end of the body we inhabit in this life. The spirit outlasts death and will seek attachment to a new body in a new "life." The transition of a soul to a new life is very important in both traditions, so followers observe specific rituals about the handling of the body at the time of dying.

Ancestor Worship

The premise of ancestor worship is that the course of life is cyclical, not linear. Those who are dead may not be seen physically, but are alive in a different world and can reincarnate in new births. Ancestor worship in various forms can be found in many parts of the world and is very strong in parts of Africa and Asia. Many Native Americans and Buddhists alike believe that the living co-exist with the dead. A central theme in ancestor worship is that the lives of the dead may have supernatural powers over those in the living world—the ability to bless, curse, give or take life. In some cultures, worship of the dead is important and includes making offerings of food, money, clothing, and blessings. In China, there is the annual observance of "sweeping the graves," and as its name denotes, it is a time for people to tend the graves of the departed ones. In Mexico, there is the Day of the Dead (Dia de los Muertos), a holiday that focuses on gathering family and friends to remember those who have died. The Day of the Dead is also celebrated by many Latinos living in the U.S. and Canada. The intent of this celebration is to encourage visits by the souls of the departed so they will hear the prayers said for them by the living. It makes sense that in cultures in which ancestor worship is common, the occurrence of organ donation and cremation may be very low.

Communication With Spiritual Leaders

It is often imperative for people to communicate with leaders from their faith community when facing death. Influential leaders from all faiths can help interpret what is happening on a spiritual level during a health crisis. For example, in the Catholic faith, a person may gain great strength and peace when the sacrament of the sick is administered by a priest. In Judaism, it is important to know the variations in practice among orthodox, conservative, and reformed traditions. Religious leaders can clarify which tenets cut across the branches of their faith in matters such as life support. In Islam, it is considered a taboo topic to talk about death with a patient; a religious leader may be a crucial intermediary between a doctor and a family about terminal illness (Coolen, 2012). Religious leaders assist individuals in making connections between their inner life or "spirit" and their communal social reasons for practicing a formal religion.

EXPRESSIONS OF GRIEF AND PAIN VARY ACROSS CULTURES

In some cultures, showing grief, including wailing, is expected of relatives at the end of a loved one's life because the more sadness and the deeper the torment displayed, the more the person is loved at the time of death. In other cultures, restraint is expected. Rules in Egypt and Bali, both Islamic countries, are opposite; in Bali, women may be strongly discouraged from crying, while in Egypt women are considered abnormal if they do not nearly incapacitate themselves with demonstrative weeping at the end of a loved one's life. A bereaved Balinese who appears to laugh off a death is behaving appropriately, based on the standards of her culture (Gire, 2002). In Japan, it is extremely important not to show one's grief for a number of reasons. The Japanese and many other Asian people believe death should be seen as a time of liberation and not sorrow. One should bear up under misfortune with strength and acceptance and certainly never do anything to make someone else uncomfortable. In Latino cultures, it may be appropriate for women to wail, but men are not expected to show overt emotion because of the notion of "machismo." In China, hiring professional wailers for funerals is still a common practice because an absence of tears indicates that a deceased person was not loved. This disgraces the family. This practice may sound quite bizarre to people from Western countries today, but it was common in Victorian England and some European countries during that era too. In keeping with the dignified behavior associated with English culture, hired mourners in Victorian England did not show obvious emotion. They wore black hats and coats that matched their somber expressions.

Attitudes About Pain

Cultural differences in response to pain compound the inherent challenges of communication for the terminally ill and others at the end of life. Although nearly all people experience pain sensations similarly, studies show there are important differences in the way people express their pain and expect others to respond to their discomfort. There are also culturally based attitudes about using pain medication. An understanding of the impact of culture on the pain experience is important in assuring effective and culturally sensitive patient care (Fortier, Anderson, & Kain, 2009).

It is well established that pain is a highly complex phenomenon that involves biological, psychological, and social variables. Patients' culturally based responses to pain are often divided into two categories, stoic and emotive. Stoic patients are less expressive of their pain and tend to "grin and bear it." They tend to withdraw socially. Emotive patients are more likely to verbalize their expressions of pain, prefer to have people around, and expect others to react to their pain to validate their discomfort. We can make the broad generalization that expressive patients often come from Hispanic, Middle Eastern, and Mediterranean backgrounds, while stoic patients often come from Northern European and Asian backgrounds. If we use such broad generalizations to help understand human behavior, however, we must always keep in mind that while culture is a framework that directs human behavior, not everyone in every culture conforms to a set of expected behaviors or beliefs. Rigid use of generalizations leads to cultural stereotyping. Any individual's experience of pain will manifest itself in emotional and behavioral responses particular to his or her culture, personal history, and unique perceptions (Davidhizar & Giger, 2004).

Self-awareness is important in comparing different expressions of pain. We are apt to believe that our own reaction to pain is "normal," and anything substantially different is abnormal. For example, a doctor or nurse raised in a family that encouraged stoicism may not know how to react to a patient who responds to pain with loud verbal complaints and may even discount such "overly expressive" reactions. There is a long tradition of stoicism in European American culture; generations of children, especially boys, would be criticized for crying like babies but applauded for keeping a stiff upper lip. A person can be described as having a high or low threshold for pain; these opposites are often correlated with strength or weakness. In any case, discounting the emotional complaints of a patient is insensitive. Pain is felt both physically and emotionally. Acute pain affects a person's ability to think straight, make decisions, and express themselves clearly even to others who speak the same language. Pain that is less intense but persists over time can lead to cycles of sleeplessness, anxiety, frustration, and even depression (Chialvo, 2008).

There is no universal language for pain, so people from different cultures will describe pain in different words. "Sharp," "throbbing," "stabbing," or "aching" makes sense to most people, but U.S. doctors and nurses might be baffled when encountering patients who explain pain in terms such as "lightning," "trees with deep spreading roots," "spider webs," or the "tones of drums and flutes" (Burhansstipanov, 1998). In many tribal cultures worldwide, stories or symbols are used when relating one's worldview. In cultures in which evil spirits are believed to cause illness and pain, patients may talk about their suffering as punishment. Indeed, given different cultural norms and language barriers, some patients will need help talking about pain in ways Western doctors and nurses can interpret. Through careful listening, encouragement, and support, health care professionals can more accurately assess pain in each individual patient.

FAMILY DYNAMICS RELEVANT TO CROSS-CULTURAL PATIENT CARE

In Western cultures, and particularly in mainstream U.S. American culture, families typically follow a nuclear model composed of parents and their children. This is markedly different from collectivist cultures that adhere to an extended family model. In cultures such as Native American, Asian, Hispanic, African, and Middle Eastern, individuals rely heavily on an extended network of reciprocal relationships with parents, siblings, grandparents, aunts, uncles, cousins, and many others. Many of these people are involved in important health decisions. The concept of family may include people who are unrelated to the patient through blood or marriage. For example, in some Hispanic families the godparents play a critical role. In American Indian families, tribal leaders, the elderly, and medicine men/women are key individuals to be consulted before important decisions at the end of life are made.

Acculturation and Heritage Consistency in Immigrants and Refugees

Families new to the U.S. encounter enormous stresses in the process of adjusting to mainstream American culture. The acculturation process creates sudden and radical shifts in family dynamics. Parents in a recently immigrated family often are aligned with the culture of the country of origin, while their offspring are likely to have adopted the dominant culture's values. This can lead to intergenerational conflicts that surface powerfully in serious health care situations. The term "heritage consistency" is used to describe how much or how little a person's lifestyle reflects his or her traditional culture. In communication at the end of life, it is important to pay attention to heritage consistency. Typically, older generations will follow cultural and religious practices more strictly than will younger ones, but not always. Avoid making assumptions. Acknowledge that it is normal for family members to agree on some things and disagree about others. Explain that optimal care depends on open dialogue.

Overcoming Language Barriers Across Generations

If there are language barriers in communicating with patients and families, interpreters should be made available whenever possible. It is important to offer interpreter services whenever a key decision maker is unable to understand English well enough to participate in a conversation. For example, the patient may be fluent in English but a spouse or parent speaks only the native language. Miscommunication increases the risk of medical errors, inappropriate treatments, emergency room visits, and unintended consent. A medical interpreter is a trained health care specialist who works with spoken language, often mediating between two languages in both directions. Understanding the nuances of two languages requires understanding the culture behind each language. Qualified medical interpreters have extensive knowledge of medical terminology as well. It is common in hospital and clinic settings for telephone interpreter services to be used, but in emotionally charged conversations it is usually best to use an in-person interpreter. In the event that professional interpretation is not possible, arranging for the family to bring a relative or friend as an interpreter is the next best option. Explain how important it is that they bring someone whom they can trust with the family's confidential medical information. Be sure they understand that young children should not be used to interpret in medical settings. Keep in mind cultural preferences about giving patients "bad news." Feeling protective, a family member may use his or her role as designated interpreter to prevent certain truths from being revealed. Similarly, it is not uncommon for family members to withhold or change information to avoid conflicts. For this reason, a representative from the community is sometimes more reliable during an exchange of medical information. The bottom line is that relying on untrained interpreters has risks, and health care professionals need to take extra care to ensure clear communication.

With or without the use of interpreter services, people should always be asked to explain what they have understood about a medical condition, prognosis, course of treatment, end-of-life care, and the like. In some cultures, it is not acceptable to ask authority figures questions. Even with patient-centered care as the ideal in U.S. health care today, physicians may still be viewed as authority figures by people from societies that emphasize status differences. Even when they do not understand or agree with what is being said, patients and family members may nod and smile to please a doctor, preserve harmony in a conversation, and avoid uncomfortable dialogue. Shame can also prevent people from admitting what they do not understand. Shame is often the reason people with low health literacy do not ask questions. End-of-life conversations are emotionally charged. It is difficult for anyone to concentrate on facts and details when they are upset.

Conversation at such difficult times should never be rushed no matter how busy health care professionals may be. Nothing can be more important than creating a safe environment so that an honest discussion of feelings may unfold.

CONCLUSIONS

In summary, the greatest fear a person can have about dying is being isolated at the end of life, and nothing feels lonelier than being unable to communicate. When someone faces a terminal medical condition, but can't give expression to the immensity of that experience, he or she will feel alone—even in a crowd of doctors, nurses, hospice staff, family, and friends. Culture and language barriers will only compound this struggle in our complex medical system. At times, health care professionals also struggle to feel understood. It isn't always clear how to be appropriate and compassionate when talking to a dying patient. Physicians and nurses, especially, may face critical medical decisions for patients daily, which is emotionally exhausting. While they are uniquely positioned to offer the dying comfort and support, talking about death and dying requires an exceedingly high level of intimacy between human beings—the very antithesis of most medical training. In general, teaching communication skills to health care professionals isn't emphasized. "Soft skills" take a back seat to medical knowledge. Communication skills that assure culturally responsive care are treated as interchangeable with cultural competency training. They are not one and the same. Future research could better define best practices for teaching the most essential communication skills that health care professionals need in difficult situations. Beyond years of experience, what makes some people more effective in end-of-life conversations? Additionally, best practices could be identified for helping doctors and nurses deal with empathy drain, a natural human response to long hours and emotional overload. This should be addressed in a very focused way during residencies. While clinical medical training standards are clearly defined and fairly uniform across educational institutions, communication skills for health care professionals are not. Taking end-of-life care as perhaps the prime example, a doctor cannot leverage her medical expertise when face-to-face with a dying patient if she can't find the words to bridge human experience. She must connect to her patient at the very moment she discloses the one separation we all fear most. It sounds far too simple, but *good communication is the essential thing that brings people through the uncertainty and fear surrounding death.* We connect through words—both purposeful and empathetic—to arrive at acceptance when the time comes to let go.

REFERENCES

Bednarz, H., Schim, S., & Doorenbos, A. (2010). Cultural diversity in nursing education: Perils, pitfalls, and pearls. *The Journal of Nursing Education, 49*, 253–260.

Bennett, M. J. (2013). *Basic concepts of intercultural communications.* Boston, MA: Intercultural Press.

Betancourt, J., Green, A., Carrillo, J. E., & Park, E. R. (2005). Cultural competence and health care disparities: Key perspectives and trends. *Health Affairs, 24*(2), 499–505.

Burhansstipanov, L. (1998). Lessons learned from Native American cancer prevention, control and supportive care projects. *Asian American and Pacific Islander Journal of Health, 6*(2), 91–99.

Campinha-Bacote, J. (2011, May 31). Delivering patient-centered care in the midst of a cultural conflict: The role of cultural competence. *OJIN: The Online Journal of Issues in Nursing, 16*(2).

Chialvo, D. (2008). Chronic pain harms the brain. Retrieved from http://www.northwestern.edu/newscenter/stories/2008/02/chronicpain.html

Coolen, P. R. (2012). *Cultural relevance in end-of-life care.* Retrieved from https://ethnomed.org/clinical/end-of-life/cultural-relevance-in-end-of-life-care#section-19

Davidhizar, R. N., & Giger, J. N. (2004). A review of the literature on care of patients in pain who are culturally diverse. *International Nursing Review, 51*. Retrieved from http://dptreference.pbworks.com/f/Review+on+culture.pdf

Fortier, M., Anderson, C. T., & Kain, Z. N. (2009). Ethnicity matters in the assessment and treatment of children's pain. *Pediatrics, 124*, 378–380.

Gire, J. T. (2002). How death imitates life: Cultural influences on conceptions of death and dying. In W. J. Lonner, D. L. Dinnel, S. A. Hayes, & D. N. Sattler (Eds.), *Online readings in psychology and culture.* Retrieved from http://www.wwu.edu/culture/gire.htm

Huff, R. M., & Kline, M. V. (2008). Health promotion in the context of culture. In *Health promotion in multicultural populations.* Retrieved from http://www.sagepub.com/upm-data/23214_Chapter_1.pdf

Liamputtong, P. (Ed.). (2013). *Stigma, discrimination, and living with HIV/AIDS: A cross-cultural perspective.* Retrieved from http://www.springer.com/social+sciences/anthropology+%26+archaeology/book/978-94-007-6323-4

Lind, R., Lorem, G., Nortvedt, P., & Hevrøy, O. (2012). Family involvement in the end-of-life decisions of competent intensive care patients. *Nursing Ethics, 20,* 61–71.

Patient Self-Determination Act, H.R. 5067 (101st) (1990).

Searight, H. R., & Gafford, J. (2005). Cultural diversity at the end of life: Issues and guidelines for family physicians. *American Family Physician, 71,* 515–522.

Shweder, R. A., Minow, M., & Markus, H. (Eds.). *Engaging cultural differences: The multicultural challenge in liberal democracies.* New York, NY: Russell Sage Foundation.

U.S. Department of Health and Human Services, Office of Assistant Secretary for Planning and Evaluation. (2008, August). *Advance directive and advance planning care: Report to Congress by N. S. Wenger, L. R. Shugarman and A. Wilkinson.* Retrieved from http://aspe.hhs.gov/daltcp/reports/2008/adcongrpt.htm

Wenger, N. S., Shugarman, L. R., & Wilkinson, A. (2008). Advance directives and advance care planning: Report to congress. Retrieved from http://aspe.hhs.gov/daltcp/reports/2008/ADCongRpt.pdf

CHAPTER SEVEN

Conversations AT THE End OF Life

ELISSA FOSTER

MAUREEN P. KEELEY

I completed my relationship with him. I didn't walk away thinking, 'Aauugh, I should have said.' 'I didn't say.' 'I could have said.' 'I wanted to say.' There wasn't anything that we didn't really say. And in the final analysis the most important, the absolutely most important things were all said; because the person who is left doesn't get stuck holding a bunch of untied knots. It's complete. You're not dragging anything along with it. We both completed the relationship. We both were able to let each other know that we didn't want it to go that way. But since it was going to go that way anyway [we made the most of that final time]. (Loved one describing her final conversations with her husband, Keeley & Yingling, 2007, pp. 17, 18)

> *She liked to be touched because she said they only touch her when they need to give her medication. So, she liked to have her hair brushed or her arms or legs rubbed, and just talking. She loved to hear about my kids. I told her once that I have a flower garden and every time I saw her after that, without fail, we talked about my garden. It was a connection for us, a bridge.* (Shyanne,[1] a hospice volunteer, describing visits to her patient, Foster, 2007, pp. 151–152)

The particular focus of this chapter is on conversation, which implies a verbal and nonverbal exchange that is personal rather than impersonal, face-to-face rather than mediated, and significant because of the nature of the interaction rather than the context. At the same time, the unique qualities of the end of life—occurring between the pronouncement of a terminal diagnosis and death—means that:

- Relationships that might otherwise be impersonal can become quite personal
- The contingencies of managing approaching death and contextual factors (related to hospitalization, in-home hospice care, nursing home care, health transitions, and so on) may greatly impact interaction
- As death becomes more imminent, nonverbal communication may be relied on more as a necessity
- Important conversations must be mediated in some way because family members and loved ones are commonly at a distance from the person who is dying

Thus, one challenge of this chapter is to draw conclusions and offer insights into end-of-life conversation while recognizing the wide range of circumstances that may be at play within such exchanges. As we discuss in more detail later in the chapter, several theoretical frameworks including functional theory, the transactional model, relational dialectics, and narrative permit us to focus on the personal, interactional, and face-to-face aspects of conversation while elucidating the particular conversational qualities resulting from the end-of-life context.

Two relational contexts in which end-of-life conversations occur are presented: close personal relationships and relationships with clinicians. The chapter concludes with general principles that guide conversation, particularly acknowledging the significant role of nonverbal communication and presence at the end of life.

THEORETICAL FRAMEWORKS FOR UNDERSTANDING END-OF-LIFE CONVERSATIONS

A number of interrelated theoretical perspectives are useful when seeking to understand the qualities of conversation at the end of life. Although this is not an exhaustive list, we have selected the following because of their consistent emphasis on emergent meaning, mutuality, and the relational dimension of communication, and we begin by reviewing functional theory, which offers insight into the influence of context on end-of-life conversations.

Functional theory. As illustrated by the two scenarios at the beginning of this chapter, the content of end-of-life conversations can be extremely varied and extend far beyond the stereotypical "death scene" conversations that loom large in film and television depictions of dying (see Robinson, this volume). A functional perspective focuses on the perceptions and meaning of social processes that individuals have pertaining to specific interactions (Shavitt & Nelson, 2001). Focusing on the communicative functions of interactions highlights the meaning and outcome that is ascribed for specific interactions and is central to understanding what is going on in a given context (McQuail, 1987). Scholars have successfully explored the functions of peoples' communication at the end of life (see Keeley, 2007; Keeley, Generous, & Baldwin, 2014), providing insight into the long-lasting impact and meaning of these conversations for family members who must go on living after the death of their loved one.

Advance care planning is a concern for families (e.g., Generous & Keeley, 2014; van Eechoud et al., 2014; see also Pecchioni and White, this volume) as well as clinicians (Almack, Cox, Moghaddam, Pollock, & Seymour, 2012). Others have noted the life-affirming value of conversations related to reminiscing or life review (Jenko, Gonzalez, & Seymour, 2007; Nussbaum, Pecchioni, Robinson, & Thompson, 2000). Relational scholars have established the significance of conversation in making space for reconciliation and mutual sense-making (Keeley & Yingling, 2007), as well as expressions of love (Keeley, 2004a). Another important dimension of end-of-life conversation serves to provide spiritual care and guidance—a function that may be fulfilled by chaplains (Considine & Miller, 2010), clinical care providers (Ragan, Wittenberg-Lyles, Goldsmith, & Sanchez-Reilly, 2008), and family members (Keeley, 2004b, 2009). Beyond the role that may be played by family members and friends who share close personal relationships with the person who is dying, those who have less frequent but regular contact (such as visiting nurses, volunteers, neighbors, and so on) may also employ conversation to serve an important function of helping to maintain social connections for the person who is dying as well as for family members (Foster, 2002, 2007).

Transactional communication. The transactional model of communication was proposed as a counterpoint to the linear, transmission model in which emphasis was placed on the message and optimizing accuracy of information transfer. In contrast, the transactional model emphasizes meaning as it emerges between communicators in a process of simultaneous and mutually influential exchange (DuPré & Foster, forthcoming). The mutuality of conversation implies more than simply turn taking; the transaction requires that both communicators attend to the other, be sensitive to verbal and nonverbal cues, and adapt to one other.

Another component of the transactional model that is particularly useful to understanding conversation at the end of life is the concept of *noise* or interference, which includes any internal (physiological, psychological, emotional) or external (physical, environmental) stimuli that interfere with the communicators' capacity to exchange meaning. A significant source of noise or interference is the uncertainty of knowing when to probe for information and when to preserve the other person's privacy. The nature of this tension and others is best explained by another theoretical framework—relational dialectics.

Relational dialectics. Before addressing the specifics of relational dialectics, it is worth defining what is implied by the relational approach to understanding human interaction. In 1967, Watzlawick, Beavin, and Jackson proposed several axioms that govern communication, one of which is that all messages consist of both a content and a relationship dimension. The content dimension conveys the information of the message, and the relational dimension constitutes the relationship between the communicators. The relational approach emphasizes what is being constructed or constituted by the message, recognizing (like the transactional model) the mutual and interdependent nature of the process (Millar & Rogers, 1976). An important factor in this approach is that the relational dimension of a message is, for the most part, implicit rather than explicit, conveyed largely nonverbally, and offers clues to emotions, the respective power or status of the communicators, implications about how one communicator intends the message to be interpreted, conversational norms, and expectations.

A number of researchers have found relational dialectics to be a powerful framework through which to understand the challenges of end-of-life communication (Foster, 2007). As a construct, relational dialectics describe the ever-changing and negotiated tensions inherent in communication between persons in an interdependent relationship, and they emphasize the tendency for opposing forces to operate simultaneously—pulling both communicators along a continuum at any given moment. The overarching dynamic in relational dialectics is of coming together (centripetal force) and coming apart (centrifugal force; Baxter & Montgomery, 1996). In the end-of-life context, this dynamic is most clearly experienced in the tension between caring for someone and sustaining quality of life (centripetal) and preparing for the end of life (centrifugal). Three of the relational dialectics related to communication at the end of life are (1) acceptance-denial (of the death), (2) openness-closedness, and (3) expression-concealment (of emotion; Keeley & Generous, 2014a).

In a study by Generous and Keeley (2014), individuals who could accept the reality that death was near were able to "acknowledge [that] the person won't be around to talk to anymore and [therefore we were] not afraid of the end" (Jane).[3] Those individuals who were in denial missed opportunities to communicate and interact with their dying loved one. For instance, Alan stated, "I didn't want to believe she was dying. I wonder if I didn't call more because I didn't want to have it confirmed that she was getting worse." The poignancy of this dialectic is that, ironically, the acceptance of the imminent separation of the relationship through death (a "coming apart" dynamic) was what facilitated the ability of the relational partner to remain engaged and connected (a "coming together" dynamic). Denial of death, although it may have arisen from a desire to "hold on" to the person who was dying ("coming together") resulted in missed opportunities and a loss of the much-desired connection ("coming apart").

Second, openness refers to not being afraid to talk about everything with the dying individual, even if it might be upsetting; thus, these individuals were striving for an authentic conversation (McQuellon & Cowan, 2000). For instance, Marisa stated that it was important to "allow the dying person to talk and express his feelings about 'everything' and to be honest with him, without yourself breaking down to the point you can no longer help him in his journey." At the other end of the dialectical tension, closedness highlights the fact that many people are closed off to communication at the end of life. This may be, in part, because death as it is generally represented in the U.S. is shrouded in loss of control, fear, and feelings of awkwardness (Seale, 1996). In addition, knowing that a loved one is dying usually causes immediate heartache and suffering for those who will survive (Moller, 1996); such emotions may make it more difficult to talk with those who are dying. For example, Brock stated, "I had to monitor the way I said things because I didn't want to say something the wrong way and offend or upset her."

Third, the dialectical tension highlighting the expression or concealment of emotions is not surprising. Some individuals are able to cry, laugh, and even share their anger together, thereby sharing their feelings with one another (Keeley & Yingling, 2007), while others continue their lifetime pattern of concealing emotions, even at the end of life (Keeley & Generous, 2014a). For instance, Victoria[*2] was able to share her anger, fears, and frustrations with her husband Kerry[*] as he was in the midst of his end-of-life journey, and he responded to each emotion honestly, also expressing his emotions as they emerged with his wife (Keeley, 2007). Conversely, James stated that "my mother was a very 'stoic' individual who *did not cry* [his emphasis]. The way she was raised was that you do not show weakness and crying was a weakness." So he honored her wishes and did not express his emotions openly in front of her.

Narrative. Scholarship on narratives has explored how people make sense of the world and the events of their lives through storytelling (e.g., Bochner, 2003, 2014), and how people who have experienced distressing events have coped with the pain through the process of telling stories (e.g., Wigren, 1994). Taking a narrative approach to communication at the end of life can illuminate people's experiences in many ways; specifically, four aspects critical to narrative theory help to explain why communication at the end of life is beneficial and necessary in U.S. society (Keeley & Koenig Kellas, 2005).

First, all human behavior is inherently narrative because communication is a fundamental part of people's lives. Narrative is privileged as *the* means by which we assess our conversations, relationships, and our place in the world; thus, the stories about death and dying shape people's communication, connections, and their roles at the end of life (Fisher, 1989).

Second, meaning-making through narrative is contextual, temporal, and complex (Somers, 1995). Death is contextual, temporal, and complex. For example, communication at the end of life is contextual because we best understand the nature of it by recognizing that it occurs within the midst of the modern "death culture" which attempts to minimize talk and stories about death (Heinz, 1999).

End-of-life communication is temporal because it is triggered by a terminal diagnosis and potentially continues until the moment of death (Keeley, 2007).

Third, end-of-life communication is complex because of the emotion, personal history, and constraints that act on it. All conversations are unique in their own right; thus, the narratives about them reveal what was most relevant and important about the end-of-life journey and/or the communication that occurred within the midst of it, for the storyteller.

Fourth, stories serve the purpose of helping us to make sense and meaning out of our lives.

The lack of stories about death in our culture can limit a person's ability to make sense of the experience, explain his or her role in the event, and experience emotional relief (Sedney, Baker, & Gross, 1994). On one hand, people who do not hear stories of death in their families may have trouble communicating about death later in life (Book, 1996). On the other hand, stories about the death of a loved one help people experience emotional relief, assign meaning to the experience, bring family members together, and facilitate communication (Sedney et al., 1994). Research highlights important connections between the telling of difficult, or traumatic, stories and the psychological and health benefits for the teller of the story (Pennebaker & Beall, 1986). This has clear implications for those interested in communication at the end of life because research suggests, and we are further convinced by our own data, that the *telling* of stories is therapeutic because it provides a release of grief and it provides individuals an opportunity to frame their end-of-life experience with their dying loved ones.

Social death and dying. As we defined the end-of-life conversation at the beginning of this chapter, the time between receiving a terminal diagnosis and the moment of death itself is marked as liminal space (Turner, 1995)—a time of transition. Researchers have described one feature of this time as the shrinking of social contacts (Seale, 1996), which may come as a consequence of reduced mobility, increasing symptoms of disease, and the need to take care of the physical contingencies of the dying process (Keeley, 2007; Nussbaum et al., 2000). Partly as a consequence of the stigmatization of dying in our culture, a process of social dying can also occur (Foster, 2007) in which communication with others across the spectrum of relationships falls away. When this happens as an involuntary and unwelcome change, there is an associated pain—a combination of loneliness and loss of identity—that accompanies the process of social dying. One antidote to this pain of social dying is to maintain connection to the fabric of social life through conversation, even about mundane matters, preserving a sense of the uniqueness and value of the person's life. In cases of extreme isolation when a patient is being cared for in an institutional setting (Lawton, 2000), a social death can occur in which the person who is dying has lost all meaningful social contact except from professionals attending to her or his physical needs (a concern expressed by the hospice patient at the beginning of the chapter).

In the sections that follow, we turn to a discussion of the particular characteristics of conversations within two different relational contexts: conversations within close personal relationships and conversations with clinicians. As outlined in the introduction, the nature of the end-of-life context means that boundaries among these different relational contexts may become permeable; however, the conversations that typically occur within each of these relational contexts is sufficiently different to allow us to outline the distinct concerns of each.

CONVERSATIONS WITHIN CLOSE PERSONAL RELATIONSHIPS

Life review. Many individuals engage with others in reminiscing or life review (Nussbaum et al., 2000) as they face death (their own or that of a loved one). A life review consists of mentally assessing one's life and may range in duration from a split second to a long reminiscence (Butler, 1971). A life review is often done through conversation with trusted others and provides opportunities to recall shared memories, to share and relive old pleasures, to reconsider and examine past sufferings (Aiken, 2001), to heal old wounds, to learn about oneself and others, to forgive (self or others), and to let go and move forward (Butler, Lewis, & Southerland, 1998). Life reviews can also confirm that one's life was well lived and establish that one's life positively impacted others (Jenko et al., 2007). Life reviews can be conducted intrapersonally or interpersonally. We argue that the life reviews conducted interpersonally through conversations with trusted individuals, whether that is with a relative stranger who has become trusted, such as a hospice volunteer, a hospice chaplain, or social worker (Ragan et al., 2008), or a loved one, have the potential for tremendous positive benefits such as confirming that the dying person's life had meaning and that she or he would be remembered.

Negotiating terminal illness. The diagnosis of a terminal illness is life changing and can also be life reducing (Ragan et al., 2008). A very sick person never has full autonomy or independence and must navigate her or his treatment and care in the midst of pain, suffering, mental fog induced by medications, and strong emotions (Hauwerwas, 2005). Very often, conversations pertaining to treatment are co-created with family members and loved ones that help negotiate choices, care options at the end of life, and other important life decisions. Not all individuals are open to these discussions, however, whether as a result of an individual's own fears or preconceptions about the correct pathway at the end of life or a cultural norm that discourages open communication about death and dying.

Communication at the end of life is often enacted in the midst of a great deal of grief. Grief for family members begins immediately upon the pronouncement of a terminal diagnosis for their loved one (Glick, Weiss, & Parkes, 1974). Discussions navigating terminal illness require that the patient and family members are willing to listen to and accept the terminal illness diagnosis (Cohen & Nirenberg, 2011). Family members' grief is a result of fears regarding the end-of-life journey that their loved one is making, and it also forestalls the tangible impact that the death will have on the surviving family members (Keeley & Yingling, 2007). This type of grief has been identified as anticipatory grief (Moller, 1996), which is characterized by disorientation and suffering of the individual, and also comes with increased feelings of attachment, closeness, tenderness, and desire to be with the loved one who is dying during whatever time is left (Parkes & Weiss, 1983).

In addition, past research regarding end-of-life communication highlights the importance of communicating one's fears, desires, and needs regarding the terminal illness as well as the death and dying process (Aiken, 2001; Metzger & Gray, 2008). These conversations about the illness, end-of-life concerns, and funeral wishes are a component of communication at the end of life (Generous & Keeley, 2014). While these instrumental details concerning the process of dying are an important part of the communication at the end of life, they are not the conversations that are the most important or memorable for those who go on living (Keeley, 2007; Keeley et al., 2014).

Memorable messages from the living's perspective. As endings draw near, such as that of an impending death, people often take the opportunity to choose and prioritize events in their lives in ways that enhance their emotional involvement and investment with their close relationships in everyday life (Carstensen, Isaacowitz, & Charles, 1999). Thus, there is often more opportunity, effort, and interest in communication at the end of life within close relationships.

A decade-long program of research conducted by Keeley and her associates exploring final conversations from the surviving family members' perspective has focused on adults (Keeley, 2007; Keeley & Yingling, 2007), children and adolescents (Keeley & Baldwin, 2012a; Keeley & Generous, 2014b), positive outcomes (Keeley & Baldwin, 2012b), challenges (Keeley & Generous, 2014a), and scale development (Generous & Keeley, 2014), and has led to a number of important findings regarding conversations within close relationships at the end of life. The primary messages reported include love, identity, religion/spirituality, routine/everyday content, difficult relationship issues (Keeley, 2007; Keeley et al., 2014), and talk about illness and death (Generous & Keeley, 2014). Children's final conversations did not include difficult relationship talk, which is thought to be because children do not have the cognitive ability to assess difficult relationships (Keeley et al., 2014). Illness and death talk was present in communication at the end of life (Generous & Keeley, 2014), but was not the conversational topic that emerged as the most important or memorable for the surviving loved ones. Perhaps survivors, upon reflection after the death of their loved one, focus on the positive conversations and the lessons learned from final conversations rather than the instrumental talk at the end of life.

CONVERSATIONS INVOLVING CLINICIANS

One of the key concerns of clinicians who care for patients and families at the end of life is how to break bad news effectively and humanely. The performative nature of communication is expressed in speech act theory (Austin, 1983), which explains that certain realities come to exist through the speaking of the words that declare them to be (e.g., "The cancer has come back," "Your mother's body is shutting down"). Thus, "breaking bad news" (Buckman, 1984, p. 1597) centers on the speech act of diagnosis, prognosis, or sharing of life-altering information, recognizing that a new reality for the patient is created through the speaking of the words. The performative nature of communication is also invoked by the many scripts or models that have been developed to assist clinicians in this profound responsibility.

One model commonly taught in the medical context for breaking bad news is SPIKES. An additional model, COMFORT, has been developed, tested, and disseminated by health communication scholars and moves somewhat away from the emphasis on scripting and the moment of "breaking bad news" to encompass what is needed of physicians during communication at the end of life. This section reviews both models and also briefly discusses empathy with a structured method for framing and delivering an empathic response.

Breaking Bad News: SPIKES. The SPIKES protocol for delivering bad news (Baile et al., 2000; Kaplan, 2010) is a standard approach to teaching clinicians how to deliver bad news. The six letters of the acronym stand for: S—Setting up the interview; P—assessing the patient's Perception (what the patient already knows about her condition); I—obtaining the patient's Invitation (making sure that the patient is ready to receive the news); K—giving Knowledge and information to the patient; E—addressing the patient's emotions with Empathic responses; S—Strategy and Summary (if the patient is ready, moving the conversation toward a plan of treatment or next steps). SPIKES is widely adopted as a protocol, probably because it encompasses process elements (specifically, making sure that the physical and emotional context of the conversation is appropriate and supportive—S, P, S), content elements (scripting—I and K), and relational elements (attending and responding to the emotional cues of the patient—E). However, scripted approaches (including others such as BREAKS; Narayanan, Bista, & Koshy, 2012) have been critiqued because they tend to reduce physician anxiety but fall short in facilitating the development and delivery of emotionally support-ive messages (Goldsmith, Wittenberg-Lyles, Villagran, & Sanchez-Reilly, 2008).

The COMFORT Model. Responding to the limitations of existing proto-cols, Villagran, Goldsmith, Wittenberg-Lyles, and Baldwin (2010) developed COMFORT—a set of competencies grounded in interaction adaptation theory (Burgoon, Stern, & Dillman, 1995; Giles, 2008; Giles, Coupland, & Coup-land, 1991) and centered on principles of relational communication (Rogers & Escudero, 2004; see also Goldsmith, Ferrell, Wittenberg-Lyles, & Ragan, 2013; Wittenberg-Lyles, Goldsmith, Richardson, Hallett, & Clark, 2013). Rather than proposing a set of steps for a single conversation, the COMFORT model de-scribes a set of competencies related to the practitioner's ongoing adaptation to the communication of the patient. "COMFORT is not a linear guide for BBN [breaking bad news] performance by clinicians, but rather a set of competencies that should occur reflexively and concurrently by patients, family members, and providers" (Villagran et al., 2010, p. 225). COMFORT facilitates a co-constructed series of encounters that meet the essential requirements of the "breaking bad news" conversation but avoid a routinized or clinician-driven orientation.

One of the least successful aspects of breaking bad news efforts by medical students (Goldsmith et al., 2008; Villagran et al., 2010) is in presenting bad news clearly and unambiguously (particularly when it comes to disclosing a terminal diagnosis), and also in communicating supportive emotional messages. In the COMFORT approach:

C—Communication—refers to communicating clear verbal (content) messages in concert with nonverbal (relational) messages that maintain a sense of immediacy and connection.

O—Orientation and Opportunity—encompasses the orientation of the patient and prac-titioner with respect to culture and health literacy, emphasizing that the clinician should adapt to the situation and recognize the absence of a shared orientation or understanding of health and illness.

M—Mindfulness—refers to the capacity to be "in the moment" with a patient and rep-resents a key difference between the COMFORT model versus the others. Although the BREAKS and SPIKES protocols emphasize that they *are not* scripts, they present step-by-step phases that suggest the "bad news conversation" should proceed in an orderly sequence. In practice, it can be difficult for practitioners and patients to remain "in the moment" with one another. Mindfulness requires attending to both the cues of the patient and one's own internal cues to respond with authenticity, even if it means "abandoning the script" (Wittenberg-Lyles, Goldsmith, & Ragan, 2010, p. 287).

F—Family—describes communicating with the patient and family as part of what is known in hospice and palliative medicine as the unit of care. Understanding how much or little a family shares with one another (the conversation characteristic) and the extent to which the family wanted to agree with one another (the conformity characteristic) (Goldsmith et al., 2013; Wittenberg-Lyles, Goldsmith, Parker Oliver, Demeris, & Rankin, 2012) can aid considerably in helping clinicians to navigate the complexity of sharing bad news and facilitating subsequent decision making.

O (the second)—has been variously labeled as Ongoing (Villagran et al., 2010), Openings (Goldsmith et al., 2013), and Oversight (Wittenberg-Lyles et al., 2010). Despite the various terms, this competency relates to the important work of communicating to ensure support beyond the exigencies of the immediate diagnosis or health transition, which often includes dialogue with the patient and family around the coordination of care and social support needs. Mindful communication that transitions a patient from direct care of health practitioners to her or his home environment is also referred to as "safety-netting" (Miller, 2004, p. 332).

R—has been variously labeled Reiterative communication (Villagran et al., 2010), Reiteration and Radically Adaptive messages (Wittenberg-Lyles et al., 2010), and Relating (Goldsmith et al., 2013). Practitioners are encouraged to view "bad news" communication with patients and family members as an ongoing process rather than as a one-time event, as patients' and family members' capacity for understanding and needs for information change over time.

T—Team structure and processes of care—speaks particularly to the context of communication in hospice and palliative care, and an important feature of the shift to a team-based approach to communication and care is that physicians are no longer assumed to be the top of a chain of command, but rather serve in a more collaborative and facilitative role.

In sum, the COMFORT approach is a set of guiding principles that can assist individual practitioners and teams to communicate effectively in the context of patients' terminal prognosis, emphasizing a nonlinear, mutually influencing, and highly individualized process.

Empathic Responses. Perhaps because COMFORT provides guidelines for teams more so than for individuals, or because it establishes a context in which empathy is supposed to emerge, the model does not address empathy as a discrete communicative function; yet empathy is an essential capacity or competency of practitioners working at the end of life. Although there is debate regarding whether empathy is innate or can be learned (Buckman, Tulsky, & Rodin, 2011), empathy can be viewed as a set of skills of attending to the emotions of another person (relational), understanding those emotions (cognitive), and responding to those emotions (communicative; Buckman et al., 2011). However, physicians are often not skilled at responding to the emotional cues of patients and tend to focus on responding to clinical questions and providing information rather than addressing expressions of feeling (Buckman et al., 2011). One approach (Suchman et al., 1997) that supports the expression of empathy in the clinical context begins with the capacity to attend to the communication of patients or family members to identify and respond to empathic opportunities (i.e., explicit expressions of emotion) or potential empathic opportunities (i.e., implied expression of emotion). Once these opportunities are identified, practitioners may respond with a potential empathic opportunity continuer that invites explicit expression of emotion, an empathic response that recognizes and validates the expression of emotion, or an empathic opportunity terminator that ignores any expression of emotion and steamrolls ahead with a pragmatic clinical agenda.

Compared with end-of-life conversations in close personal relationships, conversations involving clinicians generally revolve around care delivery and are "professionalized" to the extent that clinicians are providing care for many patients continually across the course of a career. At the same time, the best clinicians are those who can balance the demands of the clinical context with the need for individualized care and compassion. In their most positive light, the models presented here represent the best efforts of researchers to assist clinicians in striking that balance between professional and personal communication.

CONCLUSIONS: BEYOND "CONVERSATION"

Most would agree that more communication is not necessarily better, and research has demonstrated that this is particularly true in the end-of-life context (Scott & Caughlin, 2014). Pertinent critiques have also been directed at an overemphasis on cognition and "talk" to support the dying process, to the diminishment of understanding dying as a primarily bodily experience (Seale, 1996). Although the focus of this chapter is on conversation, which implies verbal exchange between interlocutors, it is important to recognize that such exchange can become extremely compromised if not impossible as death approaches, and, in some cases, the capacity to verbally communicate may leave many years before terminal time. Thus, exploring more about the role and impact of nonverbal communication is important to having a comprehensive picture of communication at the end of life. Clearly, in addition to conversation or sometimes in place of it, people communicate with one another using nonverbal behaviors during their last interactions (Manusov, Keeley, Morgan, & Barnett, 2006). Specific nonverbal cues may lead to messages of love/affection, care/assistance, comfort, companionship, connection, and emotional expression and are mostly remembered as being positive and strong (Keeley & Baldwin, 2012b). Not all nonverbal communication is positive, because it may reveal the anger, frustration, and disappointment felt by the person who is dying (e.g., throwing hospital trays, using certain gestures; Keeley & Yingling, 2007).

Perhaps one of the most simple, significant, and yet challenging orientations to communicating at the end of life is the capacity to remain mindfully present— to "be there"—for the person who is dying (Foster, 2002, 2007; Keeley & Yingling,

2007). Several factors can make such mindful presence challenging including (1) a common tendency in our culture to be uncomfortable with silence, (2) self-consciousness or a preoccupation with our own feelings, (3) intrusive thoughts and anxieties related to daily life, and (as we discussed earlier) (4) anticipatory grief. However, when one is able to overcome these sources of interference, one invites the possibility of enacting support and experiencing the death of a loved one fully, whatever that may entail. Although death is a universal experience, the moments leading up to death and the meaning that may be derived from the experience are as individual and unique as the persons involved and although there may not be one "right" way to walk the journey, the first step begins with presence and a willingness to face what comes.

NOTES

1. As explained in the book (Foster, 2007), names and identifying information related to participants were changed to protect confidentiality.
2. In the first phase of Maureen's work, most of the participants insisted on using their real first names; these individuals are marked with an *.
3. Names of other participants from Maureen's research who are quoted throughout the chapter have been replaced with pseudonyms.

REFERENCES

Aiken, L. R. (2001). *Dying, death, and bereavement* (4th ed.). Mahwah, NJ: Lawrence Erlbaum.

Almack, K., Cox, K., Moghaddam, N., Pollock, K., & Seymour, J. (2012). After you: Conversations between patients and healthcare professionals in planning for end-of-life care. *BMC Palliative Care, 11*, 15.

Austin, J. L. (1983). *How to do things with words.* London, UK: Oxford University Press.

Baxter, L. A., & Montgomery, B. M. (1996). *Relating: Dialogues and dialectics.* New York, NY: Guilford Press.

Baile, W. F., Buckman, R., Lenzi, R., Glober, G., Beale, E. A., & Kudelka, A. P. (2000). SPIKES—a six-step protocol for delivering bad news: Application to the patient with cancer. *The Oncologist, 5*, 302–311.

Blackford, J., & Street, A. (2013). Facilitating advance care planning in community palliative care: Conversation starters across the client journey. *International Journal of Palliative Nursing, 19*, 132–139.

Bochner, A. P. (2003). Perspectives on inquiry III: The moral of stories. In M. L. Knapp & J. L. Daly (Eds.), *Handbook of interpersonal communication* (3rd ed. pp. 3–101). Thousand Oaks, CA: Sage.

Bochner, A. P. (2014). *Coming to narrative: A personal history of paradigm change in the human sciences.* Walnut Creek, CA: Left Coast Press.

Book, P. L. (1996). How does the family narrative influence the individual's ability to communicate about death? *Omega: Journal of Death and Dying, 33*, 323–341.

Buckman, R. (1984). Breaking bad news: Why is it still so difficult? *British Medical Journal, 288*, 1597–1599.

Buckman, R., Tulsky, J. D., & Rodin, G. (2011). Empathic responses in clinical practice: Intuition or tuition? *Canadian Medical Association Journal, 183*, 569–571.

Burgoon, J. K., Stern, L. A., & Dillman, L. (1995). *Interpersonal adaptation: Dyadic interaction patterns.* New York, NY: Cambridge University Press.

Butler, R. N. (1971). Age: The life review. *Psychology Today, 5*, 49–55.

Butler, R. N., Lewis, M. I., & Southerland, T. (1998). *Aging and mental health* (5th ed.). St. Louis, MO: Mosby.

Carstensen, L. L., Isaacowitz, D. M., & Charles, S. T. (1999). Taking time seriously: A theory of socioemotional selectivity. *American Psychologist, 54*, 165–181.

Considine, J., & Miller, K. (2010). The dialectics of care: Communicative choices at the EOL. *Health Communication, 25*, 165–174.

Cohen, A., & Nirenberg, A. (2011). Current practices in advance care planning. *Clinical Journal of Oncology Nursing, 15*, 547–553.

DuPré, A., & Foster, E. (forthcoming). Transactional communication. In E. Wittenberg-Lyles, B. Ferrell, J. Goldsmith, T. Smith, S. Ragan, M. Glajchen, & G. Handzo (Eds.), *Textbook of palliative care communication.* Oxford, UK: Oxford University Press.

Fisher, W. R. (1989). Clarifying the narrative paradigm. *Communication Monographs, 56*, 55–58.

Foster, E. (2002). Lessons we learned: Stories of volunteer-patient communication in hospice. *Journal of Ageing and Identity, 7*, 245–256.

Foster, E. (2007). *Communicating at the end-of-life: Finding magic in the mundane.* Mahwah, NJ: Lawrence Erlbaum.

Generous, M., & Keeley, M. P. (2014). Creating the Final Conversations (FCs) Scale: A measure of end-of-life relational communication with terminally ill individuals. *Journal of Social Work in End-of-Life and Palliative Care, 10*, 257–281.

Giles, H. (2008). Communication accommodation theory. In L. A. Baxter & D. O. Braithwaite (Eds.), *Engaging theories in interpersonal communication: Multiple perspectives* (pp. 161–173). Thousand Oaks, CA: Sage.

Giles, H., Coupland, J., & Coupland, N. (Eds.) (1991). *Contexts of accommodation.* Cambridge, UK: Cambridge University Press.

Glick, I. O., Weiss, R. S., & Parkes, C. M. (1974). *The first year of bereavement.* New York, NY: Wiley.

Goldsmith, J., Ferrell, B., Wittenberg-Lyles, E., & Ragan, S. (2013). Palliative care communication in oncology nursing. *Clinical Journal of Oncology Nursing, 17*, 163–167.

Goldsmith, J., Wittenberg-Lyles, E., Villagran, M., & Sanchez-Reilly, S. (2008, January 1). *Communicating emotional support when breaking terminal bad news using the SPIKES Model: Fourth year medical student encounters.* Paper presented at the annual meeting of the National Communication Association.

Hauwerwas, S. (2005). *Naming the silences: God, medicine, and the problem of suffering.* New York, NY: T & T Clark.

Heinz, D. (1999). *The last passage.* New York, NY: New York University Press.

Jenko, M., Gonzalez, L., & Seymour, M. J. (2007). Life review with the terminally ill. *Journal of Hospice and Palliative Nursing, 9*, 159–167.

Kaplan, M. (2010). SPIKES: A framework for breaking bad news to patients with cancer. *Clinical Journal of Oncology Nursing, 14*, 514–516.

Keeley, M. P. (2004a). Final conversations: Messages of love. *Qualitative Research Reports in Communication, 5*, 35–40.

Keeley, M. P. (2004b). Final conversations: Survivors' memorable messages, concerning religious faith and spirituality. *Health Communication, 16*, 87–104.

Keeley, M. P. (2007). "Turning toward death together": Functions of messages during final conversations in close relationships. *Journal of Social and Personal Relationships, 24*, 225–253.

Keeley, M. P. (2009). Comfort and community: Two emergent communication themes of religious faith and spirituality evident during final conversations. In M. Wills (Ed.), *Speaking of spirituality: Perspectives on health from the religious to the numinous* (pp. 227–248). Cresskill, NJ: Hampton Press.

Keeley, M. P., & Baldwin, P. (2012a). Final conversations, phase II: Children and everyday communication. *Journal of Loss and Trauma, 17*, 376–387.

Keeley, M. P., & Baldwin, P. (2012b). Final conversations: Positive communication at the end-of-life. In M. Pitts & T. J. Socha (Eds.), *Positive communication in health and wellness* (pp. 190–206). New York, NY: Peter Lang.

Keeley, M. P., & Generous, M. A. (2014a, November). *Challenges of final conversations for the living.* Paper presented at the Interpersonal Communication Division of the National Communication Association, Chicago, IL.

Keeley, M. P., & Generous, M. (2014b). Advice from children and adolescents on final conversations with dying loved ones. *Death Studies, 38*, 308–314.

Keeley, M. P., Generous, M., & Baldwin, P. (2014). Final conversations phase II: Children's final conversation messages with dying family members. *Journal of Family Communication, 14*, 208–229.

Keeley, M. P., & Koenig Kellas, J. (2005). Constructing life and death through final conversations narratives. In L. M. Harter, P. M. Japp, & C. S. Beck (Eds.), *Narratives, health, and healing: Communication theory, research, and practice* (pp. 365–390). Mahwah, NJ: Lawrence Erlbaum.

Keeley, M. P., & Yingling, J. (2007). *Final conversations: Helping the living and the dying talk to one another.* Acton, MA: VanderWyk & Burnham.

Kübler-Ross, E. (1997). *Living with death and dying.* New York, NY: Simon & Schuster.

Lawton, J. (2000). *The dying process: Patients' experiences of palliative care.* London, UK: Routledge.

Manusov, V., Keeley, M. P., Morgan, S. J., & Barnett, T. L. (2006, July). *When talking is difficult: Nonverbal communication and final conversations with loved ones.* Paper presented at the biannual conference of the International Association for Relationship Research, Crete, Greece.

McQuail, D. (1987). Functions of communication: A nonfunctionalist overview. In C. R. Berger & S. H. Chaffee (Eds.), *Handbook of communication science* (pp. 327–349). Newbury Park, CA: Sage.

McQuellon, R. P., & Cowan, M. A. (2000). Turning toward death together: Conversation in mortal time. *American Journal of Hospice & Palliative Care, 17*, 312–318.

Metzger, P. L., & Gray, M. J. (2008). End-of-life communication and adjustment: Pre-loss communication as a predictor of bereavement-related outcomes. *Death Studies, 32*, 301–325.

Millar, F. E., & Rogers, L. E. (1976). A relational approach to interpersonal communication. In G. E. Miller (Ed.), *Explorations in interpersonal communication* (pp. 87–104). Beverly Hills, CA: Sage.

Miller, W. (2004). The clinical hand: A curricular map for relationship-centered care. *Family Medicine, 3*, 330–335.

Moller, D. W. (1996). *Confronting death: Values, institutions, and human morality.* New York, NY: Oxford University Press.

Narayanan, V., Bista, B., & Koshy, C. (2002). "BREAKS" protocol for breaking bad news. *Indian Journal of Palliative Care, 16*, 61–65.

Nussbaum, J. F., Pecchioni, L. L., Robinson, J. D., & Thompson, T. L. (2000). *Communication and aging* (2nd ed.). Mahwah, NJ: Lawrence Erlbaum.

Parkes, C. M., & Weiss, R. S. (1983). *Recovery from bereavement*. New York, NY: Basic Books.

Pennebaker, J. W., & Beall, S. K. (1986). Confronting a traumatic event: Toward an understanding of inhibition and disease. *Journal of Abnormal Psychology, 95*, 274–281.

Ragan, S., Wittenberg-Lyles, E., Goldsmith, J., & Sanchez-Reilly, S. (2008). *Communication as comfort: Multiple voices in palliative care*. New York, NY: Routledge/Taylor & Francis.

Rogers, L. E. & Escudero, V. (2004). *Relational communication: Interactional perspective to the study of process and form*. Mahwah, NJ: Erlbaum.

Scott, A. M., & Caughlin, J. P. (2014). Enacted goal attention in family conversations about end-of-life health decisions. *Communication Monographs, 81*, 261–284.

Seale, C. (1996). *Constructing death: The sociology of dying and bereavement*. Cambridge, UK: Cambridge University Press.

Sedney, M., Baker, J. E., & Gross, E. (1994). "The story" of a death: Therapeutic considerations with bereaved families. *Journal of Marital and Family Therapy, 20*, 287–296.

Shavitt, S., & Nelson, M. (2001). The role of attitude functions in persuasion and social judgment. In J. P. Dillard & M. Pfau (Eds.), *The persuasion handbook: Theory and practice* (pp. 137-153). Thousand Oaks, CA: Sage.

Shetty, A. A., & Shapiro, J. (2012). How to break bad news—tips and tools for resident physicians. *Journal of Medical Education Perspectives, 1*, 20–24.

Somers, M. R. (1995). The narrative construction of identity: A relational and network approach. *Theory and Society, 23*, 605–649.

Suchman, A. L., Markakis, K., Backman, H. B., & Frankel, R. (1997). A model of empathic communication in the medical interview. Journal of the American Medical Association, 277(8), 678–682.

Turner, V. (1995). *The ritual process: Structure and anti-structure*. Hawthorne, NY: Aldine DeGruyter.

van Eechoud, I. J., Piers, R. D., Van Camp, S., Grypdonck, M., Van Den Noortgate, N. J., Devuegele, M.,…Verhaeghe, S. (2014). Perspectives of family members on planning end-of-life care for terminally ill and frail older people. *Journal of Pain and Symptom Management, 47*, 876–886.

Villagran, M., Goldsmith, J., Wittenberg-Lyles, E., & Baldwin, P. (2010). Creating COMFORT: A communication-based model for breaking bad news. *Communication Education, 59*, 220–234.

Watzlawick, P., Beavin J. H., & Jackson, D. D. (1967). *The pragmatics of human communication*. New York, NY: Norton.

Wigren, J. (1994). Narrative completion in the treatment of trauma. *Psychotherapy, 31*, 415–423.

Wittenberg-Lyles, E., Goldsmith, J., Parker Oliver, D., Demeris, G., & Rankin, A. (2012). Family communication in oncology care. *Seminars in Oncology Nursing, 28*, 262–270.

Wittenberg-Lyles, E., Goldsmith, J., & Ragan, S. (2010). The COMFORT initiative: Palliative nursing and the centrality of communication. *Journal of Hospice and Palliative Nursing, 12*, 282–292.

Wittenberg-Lyles, E., Goldsmith, J., Richardson, B., Hallett, J. S., & Clark, R. (2013). The practical nurse: A case for COMFORT communication training. *American Journal of Hospice and Palliative Care, 30*, 162–166.

CHAPTER EIGHT

Family Decision Making

AND Care AT THE

End OF Life

LORETTA L. PECCHIONI

RICHARD C. WHITE

When we think of the end of life, we tend to focus on the individual who is dying; individuals, however, are nested in families. The death of one family member impacts other family members because they are interdependent—what happens to one member influences the others. Families are dynamic systems. While an individual family member may die, the family continues. In this chapter, we consider decision making by family members not only before and during the dying process of one of its members, but also after that death, as the family works to reconfigure itself.

Across the lifespan, health-related issues are central to family life (Pecchioni & Keeley, 2011). Families are the primary source of caregiving from birth to death, whether that care is the business of our daily lives, or focused during a health crisis. Habits established in childhood lay the groundwork for adulthood, potentially prolonging or negatively impacting the quality and quantity of life. Family members discuss a wide range of health-related topics, including nutrition, exercise, alcohol and substance use and abuse, sexuality and sexual health, and death and dying (Pecchioni, Overton, & Thompson, 2015). Families may discuss these topics more or less explicitly, while the behaviors that are enacted around health issues also send messages about how a particular family understands health and illness.

At the end of life, patients and family members may need to make decisions regarding the continuation or cessation of aggressive treatments (e.g., chemotherapy), the continuation or withholding of nutrition and hydration, cardiopulmonary resuscitation, and respiratory intubation (National Hospice and Palliative Care Organization, 2014a). How a particular family discusses death and dying and makes decisions at the end of life of one of its members is part of the larger family culture about health-related issues and decision making in general. Within a family, some family members may have more power to make decisions about certain topics, while others may have more power in other areas (Segrin & Flora, 2005). For example, when children are young, parents are expected to make decisions for them. As the children develop, their parents may involve them in more shared decision making or allow the children to make decisions in some areas for themselves. In general, the types of decisions that need to be made may be trivial and simple or serious and complex. For example, deciding where to have dinner as a family is a simpler decision than is deciding whether it is time for an older family member to move to a nursing home. Decisions may also be classified as instrumental, affective, or both. Instrumental choices relate to functional tasks, such as whose turn it is to clear the table after a shared family meal. Affective choices are emotion based and reflect values, roles, and feelings of the family and its individual members. Thus, whose turn it is to clear the table may be based on roles and values (e.g., daughters are expected to help with domestic housework or expectations of equity result in everyone taking a turn). Decisions regarding the end of life are usually both instrumental and affective—how to balance quality and quantity of life is a complex mix.

Communication is crucial to end-of-life decision making (Clarke, Evans, Shook, & Johanson, 2005; Hines, Babrow, Badzek, & Moss, 1997; Kopelman, 2006; Parks et al., 2011), and a lack of communication during the dying process increases problems and decreases decision making (Goldsmith, Wittenberg-Lyles, Ragan, & Nussbaum, 2011). Dying individuals and their family members, however, do not often experience effective communication during this event.

A wide range of factors impacts any family's decision-making processes during the death and dying process. First, we turn to two factors which influence whether families engage in more or less explicit decision making: cultural norms that avoid talk about death and dying, and how families rely on their shared discursive histories to manage their interactions around this topic. Then, we turn to additional factors that impact how families communicate about decisions at the end of life for one of its members, focusing on the nature of the impending death; the ability and desire of the patient to participate; the patient's preferences for which family members should be involved in decision making; family conflict dynamics; and how formal care providers interact with the family members. We then touch briefly on how the family makes decisions during bereavement and conclude with suggestions that might enable more explicit communication about end-of-life decision making.

CULTURAL NORMS

Talking about death and dying in the U.S. and many Western countries has been recognized as a cultural taboo since Kübler-Ross's (1969) classic work (see also Whitney, this volume). Western cultures, however, are not the only ones that are not receptive to these discussions (Ko, Roh, & Higgins, 2013). Callahan (2009) argued that we have limited experience with the process of dying and, therefore, do not have scripts available for addressing the various issues that arise during our dying process or that of our loved ones. As a consequence, the American way of death is one of "dying in silence" (Ragan, Wittenberg-Lyles, Goldsmith, & Sanchez-Reilly, 2008).

Even in formal caregiving settings, discomfort about having end-of-life discussions limits how frequently and thoroughly the topic is addressed. Because physicians and patients expect the other person to raise the issue, neither one initiates these conversations, so end-of-life preferences do not get addressed (Nussbaum, Pecchioni, Robinson, & Thompson, 2000). Even when formal caregivers do encourage individuals to complete living wills and other advance directives, many individuals do not do so or if they have completed this paperwork, they may not have shared their preferences with family members. In England, the End of Life Care Strategy has been developing processes for professional care providers to facilitate patient involvement in advance care planning by helping them to consider their options and preferences (Barnes et al., 2012). The study found, however, that a limited number of older patients living in the community, and being served by primary care physicians, understood their options and had completed advance care directives. In the U.S., the National Funeral Directors Association (NFDA, 2014) found that more than 95% of their survey respondents thought it was important to have their wishes followed, and yet less than 25% had talked in depth with any family members about their funeral preferences.

FAMILY DISCURSIVE HISTORY

The cultural norm to avoid the discussion of death and dying impacts family discursive histories. The difficulty of addressing these issues is intertwined with powerful, wide-ranging emotions, making discussions about end-of-life preferences inherently complex and challenging (Planalp & Trost, 2008). As a consequence, few families have had in-depth conversations about end-of-life preferences. While a Pew Research Center (2013) survey found that nearly three-fourths of respondents had thought a great deal or at least somewhat about their own wishes, and more than 60% had talked to someone (including family members as well as physicians and clergy) about those wishes, only 35% had written down those preferences in the form of a letter, will, or other advance directive. Bauer-Wu et al. (2009) found that less than two-thirds of their participants (who had advanced-stage cancer) had had any discussions about their end-of-life preferences, and more than half had not shared their preferences with family members or formal caregivers. Older patients were more likely to have had these discussions, but even they were not likely to have documented their preferences in writing. The quantity of talk, however, is less important than is the quality of those conversations. Scott (2011) found that quality of talk—measured as attention to identity goals (i.e., positive face and negative face), relational goals, and task goals—was more important than quantity of talk about end-of-life preferences with regard to concordance in predicting loved ones' preferences, completion of documentation, and relational satisfaction and closeness.

Because family members have long histories with one another, their shared experiences offer them opportunities to learn about one another's attitudes and preferences (Pecchioni, 2001; Sillars & Kalbfleisch, 1989). As patterns of interaction build up over the years, family members feel more confident in predicting the behaviors of other family members, but they may not fully understand the others' motivations and preferences (Pecchioni, 2001).

Krieger's (2014) review of different types of decision-making theories helps explain this phenomenon. Classical decision theories focus on rational, individual processes, while naturalistic decision theories acknowledge that individuals are not always thorough in considering potential options, and that they make important decisions with others. Through communicative processes, relational partners come to overlap in their cognitions and emotions about a topic and this shared cognition, or "shared mind," results in cohesion, which impacts the type and frequency of messages exchanged in making a decision. Partners who believe they are in agreement will not feel the need to express their individual opinions, whereas partners who believe they are in disagreement will feel the need to express their individual opinions and seek the partner's opinions as well.

Reliance on these assumptions about others' preferences regarding the end of life occurs, however, in the context of individuals who *would* like to be able to clearly communicate their end-of-life desires. Yet, sharing their preferences is complicated by their lack of knowledge about end-of-life medical care (Schrader, Nelson, & Eidsness, 2009). Even when people are aware that death is inevitable, planning for that death or sharing plans that have been made does not necessarily occur (Nussbaum et al., 2000). Because issues surrounding death and dying are so often avoided, explicit conversations about preferences are not likely to occur. As a consequence, family members rely on their long shared history and *assume* that they know what a family member would prefer, even though those preferences are often inaccurate (Pecchioni, 2001). Although some of this avoidance may be due to a desire to ignore death and dying, some of the avoidance may stem from the assumption that family members will know what an individual prefers based on their shared mind.

Thus, as the family becomes involved in decision making at the end of life for one of its members, their conversations occur on a continuum from more explicit to more implicit (Sillars & Kalbfleisch, 1989). At the more explicit end of the continuum, problem solving is engaged through direct and open communication in which participants identify and discuss their attitudes, beliefs, and preferences. At the more implicit end of the continuum, silent arrangements are arrived at based on years of interaction that have led the participants to believe they understand the others' preferences without open and conscious discussion. Because decision making at the end of life may create opportunities for more explicit conversations, these interactions may also bring to light differences of opinions, leading to family conflict. To avoid such conflict, a return to silent arrangements and avoidance of issues may serve as a coping mechanism for the family.

ADDITIONAL ISSUES THAT IMPACT FAMILY DECISION MAKING

Whether families have had more explicit or less explicit discussions about an individual's preferences, other factors also impact how the patient and family manage decision making at a member's end of life: the nature of the impending death; the patient's ability and desire to participate; the patient's preferences for which family members are involved in which aspects of care and decision making; how the family manages conflict; and how formal caregivers interact with the patient and family members.

Nature of the impending death. Whether families have had conversations about an individual's preferences, family decision making is impacted by the nature of the impending death. While patients and family members report a preference for having a clear diagnosis (Chan, 2011) and having this knowledge allows for more appropriate decision making (Holmberg, 2006), families do not know what questions to ask or who should address those questions (McIntyre, 2002). In spite of these desires to know that death may be imminent, when an individual is diagnosed with a life-threatening illness, but treatment options exist, the patient and family members often prefer not to consider the possibility of death and instead to focus on maintaining hope and being optimistic about the outcome—that is, survival (Nedjat-Haiem, 2011). The patient and family members are often more focused on making decisions related to managing symptoms, such as pain, side effects of treatment, and so on.

In the case of accidents, however, the stress of limited time may preclude the opportunity to process the information and work through varying options (Krieger, 2014). Time limitations may negatively impact how many family members are able to participate in decision making, especially when they are geographically dispersed. In addition, family members are not able to take the time to discuss all the options and express their opinions while also dealing with their emotional responses to the crisis. These stressors inevitably reduce the quality and quantity of decision making by the patient and family, because they are not able to fully process the needed information along with their emotional responses.

The ability and desire of the patient to participate. Patients may be more or less able to participate in decision making, and their ability may change over time. During treatment, the patient may be more or less able to fully participate because of the impact of side effects from that treatment. If the patient is comatose or cognitively impaired, he or she will not be able to participate in decision making. Depending on the age of the patient, for example, if the patient is a young child, he or she will not have the ability or will have limited ability to participate based on cognitive development (see Galvin, this volume).

Besides the patient's ability to participate in decision making, the patient's preferences will influence his or her role in that process (Krieger, 2014). Some patients prefer to have total control and to make the final decision with varying amounts of consultation with (particular) family members. Other patients may choose to abdicate decision making to an identified surrogate, whether that has been done formally (i.e., legally) or informally. Some patients may want to be more or less involved in different areas of their care. For example, pain management is often left in the control of the patient, whereas managing finances and dealing with health insurance companies may be delegated to a family member.

Of course, the patient and family may or may not be aware of the impending death. Even when they are aware, a wall may be erected which constrains their topics of conversation and impacts how explicitly they discuss decision options. In their classic study of death and dying, Glaser and Strauss (1966) identified four dying contexts: closed, suspicion, mutual pretense, and open discussion. Mutual pretense is the most common (Glaser & Strauss, 1977) and is maintained by avoiding topics such as the patient's prognosis, discussing future plans as if the patient will participate in them, and sticking to safe topics and small talk (McKenzie, 1980). The patient and family members assume that others do not want to engage in conversations about death and so do not raise the topic to try to protect the others from painful emotions. Thus, engaging in mutual pretense will "create and enact many, many layers of denial" (Goldsmith et al., 2011, p. 445). Inevitably, this type of denial impacts decision making because the need for decisions is ignored or decisions that are made reflect this mutual pretense that death is not inevitable.

Patient preferences for which family members are involved in decision making. For family members to be involved, they must be informed about the situation and "invited" into the conversation. The patient may choose to reveal different levels of information to various family members. Even a family member who is informed about a life-threatening illness may not be invited into the decision-making process. For example, a parent may inform his or her children, but make decisions with the spouse.

Because family members have distinct relational roles, they are likely to have had different types of conversations. Spouses have the legal ability to make decisions for each other when one is incapable of doing so; therefore, formal caregivers turn to them first when decisions need to be made. Even if a couple has not had explicit conversations or signed legal documents, they are more likely to have had discussions about others' situations and their own preferences in light of those experiences (Nussbaum et al., 2000). Hinton (1981) found that spouses were about evenly divided among open (those who talked openly about a range of issues), mixed (those who talked openly about some issues while avoiding other topics), and closed (those who avoided nearly all of these issues) styles.

Older adults who have children may have also had these conversations with them, or have had some conversations with some of their children and other conversations with other children because of expectations regarding who will become the surrogate decision maker, assuming that those types of decisions have been made and formalized through a health care power of attorney or health care proxy (Nussbaum et al., 2000). Oldest daughters and/or more geographically proximate children are more likely to be considered as surrogate decision makers, so these conversations are more likely to have occurred, whereas other children may not have been included. Individuals with young children, however, are unlikely to have had these conversations with these children. Often family members try to protect children from bad news, and yet even young children know that something is going on and are more capable of dealing with these issues than they are given credit for (FitzSimmons, 1994).

Individuals who are not married and/or do not have children may have to consider other family members as their surrogates. They may turn to siblings, nieces and nephews, cousins, or friends who are not relatives. Little research has been conducted on how these family members or friends negotiate decision making at the end of life. The assumption is that without legal standing, these individuals may be precluded from being involved by formal caregivers.

Which family members are involved in decision making at the end of life is likely to reflect long-standing patterns of interaction within the family. Being able to share in problem solving and engage in collaborative decision making depends on the family's existing rules and roles (King & Quill, 2006). Those families that have interaction patterns that encourage shared problem solving and collaborative decision making are more able to call on those skills as they address end-of-life decisions for one of its members. A family with a history of suppressing the expression of emotions will have difficulty coming to terms with the reality of the loved one's impending death and will avoid the related decision making. These problems may be exacerbated if the person who is dying is also the authority figure in the family. In this case, the other family members are less likely to have the skills to make decisions or the willingness to challenge that authority figure if they disagree with him or her.

Family conflict dynamics. Although family members tend to have decision-making styles in common, not all members will adopt the same style (Segrin & Flora, 2005). No matter which family members are involved in end-of-life decision making, some family members may encourage more open discussion, ask questions, and offer their opinions. Other family members may try to avoid the topic by redirecting the discussion or selecting more ambiguous language. When different family members have different understandings or prioritize different goals, conflict is likely to arise. These conflicts, however, may also reflect long-standing tensions within the family, and complicate and delay any decision making (King & Quill, 2006).

In addition to differences among family members, the patient and family members may have different goals. Patients tend to prefer decisions that allow them to die with dignity by managing their pain and focusing on the quality of life during their last days. For example, individuals with a recurrence of cancer may forgo treatment because of the negative side effects they suffered during the first round of treatments. Families, however, tend to focus on quantity over quality of life (King & Quill, 2006), and resist the withdrawal of treatment or insist on aggressive, though medically futile, treatments (Goldsmith et al., 2011).

Whether differences arise based on long-standing issues (King & Quill, 2006; Kopelman, 2006; Kramer, Boelk, & Auer, 2006) or because different individuals have different goals, conflict among family members may arise as they struggle with making decisions as one of their members is dying (Goold, Williams, & Arnold, 2000; Kramer, 2013). Although one goal of advance care planning is to avoid conflict at the end of life (Parks et al., 2011), having a written document does not guarantee that conflict will not arise (Kramer, Kavanaugh, Trentham-Dietz, Walsh, & Yonker, 2009). Because of the potential for conflict among family members, patients may choose to try to help them avoid this conflict by involving some members while excluding others, only to exacerbate long-standing issues.

Interactions between family members and formal health care providers. Although most individuals want to have family members involved in the decision-making process, formal health care providers may find sharing that information difficult. One reason for this difficulty is legal, based on the HIPAA Privacy Rule (U.S. Department of Health and Human Services, 2009). Health-related information is private information; that is, the information about a patient's health status is legally his or her own information. For the patient and family members to make decisions, they must have information, and most often they turn to the formal health care providers for that information (Nussbaum et al., 2000). Formal care providers, however, must consider who is allowed to have information based on their legal status through marriage and/or a health care power of attorney, living will, or other documents. Therefore, formal care providers are legally limited with whom they may share information. Patients and their family members, however, often have much less restrictive attitudes toward who is considered to be in a caregiving role and, therefore, should receive information from formal caregivers (Hauser & Kramer, 2004).

In addition, if the patient has signed legal documents, such as an advance care directive, physicians and health care proxies are legally required to follow that document, despite any preferences expressed by family members even when they may argue for voiding those documents (Winter & Parks, 2008). Potentially more complicated are conversations about the patient's preferences when the physician and patient have had these discussions, but those decisions have not been shared by the patient with the family through formal or informal means. The formal care provider and family members may have very different understandings of the patient's preferences, but the physician must follow his or her understanding of those guidelines rather than follow the demands of family members.

Besides these legal limitations, formal care providers may not have the communicative skills to deliver bad news in a compassionate fashion, or to provide the needed information as well as be nurturing. Interactions among the physician, patient, and companion are complicated communicative events during routine health interactions (Gutierrez, 2013; Nussbaum et al., 2000), so it is not surprising that discussions about the end of life may be even more complicated for health care providers when they are interacting with multiple individuals who may have different perspectives and goals (Goldsmith et al., 2011).

Physicians could be of greater service to patients and their families if they encouraged advance care planning, promoted more effective communication among all parties, and demonstrated empathy for the family members' emotions and grief (Rabow, Hauser, & Adams, 2004). Attending to this range of patient and family needs, however, is neither why medical personnel are hired nor the focus of their training. However, when family conflict arises, medical personnel are expected to intervene to resolve these issues (Boelk & Kramer, 2012).

Because physicians know they have poor skills at breaking bad news and talking about death, discussing advance directives, and coordinating care, physicians may make decisions without collaborating with the patient and family (Back, Arnold, Tulsky, Baile, & Fryer-Edwards, 2003; Jackson et al., 2008; Wittenberg-Lyles, Goldsmith, Ragan, & Sanchez-Reilly, 2010a, 2010b). Especially when the dying person is institutionalized in a nursing home or hospital, physicians may limit both the patient's and the family's involvement in decision making (Larochelle, Rodriguez, Arnold, & Baranato, 2009). As a consequence, the family may have few opportunities to be involved (Nussbaum et al., 2000).

Holst, Lundgren, Olsen, and Ishøy (2009) address how difficult it may be in hospice care to balance the needs of all parties, even in the best of circumstances. The decision-making process, however, becomes particularly challenging if there are factions within the family advocating for different courses of action or bringing their long-standing issues with each other into the process. For example, if a patient has children with more than one partner, the children and their other parent may have different views of what the patient wants and of their relative rights to help make decisions. These factions may try to play different staff members against each other; therefore, Holst et al. (2006) recommend written agreements that are shared widely.

MOVING TOWARD MORE EXPLICIT DECISION MAKING

Whether family members have had discussions about end-of-life issues, involvement with hospice care is likely to increase the opportunities for and openness of these conversations. Hospice care serves both the patient who is dying and his or her family members and friends with its primary goals being the management of physical, emotional, social, and spiritual pain (Ragan et al., 2008). Although we tend to acknowledge the physical pain often associated with fatal illnesses, individuals who are aware of their impending death may experience emotional and social pain as they realize that their loved ones are suffering because of their impending death. Their family members also experience emotional and social pain as they observe a loved one's suffering and ponder a future without that person.

As the hospice movement grows in the U.S., more individuals and their families are likely to take advantage of its services (see Egbert, this volume). In spite of the benefits of the hospice experience, however, a resistance to the move to hospice care exists because it is seen as a marker of death (Goldsmith et al., 2011) as patients, families, and doctors may all find it difficult to accept that a patient is dying (Callahan, 2009). This resistance often delays admission to hospice services. In 2012, the median stay in hospice was 18.7 days, and nearly two-thirds of those admitted died in less than 30 days (National Hospice and Palliative Care Organization, 2014a).

To provide individually tailored care, hospice staff attempt to learn about the patient's physical and emotional needs, social and cultural setting, along with family dynamics and expectations (Holst et al., 2009; King & Quill, 2006). Therefore, one of the key aspects of hospice with regard to family decision making is the family meeting, or series of meetings, facilitated by trained hospice staff members (King & Quill, 2006; Levin, Moreno, Silvester, & Kissane, 2010). In these family meetings, hospice staff want to learn about the family's understanding of their loved one's prognosis and treatment options; the family's values; and the patient's preferences and the family's understanding of those preferences (King & Quill, 2006). The hospice staff then help to guide the family through the process of developing a care plan that is tailored to individual needs (Goldsmith et al., 2011).

During the process of developing the individualized care plan, hospice staff members find opportunities to generate more explicit communication between the patient and family members (Goldsmith et al., 2011). For example, metaphors and strategic ambiguity are often used to avoid talking explicitly about the fact that death is imminent and to suppress feelings. Unpacking these metaphors and reducing ambiguity lead to more explicit communication styles. In spite of attempts to increase the explicitness of communication, the topics that arise in hospice care tend to focus on physical needs and caregiving issues, with some attention paid to issues regarding family dynamics, while conversations about death and dying continue to be avoided (Brownlee & Bruening, 2010).

Because spirituality is often considered such a personal experience and different family members may have different beliefs, hospice workers often find it difficult to navigate the spiritual needs of their clients (Considine & Miller, 2010). Spirituality, however, provides a vital source of comfort for believers; therefore, hospice staff must try to balance between leading and following the patient and family in discussions about their spiritual pain and needs. A key factor may well be the simple acknowledgment that different individuals have different spiritual needs and beliefs and that the patient and family should make room for these differences as they manage the end of life of one of its members.

With a wide range of family dynamics in mind, the DECIDE model helps to organize the different types of interactions that are likely to arise throughout this decision-making process and an approach for balancing these multiple needs and goals. Krieger (2014) identifies five styles based on the desire of the patient for autonomy or interdependence and the desire of the family member (or members) to support autonomy or interdependence during decision making. These styles are independent, isolated, collaborative and delegated, and demanding. The independent style emphasizes the patient's autonomy and the family members work to facilitate autonomy by not attempting to influence them or other caregivers. In the isolated style, the patient desires interdependence by seeking support and input from family members; however, the family members ignore or rebuff these attempts because they want the patient to be responsible for decisions. In the collaborative and delegated styles, both the patient and family members desire interdependence and either work as full partners during decision making or the patient delegates his or her rights and responsibilities to a particular family member. In the demanding style, the patient desires autonomy while the family desires interdependence and thus offers unsolicited support. These different styles highlight complex relational dynamics and provide a means for identifying the source of at least some types of conflict that could then be more effectively mediated.

FAMILY ADJUSTMENTS FOLLOWING THE DEATH OF A MEMBER

The loss of a family member is important to family members individually and as a unit during and after the loved one's death (Goldsmith et al., 2011). At the time of the death, many decisions need to be made and action taken. Initial decisions, such as funeral plans (e.g., burial or cremation, plot location) and managing the estate, may be addressed by final arrangement plans and/or wills (Callahan, 2009; NFDA, 2014). At least one person needs to know about insurance policies, survivors' pension benefits, bank accounts, and the location of documents such as deeds; however, these topics are not common among final conversations (Keeley, 2007).

Bereavement is a complex process (see also Toller, this volume), so we will limit our discussion here to its impact on family decision making. The overall success of bereavement may depend on the family's adaptive resources (King & Quill, 2006) and acceptance of an expected loss through pre-loss communication with the now-deceased family member (Metzger, 2008). If they had strong skills prior to the loss of the loved one, they will be able to call on those skills to help them adjust and adapt to the new configuration of their individual and family lives. One of the benefits of hospice care is that survivors whose loved one died in hospice report less complicated grief because the staff helped them to develop skills and to look to the future and anticipate reconfiguring the survivors' lives (Bakitas et al., 2009; Zhang et al., 2009).

One of the greatest challenges of family bereavement is that a complex mix of emotions is being felt, which often makes decision making more difficult as family members do not want to make decisions or feel capable of making decisions (Nussbaum et al., 2000). In addition, not all members of the family will express their grief in the same manner or on the same timetable (Nussbaum et al., 2000). These differences may lead to conflict among family members as they fail to understand each other's grieving process and negatively impact effective decision making as they focus on their differences rather than on their shared histories. If the person who died was a key source of decision making, the family may struggle to develop the skills to process their options (Nussbaum et al., 2000). Creating opportunities for shared grief may help the family to move through the bereavement process (Callahan, 2009), not only because it helps them to manage their emotions, but because it also reinforces their ability to work as a unit.

While the loss of a loved one affects the whole family, the degree of impact will depend on individual relationships with that person. Because family roles are defined in relationship to other family members (e.g., spouse, parent-child, grand-parent-grandchild), the loss of a family member affects the relational and social roles that were intertwined with that loved one (Keeley, 2007). Not surprisingly, the loss of a long-term spouse will have greater impact than will the loss of a grandparent with whom a grandchild was not particularly close (Nussbaum et al., 2000). For widowed individuals, the loss of the partner has a number of conse-quences, but one of most importance for our purposes in this chapter is that they have been making decisions during their shared lifetime with this partner and they may find it difficult to make decisions or to find a new partner for decision making. If the surviving spouse has adult children, they are likely to become more involved in decisions, but the domains of these decisions may be quite different from those that occurred with the spouse. For older individuals, maintaining their indepen-dence in their home may become more difficult as they no longer have the spouse to assist them in day-to-day household activities. Therefore, older adults who are widowed will move either to cohabit with children or to an institutional setting such as assisted living or a nursing home. Making these types of major decisions while also mourning the loss of a loved may be particularly challenging when seen as an abandonment of shared memories as well.

Besides the impact on individuals, the family must work to reconfigure itself after the death of a loved one. While the impact of the loss of a loved one ripples through all types of family dynamics and functioning, we will limit our focus here to the decision-making process. The role the deceased played in the family impacts future decision-making processes. For example, if the deceased person was the pri-mary decision maker, the family will need to adjust who makes decisions with and for the surviving members. Just as a widowed individual may now have to make decisions without the deceased partner, other family members may need a new source of advice and assistance when making decisions. For example, an adult child with young children may have relied on the advice of the now-deceased parent when making child-rearing decisions. With that source of information, wisdom, and support now absent, new sources must be developed.

CONCLUSIONS

Although conversations about the end of life are challenging—especially when talking with loved ones about their future deaths—they are worth the time and effort. Having these discussions and, preferably, putting preferences in writing help to ensure that the patient's wishes are followed. Not only does this serve the person who is dying, it also serves the survivors by reducing the stress and burden for family caregivers as they make decisions during an emotional time. This reduces the potential for conflict among family members. When end-of-life decisions are guided by the values of the individual who is dying, everyone involved may feel more confident that they have shown respect for their loved one and are then better able to reflect on their own preferences for the end of life.

The importance of having planned for and shared one's preferences with regard to the end of life seems evident for all concerned. Encouraging those conversations, however, continues to be a challenge. Future research should examine ways not only to encourage such conversations, but also to facilitate the formal documentation of these preferences.

Conversations among loved ones regarding their preferences to guide end-of-life decision making are easier when they occur before their need arises. The National Hospice and Palliative Care Organization (2014b) recommends that individuals and families take advantage of "conversation triggers" that serve as an opening for these discussions. Opportunities arise from many sources: the death of a friend or colleague; the media, including television talk shows, dramas and comedies, movies, and newspaper or magazine articles or books about illness; sermons; financial planning; annual medical checkups; and family occasions such as baptisms, marriages, and (especially) funerals. In a culture that avoids conversations about death and dying, providing examples of *how* to initiate those discussions seems vital.

Once a family member has entered hospice care, hospice staff have the training and tools to help guide the patient and family through the process. For example, King and Quill (2006) developed and refined (Wilkins, Quill, & King, 2009) a tool that helps to assess a family's strengths based on their relational abilities and offer strategies for intervention when a family exhibits behaviors reflecting serious disruption. Research on the implementation of such strategies, including identifying who might be in a position to make these assessments and assist the family through the process, is needed. In addition, extending this training to begin earlier in the caregiving process might be beneficial. If physicians do not engage in these discussions with the patients during regular exams, who in the health care system might do so?

REFERENCES

Back, A., Arnold, R. M., Tulsky, J. A., Baile, W. F., & Fryer-Edwards, K. (2003). Teaching communication skills to medical oncology fellows. *Journal of Clinical Oncology, 21*, 2433–2436.

Bakitas, M., Lyons, K., Hegel, M., Balan, S., Brokaw, F., Seville, J., & Ahles, T. (2009). Effects of a palliative care intervention on clinical outcomes in patients with advanced cancer. *JAMA, 302,* 741–749.

Barnes, S., Gardiner, C., Gott, M., Payne, S., Chady, B., Small, N., & Halpin, D. (2012). Enhancing patient-professional communication about end-of-life issues in life-limiting conditions: A critical review of the literature. *Journal of Pain and Symptom Management, 44,* 866–879.

Bauer-Wu, S., Yeager, K., Norris, R. L., Qin, L., Habin, K. R., Hayes, C., & Jurchak, M. (2009). Communication and planning at the end-of-life: A survey of women with advanced stage breast cancer. *Journal of Communication in Healthcare, 2,* 371–386.

Boelk, A. Z., & Kramer, B. J. (2012). Advancing theory of family conflict at the end of life: A hospice case study. *Journal of Pain and Symptom Management, 44,* 655–670.

Brownlee, A., & Bruening, L. M. (2010). Methods of communication at end of life for the person with amyotrophic lateral sclerosis. *Topics in Language Disorders, 32,* 168–185.

Callahan, D. (2009). Death, mourning, and medical progress. *Perspectives in Biology and Medicine, 52,* 103–115.

Chan, W. C. (2011). Being aware of the prognosis: How does it relate to palliative care patients' anxiety and communication difficulty with family members in the Hong Kong Chinese context? *Journal of Palliative Medicine, 14,* 997–1003.

Clarke, P., Evans, S. H., Shook, D., & Johanson, W. (2005). Information seeking and compliance in planning for critical care: Community-based health outreach to seniors about advance directives. *Health Communication, 18,* 1–22.

Considine, J., & Miller, K. (2010). The dialectics of care: Communicative choices at the end of life. *Health Communication, 25,* 165–174.

FitzSimmons. E. (1994). One man's death: His family's ethnography. *Omega: Journal of Death and Dying, 30,* 23–39.

Glaser, B. G., & Strauss, A. L. (1966). *Awareness of dying.* Chicago, IL: Aldine.

Glaser, B. G., & Strauss, A. L. (1977). The ritual drama of mutual pretense. In S. H. Zarit (Ed.), *Readings in aging and death: Contemporary perspectives* (pp. 271–276). New York, NY: Harper & Row.

Goldsmith, J., Wittenberg-Lyles, E., Ragan, S., & Nussbaum, J. F. (2011). Life span and end-of-life health communication. In T. L. Thompson, R. Parrott, & J. F. Nussbaum (Eds.), *The Routledge handbook of health communication* (pp. 441–454). New York, NY: Routledge.

Goold, S. D., Williams, B., & Arnold, R. M. (2000). Conflicts regarding decisions to limit treatment: A differential diagnosis. *JAMA, 283,* 909–914.

Gutierrez, K. M. (2013). Prognostic categories and timing of negative prognostic communication from critical care physicians to family members at end of life in an intensive care unit. *Nursing Inquiry, 20,* 232–244.

Hauser, J., & Kramer, B. (2004). Family caregivers in palliative care. *Clinics in Geriatric Medicine, 20,* 671–688.

Hines, S. C., Babrow, A. S., Badzek, L., & Moss, A. H. (1997). Communication and problematic integration in end-of-life decisions: Dialysis decisions among the elderly. *Health Communication, 9,* 199–217.

Hinton, J. M. (1981). Sharing or withholding awareness of dying between husband and wife. *Journal of Psychosomatic Research, 25,* 337–343.

Holmberg, L. (2006). Communication in action between family caregivers and a palliative home care team. *Journal of Hospice and Palliative Nursing, 8,* 276–287.

Holst, L., Lundgren, M., Olsen, L., & Ishøy, T. (2009). Dire deadlines: Coping with dysfunctional family dynamics in an end-of-life care setting. *International Journal of Palliative Nursing, 15,* 34–41.

Jackson, V., Mack, J., Matsuyama, R., Lakoma, M. D., Sullivan, A. M., Arnold, R. M.,…Block, S. D. (2008). A qualitative study of oncologists' approaches to end-of-life care. *Journal of Palliative Medicine, 11,* 893–906.

Keeley, M. (2007). "Turning toward death together": The functions of messages during final conversations in close relationships. *Journal of Social and Personal Relationships, 24,* 225–253.

King, D., & Quill, T. (2006). Working with families in palliative care: One size does not fit all. *Journal of Palliative Medicine, 9,* 704–715.

Ko, E., Roh, S., & Higgins, D. (2013). Do older Korean immigrants engage in end-of-life communication? *Educational Gerontology, 39,* 613–622.

Kopelman, A. E. (2006). Understanding, avoiding, and resolving end-of-life conflicts in the NICU. *The Mount Sinai Journal of Medicine, 73,* 580–586.

Kramer, B. J. (2013). Social workers' roles in addressing the complex end-of-life care needs of elders with advanced chronic disease. *Journal of Social Work in End-of-Life and Palliative Care, 9,* 308–330.

Kramer, B. J., Boelk, A. Z., & Auer, C. (2006). Family conflict at the end of life: Lessons learned in a model program for vulnerable older adults. *Journal of Palliative Medicine, 9,* 791–801.

Kramer, B. J., Kavanaugh, M., Trentham-Dietz, A., Walsh, M., & Yonker, J. A. (2009). Predictors of family conflict at the end of life: The experience of spouses and adult children of persons with lung cancer. *The Gerontologist, 50,* 215–225.

Krieger, J. L. (2014). Family communication about cancer treatment decision-making. In E. Cohen (Ed.), *Communication Yearbook 38* (pp. 278–305). Thousand Oaks, CA: Sage.

Kübler-Ross, E. (1969). *On death and dying.* New York, NY: Macmillan.

Larochelle, M. R., Rodriguez, K., Arnold, R. M., & Baranato, A. E. (2009). Hospital staff attributions of the causes of physician variation in end-of-life treatment intensity. *Palliative Medicine, 23,* 460–470.

Levin, T. T., Moreno, B., Silvester, W., & Kissane, D. W. (2010). End-of-life communication in the intensive care unit. *General Hospital Psychiatry, 32,* 433–442.

McIntyre, R. (2002). *Nursing support for families of dying patients.* London, UK: Whurr.

McKenzie, S. C. (1980). *Aging and old age.* Glenview, IL: Scott, Foresman.

Metzger, P. J. (2008). End-of-life communication and adjustment: Pre-loss communication as a predictor of bereavement-related outcomes. *Death Studies, 32,* 301–325.

National Funeral Directors Association. (2014). *2014 Consumer Awareness and Preferences Study.* Brookfield, WI: Author.

National Hospice and Palliative Care Organization. (2013). *NHPCO's facts and figures: Hospice care in America, 2013 edition.* Retrieved July 14, 2014, from http://www.nhpco.org/

National Hospice and Palliative Care Organization. (2014a). Communicating your end-of-life wishes. Retrieved July 14, 2014, from http://www.nhpco.org/

National Hospice and Palliative Care Organization. (2014b). Conversations before the crisis. Retrieved August 2, 2014, from http://www.nhpco.org/outreach-materials/caring-connections-materials

Nedjat-Haiem, F. (2011). Getting to end-of-life discussions in advanced cancer care: Barriers and attitudes that limit end of life communication for disadvantaged Latinos. *Dissertation Abstracts International,* section A, 71.

Nussbaum, J. F., Pecchioni, L. L., Robinson, J. D., & Thompson, T. (2000). *Communication and aging* (2nd ed.). Mahwah, NJ: Lawrence Erlbaum.

Parks, S. M., Winter, L., Santana, A. J., Parker, B., Diamond, J. J., Rose, M., & Myers, R. E. (2011). Family factors in end-of-life decision-making: Family conflict and proxy relationship. *Journal of Palliative Medicine, 14*, 179–184.

Pecchioni, L. L. (2001). Implicit decision-making in family caregiving. *Journal of Social and Personal Relationships, 18*, 219–237.

Pecchioni, L. L., & Keeley, M. P. (2011). Insights about health from family communication theories. In T. L. Thompson, R. Parrott, & J. Nussbaum (Eds.), *The Routledge handbook of health communication* (2nd ed., pp. 363–376). New York, NY: Routledge.

Pecchioni, L. L., Overton, B. C., & Thompson, T. L. (2015). Families communicating about health. In R. West & L. Turner (Eds.), *The Sage family communication handbook* (pp. 306–319). Thousand Oaks, CA: Sage.

Pew Research Center. (2013). *Views on end-of-life medical treatments.* Washington, DC.

Planalp, S., & Trost, M. R. (2008). Communication issues at the end of life: Reports from hospice volunteers. *Health Communication, 23*, 222–233.

Rabow, M., Hauser, J., & Adams, J. (2004). Supporting family caregivers at the end of life: "They don't know what they don't know." *JAMA, 291*, 483–491.

Ragan, S., Wittenberg-Lyles, E. M., Goldsmith, J., & Sanchez-Reilly, S. (2008). *Communication as comfort: Multiple voices in palliative care.* New York, NY: Routledge.

Schrader, S., Nelson, M., & Eidsness, L. (2009). Dying to know: A community survey about dying and end-of-life care. *Omega, 60*, 33–50.

Scott, A. (2011). Family conversations about end-of-life health decisions. *Dissertation Abstracts International*, section A, 72.

Segrin, C., & Flora, J. (2005). *Family communication.* Mahwah, NJ: Lawrence Erlbaum.

Sillars, A. L., & Kalbfleisch, P. J. (1989). Implicit and explicit decision-making styles in couples. In D. Brinberg & J. Jaccard (Eds.), *Dyadic decision making* (pp. 179–215). New York, NY: Springer.

U.S. Department of Health and Human Services. (2009). Health Insurance Portability and Accountability Act (HIPAA) Privacy Rule. Retrieved from http://www.hhs.gov/ocr/privacy/hipaa/adminstrative/privacyrule/index.html.

Wilkins, V. M., Quill, T. E., & King, D. A. (2009). Assessing families in palliative care: A pilot study of the Checklist of Family Relational Abilities. *Journal of Palliative Medicine, 12*, 517–519.

Winter, L., & Parks, S. M. (2008). Family discord and proxy decision makers' end-of-life treatment decisions. *Journal of Palliative Medicine, 11*, 1109–1114.

Wittenberg-Lyles, E., Goldsmith, J., Ragan, S., & Sanchez-Reilly, S. (2010a). *Dying with COMFORT: Family narratives and early palliative care.* Cresskill, NJ: Hampton Press.

Wittenberg-Lyles, E., Goldsmith, J., Ragan, S., & Sanchez-Reilly, S. (2010b). Medical students' views and ideas about palliative care communication training. *American Journal of Hospice and Palliative Medicine, 27*, 38–49.

Zhang, B., Wright, A. A., Huskamp, H. A., Nilsson, M. Maciejewski, M. L., Earle, C. C.,…Prigerson, H. G. (2009). Health care costs in the last week of life: Associations with end-of-life conversations. *Archives of Internal Medicine, 169*, 480–488.

CHAPTER NINE

Family Communication
AS A Child Is Dying

KATHLEEN A. GALVIN

The death of a child is perceived as a death out of season, a monstrosity, an outrage against the natural order of things. (Viorst, 1986)

Parents never envision talking with their terminally ill children about death. Yet, when children battle a potentially fatal childhood illness, parents struggle to decide whether, when, and under what conditions they will begin an ongoing conversation about death with their 5- or 15-year-old. In addition, they confront related issues—whether, when, and how to engage their other children and extended family members in these conversations. Conversely, terminally ill children wonder whether, when, and how to share their questions and feelings with family members. If such conversations occur, no family member escapes unscathed from the pain of the heart-wrenching talks but few regret those conversations.

Although only a small number of U.S. families experience the death of a child or adolescent, when a family loses one of their youngest members, the loss ripples through generations (Ward, DeSantis, Robbins, Kohler, & Jemal, 2014). Few communication scholars have addressed the impact of a child's death; fewer still have examined interactions between and among family members as a child faces death. This chapter explores the question, What communication practices characterize family communication as a child or adolescent faces death? Before addressing family communication as a child confronts death, a brief overview of certain potentially lethal diseases and their impacts is provided.

CHILDHOOD CANCER AND OTHER LIFE-THREATENING DISEASES

Childhood cancer remains the leading disease-related cause of death in U.S. children ages 5 to 14. Approximately 1 in 285 U.S. children will be diagnosed with cancer before the age of 20; their overall 5-year survival rate is approximately 80%. Approximately 1 in 530 young adults between the ages of 20 and 39 is a cancer survivor (Ward et al., 2014).

Sickle cell disease is the most common life-shortening childhood genetic disease. Approximately 1,000 infants are born with sickle cell disease every year. A majority of patients, 60% to 80%, are African Americans (1 in 500) or Latino (1 in 1,000 to 1,400) (U.S. National Library of Medicine, 2012).

Cystic fibrosis, the most common genetic disease in the U.S., is the second most common life-shortening childhood genetic disorder, affecting 30,000 children and adults in the U.S. (Cystic Fibrosis Foundation, 2014). Approximately 1,000 new cases are diagnosed each year (American Lung Association, 2010). Other disorders that may lead to childhood death include AIDS, lissencephaly, asthma, meningitis, and multiple sclerosis.

Children and adolescents encounter death in other ways: frequently, these deaths are sudden and immediate. Accidents represent the major cause of death in children from ages 1 to 24 (MedlinePlus, 2012). Along the age continuum, infants are more likely to die of developmental and genetic conditions and SIDS, whereas for children ages 1 to 14 cancer is the third most common cause of death. In addition, adolescents/young adults between the ages of 15 and 24 are more likely to die as a result of homicide and suicide; in most of these cases, family members do not experience final conversations. This chapter focuses extensively on childhood cancer in American and Western European families because this disease affects the greatest number of children and represents the largest number of communication-oriented research studies.

FOUNDATIONAL FAMILY COMMUNICATION-ORIENTED RESEARCH

Early studies of parents' ongoing communication with dying children gained visibility through the scholarship of three social scientists. Glaser and Straus (1965) depict how parents and ill children enacted protection charades involving a pretense strategy: "When something happens, or is said that tends to expose the fiction that both parties are attempting to sustain (i.e. that the patient is not dying, is going to get better) then each must pretend that nothing has gone awry" (Glaser & Strauss, 1965, p. 73). This mutual avoidance strategy prevented family members' disclosure about a child's serious health issues or imminent death. Glaser and Strauss's grounded theory approach to studying childhood death remains a major scholarly contribution.

As a pioneer of the area, Bluebond-Langner (1978) conducted ethnographic research on family communication and dying in a hospital ward serving young leukemic patients ages 3 through 9. These early scholars revealed the difficult and convoluted family communication patterns that develop as a child faces death. Bluebond-Langner's early research shattered the following comforting myths: (1) children do not comprehend the gravity of their illness and (2) they do not understand that they are dying. Her observations of children's interactions on a leukemia ward revealed that patients obtained their information about death by observing dying peers, talking with peers about conceptions of death, and eavesdropping on conversations of medical professionals and family members. Her research revealed that "kids realize dying is not an appropriate topic with parents but see it as appropriate with other children" (p. 10).

These observations revealed the painful pretense maintained by dying children and their parents. Children frequently discussed their health conditions in their communal bathroom, thereby preventing adults from overhearing them. Some quizzed the nursing staff about how their illness compared with that of a recently deceased child. As certain young, relapsed patients moved through the five stages of leukemia, they became less likely to talk about treatments with their parents and more skilled at identifying the taboos about discussing their disease. These children became adept at continual eavesdropping, reading parental nonverbal cues, and pretending to sleep while doctors discussed their conditions with their parents. Nearing the end of their lives, some children became fearful of wasting time and began asking direct questions or making statements about their perceived short-term prognosis. Unfortunately, these efforts seldom broke the silence. Most parents and offspring enacted pretense performances until a child's last breath.

Over ensuing decades, changes in medical practices and normative family communication patterns served to alter family interaction patterns as a child confronts death. Today, in many Western nations, effective pediatric care is characterized by three assumptions: (1) shared knowledge exists among the child, family, and medical professionals; (2) relationships reflect mutual respect, caring, and trust among all involved; and (3) supportive shared decision making occurs among the child (depending on age), members of the family, and the medical team (Mack & Liben, 2012). Open communication serves as the goal; frequently difficult and necessary conversations occur between and among family members. Even so, some parents still resist full disclosure and some children and adolescents choose to protect their parents, enacting a "context of painful pretense" (Bluebond-Langner & Nordquist Schwallie, 2008, p. 166). Often this practice reflects a family's cultural or religious norms and members' implicit or explicit communication rules.

CHILDREN'S FAMILY COMMUNICATION PATTERNS

Children with life-threatening illnesses, even young children, frequently exhibit some level of awareness that they are dying although they may not express this cognizance directly in order to protect other family members. This awareness comes as a result of "reading physiological cues as their bodies change and the visual or auditory cues from the reactions of parents and medical staff members" (Beale, Baile, & Aaron, 2005, p. 3629). Often, children do not have an opportunity to discuss death because parents prevent such discussions (Black, 1998) because of protectiveness, cultural norms, or fear of facing the truth. However, recent studies reveal that children wish to be informed about their health status and future treatments (Wolfe, Friebert, & Hilden, 2002).

When children become concerned about the fatal nature of their disease, they may articulate their fears in multiple ways—verbally or nonverbally, directly or indirectly. If such concerns are not recognized and addressed openly, some will enact their fears through recognizable behaviors. Adolescents are often aware of the limited time they have left and may express their anxiety by regressing into a fetal position or expressing fears that their treatments will not be successful (Beale et al., 2005). If such strategies do not affect the way the information is provided by parents and doctors, teenagers may express rage, raise concerns about sexuality and appearance, and display heightened time awareness. Young children who become aware of physiological changes communicate their fears through drawings and behavioral indicators such as crying, becoming lethargic, making angry outbursts, and refusing to eat or cooperate during medical procedures.

As the end approaches, a child may turn inward, withdrawing from engagement with others. Such communication barriers frequently affect family members, not only at the moment, but also over the ensuing time period. Therefore, confronting issues about how best to communicate effectively with dying children is "seminal because providing information and actively addressing their concerns can enhance the cooperation of the child, reduce anxiety, and lighten the burden of secrecy" (Beale et al., 2005, p. 3629). Open family communication prevents painful regrets that can significantly impede members' recovery processes.

PARENTAL COMMUNICATION WITH DYING CHILDREN

The death of a child shatters the societal expectation that children outlive their parents. When parents "find themselves watching their child face the threat of death, imminent or not, any sense of order is shattered" (Sourkes et al., 2005, p. 350). In this situation, a parent's responsibilities involve shepherding a seriously ill child, and any siblings, through the excruciating process of living in the present while preparing for an unfathomable loss.

Given the sensitivity of these issues and the difficulty of gaining access to affected family members, very few communication research studies address dying children and their families. One major retrospective Swedish study examined parental communication about death when a child had a malignant disease (Kreicbergs, Valdimarsdottir, Onelov, Henter, & Steineck, 2004). Researchers asked 449 parents who lost a child to describe their communication with that child about death. Of the 429 parents who provided communication information, 147 (34%) reported talking about death with their child and 282 (66%) revealed that they had not discussed the topic. None of those who talked about death regretted it, whereas 69 (27%) of those who did not talk about it regretted their decision. Although 73% of parents reported talking about death with their children, 63% of those children were not told their illness was incurable. Occasionally, a physician also participated in the family conversation. Parents who sensed that their child was aware of his or her imminent death and parents of older children were more likely to discuss death with their offspring. Not surprisingly, religious parents were more likely to discuss death. Finally, most parents (76% or 326 respondents) talked with each other at some point about their child's forthcoming death.

Studies reveal that children wish to be informed by their parents about their illness and treatment plans, yet unsubstantiated beliefs exist regarding the impact of communicating about death with a child (Wolfe et al., 2002). Common myths, as above, include (1) the child cannot comprehend the concept or (2) the child will become severely depressed. These beliefs may reflect the need for grieving adults to protect themselves when they cannot find the words to initiate conversations about death with a beloved child. Given that ongoing research indicates that children often understand their medical status but pretend to be ignorant of their impending death in order to protect their parents, open and honest conversations represent an opportunity for honest disclosures and loving interactions.

Unfortunately, the nature of the treatments may compromise the context for such conversations. Talking with a child at the end of life becomes especially complicated when health practitioners use aggressive, toxic therapies. Researchers who queried parents about their hospitalized children's last weeks found that children dying of cancer experienced fatigue, pain, breathlessness, and poor appetite during their last month (Wolfe et al., 2000). Parents reported that 89% of the children suffered "a lot" or "a great deal" from at least one symptom, circumstances that prevented meaningful conversations. These authors called for greater attention to symptom control and the child's overall well-being in order to facilitate a more peaceful death; they asserted that hospice care provided a "greater likelihood that parents would describe their child as calm and peaceful during the last month of life" (Wolfe et al., 2000, p. 332). Clearly, context may affect family members' ability to discuss death with a desperately ill child.

Hospice represents a type of palliative care (see Egbert, this volume) provided to patients expected to live six months or less and who no longer receive treatment for their illness. Within a hospice context, many children die either at home or in a hospice facility. This context encourages open family communication involving the dying child. Parents are encouraged to ask open-ended questions, look for hidden meanings in their child's questions or comments, talk about the child's thoughts and feelings, and reassure the child that he or she will not die alone (American Society of Clinical Oncology, 2014).

As parents watch their children fade, the rest of their world continues to spin. Other people and commitments require attention. Parents struggle to decide where to invest their time. One parent whose 8-year-old son battled cancer captures this experience, saying, "In this fragmented world I tried desperately to negotiate numerous dialectical tensions: public—private, home—work, sick child—healthy child, order—chaos" (Manning, 2008, p. 244).

DECISION MAKING AS A CHILD FACES DEATH

Little is known about parental decision making when children are dying (Heinze & Nolan, 2012). As parents manage their children's medical care, they struggle with decisions about how much to engage their affected child, siblings, and other members of the extended family in these conversations. One of the most challenging questions remains, "Should I talk with my child about death?" If the patient is an adolescent, a parent may also ask, "To what extent should I involve my teenager in end-of-life decision making?"

Family decision making when a child confronts death challenges every affected parent. Based on their meta-ethnography of the extant research on parental decision making for children with cancer at the end of life, Heinze and Nolan (2012) identified three emerging themes: communicating, extending time, and understanding the prognosis. The authors explained that parents wanted direct and honest communication from medical professionals and equated clear and compassionate communication with excellent care. Parents emphasized their need for emotional support and their desire for "comfort, emotion, sincerity, verbalizations of caring, and reassurance" (Heinze & Nolan, 2012, p. 342). They also wished to extend the time they have with their dying children. Finally, they expressed their need for a straightforward understanding of their child's medical state instead of receiving contradictory messages from different medical professionals. For most parents, determining the circumstances of their child's death represents the most painful and significant decision of their lives.

Disagreements between an older child and parent may arise when discussing life-prolonging possibilities. Today, many Western nations rely on the concept of "shared decision making" when confronting major medical issues. This approach, a middle ground between paternalism (physician controlled) and informed choice (patient/family controlled), entails information transparency among the medical professionals, parents, and children, according to their age and comprehension (Makoul & Clayman, 2006). The role of children in treatment decision making has changed over time. Currently, "pediatric societies in North America, as well as the United Kingdom and Europe take the position that children should be part of the decision-making process" (Bluebond-Langner, Belasco, & DeMesquita Wander, 2010, p. 330). This shift alters the traditional assumption of parental decision making when a child battles illness.

In cases involving young children, parents now share decision making with physicians; in cases involving adolescents, the patient may participate in decision making by providing assent. This approach supports older children's involvement, especially when "the clarity of the 'right choice' fades, where treatment preferences are based upon personal values and 'quality of life' issues" (McCabe, 1996, p. 506).

Aware that their recovery chances range from minimal to none, some children protect their parents from their fears and doubts. Therefore, some children enact the mutual pretense strategy desiring not to challenge their parents (Bluebond-Langner et al., 2010). Other children reveal a desire for some control over the process, such as a 10-year-old who writes about being caught between "kind of wanting to go up to heaven" while also reflecting on how much her family would miss her (Sourkes et al., 2005, p. 368). Certain older adolescents, under the age of 18, may be excluded from end-of-life discussions; their parents and medical professionals manage the case without requesting or permitting the patient's involvement. During end-of-life care, medical ethicists may become involved in order to reach a decision about the appropriateness of involving the patient in decision making (Galvin & Liu, 2014).

Occasionally, grieving parents, their terminally ill child, and medical personnel become embroiled in painful disagreement regarding medical decision making, creating even more painful family interactions. "Shuttle Diplomacy" represents a resource to help facilitate family decision making. This mediation model is "applicable to the issue of involving chronically and terminally ill children in treatment decisions" (Bluebond-Langner & Nordquist Schwallie, 2008, p. 168). It maps out a plan for negotiations when children voice their opinions related to treatment possibilities and outcomes (Bluebond-Langner, DeCicco, & Belasco, 2005), assuming that all parties—physician, parent(s), and child—need to be respected and that children have a right, if they wish to become involved, to know about the procedures they would undergo. A highly structured process, this model attempts to identify seriously ill children's perspectives and incorporate them into the decision-making process.

Mature minors are adolescents capable of fully comprehending the nature and consequences of proposed medical treatments, who represent a special decision-making category (Kuther, 2003). Focusing on competency as a major determinant, Derish and Vanden Heuvel (2000) recommended involving certain mature adolescents in end-of-life decisions, asserting that mature minors are particularly vulnerable to receiving end-of-life treatments that they did not choose to accept.

AYAs: ADOLESCENT AND YOUNG ADULT ISSUES

Recent changes in the conception of adolescence have impacted medical decision making. In recent decades, the notion of adolescence has been extended as the result of widespread continuing education and training beyond secondary school as well as later entry into marriage and parenthood. Developmental theorist Arnett (2000, 2011) proposed a new life stage of "emerging adulthood" characterized by identity exploration, instability, a focus on self, feeling in-between, and considering possibilities. He argues that contemporary young people remain more dependent on their families for support, financial and otherwise, than in previous decades. Hence, modern-day parents tend to be more involved in medical decision making and the medical care of their older adolescent and young adult offspring than in previous generations.

Family challenges surface when adolescents or young adults face the probability of death at the same time their independent lives are taking shape. In the U.S., the category of young adult oncology usually includes individuals 15 to 39 years of age; in European countries, the age range tends to be 13 to 24 (Adolescent and Young Adult Oncology Progress Review Group, 2006). Adolescent oncology patients between 15 and 19 most commonly battle lymphomas, germ cell tumors, and leukemias. Some of the most complex treatment issues involve the desires of older high school and younger college-age students to become involved in their care decisions, possibly usurping their parents' decision-making power.

Teenagers confronting a deadly cancer encounter unique circumstances as they struggle to share age-appropriate developmental experiences while confronting significant physical and psychological challenges. Essentially, they find themselves "caught between childhood and adulthood both medically and developmentally" (Howk & Wasilewsku-Masker, 2011, p. 11). Because adolescents tend to envision themselves as invulnerable, they may minimize or ignore symptoms as they prioritize current commitments or pleasures. Teenagers may attribute their fatigue or physical changes to other causes. Yet, at this age of increased vulnerability to stress, a cancer diagnosis presents teenagers with "major developmental challenges beyond those faced by other young people" (Adolescent and Young Adult Oncology Progress Review Group, 2006, p. B41).

Adolescents' desire to socialize and maintain friendships interfaces with their medical care. A study of cancer patients between the ages of 13 and 19 revealed adolescents' need to manage the following four areas of their lives (Lam, Cohen, & Roter, 2013). First, affected teenagers seek to avoid isolation through participating physically and socially in normative adolescent life, while remaining responsive to medical concerns or prohibitions. Second, many grapple with the change in peers' social perceptions of them because of others' constant awareness of their condition. Managing a multitude of these interpersonal interactions creates a high level of stress. Third, teen patients struggle with the physical effects of cancer treatments, such as loss of weight, hair, or limbs; these losses not only affect everyday life but also call attention to the ailing peer in undesirable ways. Finally, adolescents have health communication expectations, such as participating in discussions of their condition with professionals or others. Many affected teenagers report enacting coping strategies such as joking about the cancer and seeking out a support community of peers battling cancer in order to manage these challenges.

In their search for support, many seriously ill teens or young adults turn to online communities to find a therapeutic peer community. As a result of discussions between a team of cystic fibrosis medical specialists and 18 affected teenagers who reported having no friends battling this disease, an online discussion group was formed. Members participated in an Internet-based or WebTV support system for five months (Johnson, Ravert, & Everton, 2001), after which time the researchers concluded that the social and expressive characteristics of the group involvement held promise as a support vehicle. Similarly, many AYA (Adolescent/Young Adult) cancer patients join Stupid Cancer, an online/offline community for interactional support (National Cancer Institute, n.d.). Not surprisingly, these adolescents need support to deal with their feelings of anger as they grieve the loss of relationships that are just beginning to form; however, parents may struggle with their teenagers' reliance on this type of support.

Cancer treatments shatter many teenagers' age-appropriate goals of gaining privacy and achieving autonomy. Adolescent patients need others to respect their privacy and their desire to control with whom their medical information is shared. At the same time, parents struggle to shield their teenagers from bad news even when adolescents ask to hear the truth. Sometimes parents' intrinsic desire to protect their children leads them to request that health care professionals limit the medical information that the patient hears (Howk & Wasilewski-Masker, 2011).

Many parents feel ill equipped to hold an honest conversation with their adolescent about death. They may be insecure about what words to use and how to respond to questions their children may have; avoidance of these conversations and questions appears as a preferable alternative. In many cases, parents do not know other parents who have experienced such potential loss, or their denial of death remains powerful (Howk & Wasilewski-Masker, 2011).

Because adolescents understand the permanent and irreversible nature of death, health professionals confront an ethical dilemma when parents request that older teenagers be denied accurate information regarding the serious nature of their conditions. Most medical professionals believe that teenagers are equipped to provide input into their plan of care and making decisions, such as whether to continue curative treatment or pursue palliative care (Howk & Wasilewski-Masker, 2011). To deny an adolescent the opportunity to participate in his or her care decisions often creates an ethical minefield.

Because certain treatments for life-threatening cancer involve fertility-threatening radiation treatments, health care professionals may present parents and older adolescents with fertility-preservation options that must occur before the cancer treatment commences. In cases of adolescent males, sperm banking provides a fast and highly effective method of preserving fertility for those who have reached puberty. In cases of adolescent females confronting fertility-threatening cancer, the issues are more complicated and involve complicated family discussion (Galvin & Clayman, 2010). Female fertility preservation efforts involve hormonal intervention followed by in vitro fertilization and embryo cryopreservation (Woodruff, 2010). Such decision making is compounded by the possibility of the child's death at some future point, leaving other family members to make decisions regarding the future of the banked sperm or eggs.

One of the few studies of later adolescents and young adults with advanced cancer (ages 20 to 40) examined the relationship between grief due to cancer-related losses and life disruption due to cancer symptoms (Trevino, Fasciano, & Prigerson, 2013; Trevino, Maciejewski, Fasciano, & Prigerson, 2011). In addition to the expected fatigue and pain, the authors suggest that grief constitutes a unique burden for young adults because the disease may interfere with the patients' ongoing romantic relationships, pursuit of further education, and career plans as well as their family interactions. Many young adults confront their inability to reach their long-term life goals, such as achieving a professional career or becoming a parent, because of early-onset menopause or compromised fertility. These authors advance the benefits of social networking on the Internet to reduce feelings of isolation. As teenagers and young adults continue to outpace their parents in technological skills, younger patients often become more knowledgeable about their diseases and their treatment opportunities, a reality that changes family decision-making practices.

SIBLINGS OF DYING CHILDREN

Siblings of a child or adolescent diagnosed with life-limiting cancer find themselves caught in a web of stressors including anxiety, fear, and change. The extent to which the experience dominates their lives depends, in part, on their age, relationship to the affected sibling, family communication practices, and the family structure. The following themes dominate their lives: loss, gains, intense feelings, and an ongoing sense of unmet needs (Wilkins & Woodgate, 2005). Whereas some siblings are involved in relevant family conversations, others fade into the background. Bluebond-Langner (1996) reported that "well siblings' understanding of themselves and others is linked to their parents' responses and to their ill sibling's condition and illness experience" (p. xiii).

Especially for younger children, the loss of time with parents when a sibling is critically ill looms large as parental substitutes become more actively involved in their everyday lives. Even when present, parents may be distracted by worries about their critically ill child and therefore less emotionally available to their other children. Older siblings often find themselves performing housework tasks or caretaking younger siblings. Conversely, many siblings experience emotional growth as they respond to their affected brother's or sister's needs.

These circumstances generate a wide range of intense feelings, often involving sadness, loneliness, rejection, anxiety, anger, jealousy, and guilt at various points as parents and other relatives become consumed by the dying child's needs (Wilkins & Woodgate, 2005). Confounding this issue further, family interaction patterns shift because of the decreasing time available for sibling-parent conversations, a reality that leads to communication breakdowns. Based on his early study of siblings of pediatric cancer patients ages 7 to 18, Koch (1985) identified the following five patterns of the siblings' response to the family changes: (1) an increase in negative affect (sad, angry); (2) the emergence of rules prohibiting emotional expression; (3) health and behavior problems; (4) role changes; and (5) increased closeness. Many siblings revealed their sorrow about the diagnosis or wished they could experience the pain in the affected child's place. Even given their discussion of multiple problems, siblings identified increased family closeness as a positive outcome.

When children are able to talk about what is "going on" in the family, overall communication occurs more freely. For example, a study of sibling communication with children and their dying sibling found that mothers who talked more freely with dying children also did so with the siblings (Graham-Pole, Wass, Eyeberg, Chu, & Olejnik, 1989).

These overall findings continue into the present. As one child in a family battles life-limiting cancer, parents struggle to find a balance between involving and protecting their other children. Often, adults attempt to protect siblings from some of the stress and pain but, in many cases, siblings read this as exclusion (Chalmers, 2010). Frequently, siblings know more than parents realize because they overhear comments or discussions that lead to anxiety and confusion. Essentially, siblings need straightforward information in language they can understand. According to Chalmers (2010), when adults do the following, siblings will cope more effectively: (1) reassure them they will be taken care of, (2) acknowledge their grief, and (3) validate their experiences and feelings.

Siblings pay a particularly high price as the death of a brother or sister approaches; many report feelings of loneliness, sadness, anxiety, depression, guilt, and shame (Hancock, 2011). Some siblings act out their behavioral and emotional stress, which contributes to family problems. Often, this acting-out behavior signals a need for attention. Because siblings of dying children have a high risk of developing psychological disturbance (Black 1998), they are more likely to struggle with normative everyday interactions. In recent years, Internet resources for siblings of patients battling chronic and life-threatening medical conditions, such as Starbright World, serve to create online support communities (Llenas, 2013).

Siblings frequently experience a sense of belonging when they become involved in the ill sibling's care. Behaviors such as giving a foot massage help a sibling to feel included and useful (Chalmers, 2010). Although some siblings are at risk for emotional and behavioral difficulties, others experience emotional growth as they become more compassionate. Siblings with greater empathy tend to experience fewer difficulties in psychological adjustments than those with lower empathy levels (Labay & Walco, 2004).

After a child dies, the bereaved siblings experience a "double loss" due to the death and the unavailability of parents who are overwhelmed with grief (Gerhardt et al., 2012, p. 210). After the death of an infant or young child, it is not unusual for a surviving child to become more "special" or for the child closest to the deceased child to feel obligated to make up for the family's loss (McGoldrick, Gerson, & Petry, 2008). Siblings carry this experience of a sibling's death throughout their lives

PERINATAL LOSS AND COMMUNICATION

A seldom-addressed area of family grief and communication involves perinatal loss—the death of a fetus during a pregnancy of 22 weeks or more (miscarriage) or a stillbirth or neonatal death. Many outsiders presume the impact of this loss will be minimal. The opposite, however, is frequently true; if family members and friends are not attuned to this grief, it becomes disenfranchised.

Given the significant changes in pregnancy care in the past decades, parental connections to an unborn child have deepened in multiple ways. Medical tests indicate the fetus's gender early in the pregnancy. This information permits parents to refer to the fetus by his or her gender and planned name; it may influence their plans for decorating the baby's space or purchasing clothes and toys. Parents frequently address a fetus by his or her proposed name and assign the fetus personal characteristics, such as "feisty" or "easygoing."

Today, many family members consider that they "met the new addition" through the magic of technology. "The most controversial aspect of ultrasound imaging is what this 'window' says about the fetus as a person" (Mitchell, 2001, p. 6). Most parents listen to their offspring's heartbeat while watching their child(ren) sucking a thumb or yawning. Images of the child in utero appear in photos proudly shared with other family members. Some parents who experience seeing the beating heart and thumb-sucking behavior view this as a demonstration that "the fetus is aware of its surroundings and has the potential for or actually possesses distinctive human consciousness and personhood" (Mitchell, 2001, p. 6).

Today, a fetal death creates a powerful sense of loss because of the depth of bonding and constructed personal identity, in part, through ultrasound viewing experiences of parents, and often siblings and grandparents, which established him or her as a family member. On occasion, parents confront making a tragic decision, such as removing a severely ill newborn from life support; little is known about such decision-making conversations.

Perinatal death not only results in the loss of life; it also shatters a family's hopes and dreams for the future. Such an experience evokes strong feelings of guilt about what might have, or should have, been done to prevent the loss. But, unlike the death of a child who has been an active presence in the family, outsiders may perceive perinatal death as a non-event, raising doubts in the family members' minds about whether they ought to be feeling as they do and whether society sanctions their grief (Silverman & Baglia, 2015). Given the difficulty of grieving a perinatal death, this loss may remain unresolved for a long time, although current research efforts explore the impact of creating a memory scrapbook (Willer, in progress).

Perinatal loss often impacts familial identity. If the partners are childless, perinatal loss threatens their newfound family identity. In many homes, parents face the communication challenge of explaining what happened to their promised sister or brother. The absence of social sanctions for the grief, as well as the other children's inability to understand the meaning of death, may strain parenting abilities and threaten family equilibrium.

CONCLUSIONS

Although a substantial literature addresses the impact of caring for a dying child on parents and siblings, little is known about the roles and interactional patterns of (1) extended family members such as grandparents, stepparents, and stepsiblings, (2) single parents, or (3) gay, lesbian, bisexual, and transgender parents (GLBT). For example, grandparents of children who died of cancer experience "silent grief" because "their grief is silent and has no cultural framework" (Nehari, Grebler, & Amos, 2008, p. 53). The concept of unacknowledged grief extends to the experiences of myriad family members, linked through combinations of biology, law, and commitment.

Currently, communication scholars are breaking new ground through their examinations of the role of narrative in healing (Silverman & Baglia, 2015), the use of online communities of young adults with cancer (Donovan, LeFebvre, Tardiff, Brown, & Love, 2014), and the struggle with uncertainty experienced by numerous adolescent and young adult cancer patients (Donovan, Brown, LeFebvre, Zaitchik, & Love, in press). Communication scholars committed to explorations of palliative care and communication among adolescent and young adult patients and their family members need to partner with medical professionals, family therapists, and social workers to gain access to young patients and their families undergoing an extraordinarily painful period of their lives. In addition, there is much to be learned about their needs and concerns about their future and their ties to family and friends, the writings, artwork, and interpersonal interactions of adolescents and young adults through the use of new media. No longer does the hospital room or a bedroom limit the communication of desperately ill children.

In the end, family members live with the memories of the familial messages exchanged, face-to-face or through mediated contexts, over the period of an increasingly debilitating illness. When a child dies, the loss reverberates throughout generations. Stories serve as markers of healing; sudden tearful silences serve as reminders of unresolved grief. The death of a child truly is an outrage (Viorst, 1986).

REFERENCES

Adolescent and Young Adult Oncology Progress Review Group. (2006). *Closing the gap: Research and care imperatives for adolescents and young adults with cancer* (NIH Publication No. 06-6067). Washington, DC: U.S. Department of Health and Human Services.

American Lung Association. (2010). Cystic fibrosis (CF). In *State of lung disease in diverse communities*. Retrieved from http://www.cff.org/AboutCF?

American Society of Clinical Oncology. (2014). *Caring for a terminally ill child: A guide for parents*. Retrieved from http://www.cancer.net/navigating-cancer-care/advanced-cancer/caring-terminally-ill-child-guide-parents

Arnett, J. J. (2000). Emerging adulthood: A theory of development from the late teens through the twenties. *American Psychologist, 55*, 469–480.

Arnett, J. J. (2011). Emerging adulthood(s): The cultural psychology of a new life stage. In L. A. Jensen (Ed.), *Bridging cultural and developmental approaches to psychology: New synthesis in theory, research, and policy* (pp. 255–275). New York, NY: Oxford University Press.

Beale, E. A., Baile, W. F., & Aaron, J. (2005). Silence is not golden: Communicating with children dying from cancer. *Journal of Clinical Oncology, 23*, 3629–3631.

Black, D. (1998). The dying child. *BMJ: British Medical Journal, 316*, 1376–1378.

Bluebond-Langner, M. (1978). *The private worlds of dying children.* Princeton, NJ: Princeton University Press.

Bluebond-Langner, M. (1996). *In the shadow of illness: Parents and siblings of the chronically ill child.* Princeton, NJ: Princeton University Press.

Bluebond-Langner, M., Belasco, J. B., & DeMesquita Wander, M. (2010). "I want to live, until I don't want to live anymore": Involving children with life-threatening and life-shortening illnesses in decision-making about care and treatment. *Nursing Clinics of North America, 45*, 329–343.

Bluebond-Langner, M., DeCicco, A., & Belasco, J. (2005). Involving children with life shortening illnesses in decisions about participation in clinical research: A proposal for shuttle diplomacy and negotiation. In E. Kodish (Ed.), *Ethics and research with children: A case-based approach* (pp. 241–246). New York, NY: Oxford University Press.

Bluebond-Langner, M., & Nordquist Schwallie, M. (2008). "It's back": Children with cancer talking about their illness when cure is not likely. In C. Commachio, J. Golden, & G. Weitz (Eds.), *Healing the world's children: Interdisciplinary perspectives on child health in the twentieth century* (pp. 161–175). Montreal, Quebec, Canada: McGill-Queen's University Press.

Chalmers, A. (2010). When a sibling is terminally ill: Supporting children. *Child Bereavement UK.* Retrieved from http://www.childbereavementuk.org

Cystic Fibrosis Foundation. (2014, June 16). About CF. Retrieved from http://www.cff.org/AboutCF/?

Derish, M. T., & Vanden Heuval, K. (2000). Mature minors should have the right to refuse life-sustaining medical treatment. *Journal of Law, Medicine and Ethics, 28*, 109–124.

Donovan, E. E., Brown, L. E., LeFebvre, L., Zaitchik, S., & Love, B. (in press). "The uncertainty is what is driving me crazy": The tripartite model of uncertainty in the adolescent and young adult cancer context. *Health Communication.*

Donovan, E. E., LeFebvre, L., Tardiff, S., Brown, L. E., & Love, B. (2014). Patterns of social support communicated in response to expressions of uncertainty in an online community of young adults with cancer. *Journal of Applied Communication Research, 42*, 432–455.

Galvin, K. M., & Clayman, M. L. (2010). Whose future is it? Ethical family decision-making about daughters' treatment in the oncofertility context. In T. K. Woodruff, L. Zoloth, L. Campo-Engelstein, & S. Rodriguez (Eds.), *Oncofertility: Ethical, legal, social, and medical perspectives* (pp. 429–445). New York, NY: Springer.

Galvin, K. M., & Liu, E. (2014). Disturbing arguments: Treatment decision-making when a female adolescent confronts fertility-threatening cancer. In C. H. Palczewski (Ed.), *Disturbing argument* (pp. 136–142). New York, NY: Routledge.

Gerhardt, C. A., Fairclough, D., Grossenbacher, J. C., Barrera, M., Gilmer, M. J., Foster, T. L., & Vannata, K. (2012). Peer relationships of bereaved siblings and comparison classmates after a child's death from cancer. *Journal of Pediatric Psychology, 37*(2), 209–219.

Glaser, B., & Strauss, A. (1965). *Awareness of dying: A study of social interaction.* Chicago, IL: Aldine.

Graham-Pole, J., Wass, H., Eyeberg, S., Chu, L., & Olejnik, S. (1989). Communicating with dying children and their siblings: A retrospective analysis. *Death Studies, 13*, 465–483.

Hancock, L. (2011). The camp experience for siblings of pediatric cancer patients. *Journal of Pediatric Oncology Nursing, 28*, 137–142.

Heinze, K. E. K., & Nolan, M. T. (2012). Parental decision-making for children with cancer at the end of life: A meta-ethnography. *Journal of Pediatric Oncology Nursing, 29*, 337–345.

Howk, T., & Wasilewski-Masker, K. (2011). Palliative care for adolescents and young adults: A pediatric perspective. *Journal of Adolescent and Young Adult Oncology, 1*, 11–12.

Johnson, K. B., Ravert, R. D., & Everton, A. (2001). Hopkins Teen Central: Assessment of an Internet-based support system for children with cystic fibrosis. *Pediatrics, 107*, 1–8.

Koch, A. (1985). "If only it could be me": The families of pediatric cancer patients. *Family Relations, 34*, 63–70.

Kreicbergs, U., Valdimarsdottir, U., Onelov, E., Henter, J-I., & Steineck, G. (2004). Talking about death with children who have severe malignant disease. *New England Journal of Medicine, 351*, 1175–1185.

Kuther, T. L. (2003). Medical decision-making and minors: Issues of consent and assent. *Adolescence, 38*, 343–358.

Labay, L. E., & Walco, G. (2004). Brief report: Empathy and psychological adjustment in siblings of children with cancer. *Journal of Pediatric Psychology, 29*, 309–314.

Lam, C. G., Cohen, K. J., & Roter, D. L. (2013). Coping needs in adolescents with cancer: A participatory study. *Journal of Adolescent and Young Adult Oncology, 2*, 10–16.

Llenas, B. (2013, July 28). Social media gives voice, hope to young cancer patient. Fox News. Retrieved from http://www.foxnews.com/health/2013/07/28/social-media-gives-voice-hope-to-young-cancer-patient/

Mack, J. W., & Liben, S. (2012). Communication. In A. Goldman, R. Hain, & S. Liben (Eds.), *Oxford textbook of palliative care for children* (2nd ed., pp. 23–34). New York, NY: Oxford University Press.

Makoul, G., & Clayman, M. L. (2006). An integrative model for shared decision-making in medical encounters. *Patient Education and Counseling, 60*, 302–312.

Manning, L. D. (2008). Parenting and professing in cancer's shadow. *Women's Studies in Communication, 31*, 240–248.

McCabe, M. A. (1996). Involving children and adolescents in medical decision-making: Developmental and clinical considerations. *Journal of Pediatric Psychology, 21*, 505–516.

McGoldrick, M., Gerson, R., & Petry, S. (2008). *Genograms: Assessment and intervention* (3rd ed.). New York, NY: Norton.

Medline Plus. (2012, August 1). *Death among children and adolescents.* U.S. National Library of Medicine, NIH National Institutes of Health. Retrieved from http://www.nlm.nih.gov/medlineplus/ency/article/001915.htm

Mitchell, L. M. (2001). *Baby's first picture: Ultrasound and the politics of fetal subjects.* Toronto, Ontario, Canada: University of Toronto Press.

National Cancer Institute. (n.d.). Organizations and resources. Retrieved November 18, 2014, from http://www.cancer.gov/cancertopics/aya/resources

Nehari, M., Grebier, D., & Amos, T. (2008). The silent grief. *Bereavement Care, 27*(3), 51–54.

Silverman, R. E., & Baglia, J. (Eds.). (2015). *Communicating pregnancy loss: Narrative as a method for change.* New York, NY: Peter Lang.

Sourkes, B., Franke, L., Brown, M., Contro, N., Benitz, W., Case, C.,...Sunde, C. (2005). Food, toys, and love: Pediatric palliative care. *Current Problems in Pediatric Adolescent Health Care, 35,* 350–386.

Trevino, K. M., Fasciano, K. F., & Prigerson, H. G. (2013). Patient-oncologist alliance, psychosocial well-being, and treatment adherence among young adults with advanced cancer. *Journal of Adolescent and Young Adult Oncology, 31,* 1683–1689.

Trevino, K. M., Maciejewski, P. K., Fasciano, K., & Prigerson, H. G. (2011). Grief and life disruption in young adults with advanced cancer. *Journal of Adolescent and Young Adult Oncology, 1,* 168–172.

U.S. National Library of Medicine. (2012). *Genetics home reference: Your guide to understanding genetic conditions.* Retrieved November 18, 2014, from http://ghr.nlm.nih.gov

Viorst, J. (1986). *Necessary losses: The loves, illusions, dependencies, and impossible expectations that all of us have to give up in order to grow.* New York, NY: Fireside.

Ward, E., DeSantis, C., Robbins, A., Kohler, B., & Jemal, A. (2014). Childhood and adolescent cancer statistics, 2014. *CA: A Cancer Journal for Clinicians, 64,* 83–103.

Wilkins, K. L., & Woodgate, R. L. (2005). A review of qualitative research on the childhood cancer experience from the perspective of siblings: A need to give them a voice. *Pediatric Oncology Nursing, 22,* 305–319.

Willer, E. (in progress). Scraps of the Heart Project. University of Denver. Retrieved from https://www.indiegogo.com/projects/the-scraps-of-the-heart-project

Wolfe, J., Friebert, S., & Hilden, J. (2002). Caring for children with advanced cancer: Integrating palliative care. *Pediatric Clinics of North America, 49,* 1043–1062.

Wolfe, J., Grier, H. E., Klar, N., Levin, S. B., Ellenbogen, J. M., Salem-Schatz, S.,...Weeks, J. C. (2000, February 3). Symptoms and suffering at the end of life in children with cancer. *New England Journal of Medicine, 342,* 326–332.

Woodruff, T. K. (2010, August). *The Oncofertility Consortium—addressing fertility in young people with cancer* (Vol. 7). Retrieved from http://www.nature.com/nrclinonc

CHAPTER TEN

Hospice Care AND Communication

NICHOLE EGBERT

The predominant medical paradigm is the biomedical model whereby health is seen as the absence of disease. Although historically the reductionist biomedical model was effective in combating infectious diseases and pathogens, modern medicine has had to shift its focus to assisting patients who suffer with chronic conditions (Havelka, Lučanin, & Lučanin, 2009). The goal of the biomedical approach to any health issue remains the same, however—to extend life and delay death. Health professionals in modern hospitals are highly trained to cure illness and disease using tools of medicine and technology. However, except for the very few palliative care specialists, clinicians may succeed in extending the length of life to the detriment of quality of life. The predominant biomedical approach has failed in many ways to relieve patients' suffering with chronic illness—suffering that is experienced on physical, social, emotional, and spiritual levels (e.g., Kaut, 2002). The aim of this chapter is to consider how communication in hospice settings has been used to reinforce the traditional biomedical model or extend beyond it in the delivery of effective hospice care to patients.

TRADITIONAL AND EMERGENT MODELS OF PATIENT CARE

In 1977, Georg Engel introduced the "biopsychosocial model of medicine" (or BPS model; Engel, 1977), which criticized the reductionist biomedical model for its separation of mind and body, privileging the view of the body as machine (for a recent overview, see Borrell-Carrió, Suchman, & Epstein, 2004). Engel argued that health would be better achieved by giving equal weight to the patient's narrative and emotions in treatment. According to this model, "the patient does not exist as an independent, atomistic machine; rather, the social existence of patient and the reality that relationships can enhance, or impair, quality of life are taken into account" (Tracy, 2014, p. 260). In the present day, although the philosophy of the biopsychosocial model is often extolled, modern health care practitioners are still typically trained in the highly technical, scientific, and reductionist paradigm of the biomedical model that Engel critiqued many decades earlier. Unfortunately, the ramifications of this approach are felt most keenly when patients are at the end of life.

Alternatively, the philosophy of hospice care embraces the biopsychosocial model by balancing the personhood of the patient with the science of medicine to reduce suffering. Connor (1998) defined hospice as

> a coordinated program providing palliative care to terminally ill patients and supportive services to patients, their families, and significant others 24 hours a day, seven days a week. Comprehensive/case managed services based on physical, social, spiritual, and emotional needs are provided during the last stages of illness, during the dying process, and during bereavement by a medically directed interdisciplinary team consisting of patients/families, health care professionals and volunteers. Professional management and continuity of care is maintained across multiple settings including homes, hospitals, long term care and residential settings. (pp. 3–4)

Hospice care is one form of palliative care, which is defined as

> specialized medical care for people with serious illnesses. It is focused on providing patients with relief from the symptoms, pain, and stress of a serious illness—whatever the diagnosis. The goal is to improve quality of life for both the patient and the family. (Center to Advance Palliative Care, 2014, para. 1)

In hospice care, medicine and science are tools for palliation instead of cure. In addition, the team-based approach to patient care includes not only clinical staff, but also social workers, members of the clergy, and even family caregivers and hospice volunteers. In this way, the interdisciplinary hospice team collaborates to achieve the best mix of services to try to keep the patient comfortable physically, mentally, socially, and spiritually. Hospice care has become the model for holistic care at the end of life, perhaps paving the way for an updated patient care model that incorporates spirituality as well—the biopsychosocial-spiritual model of health care (Sulmasy, 2002).

Just as medicine is a tool for the delivery of effective palliative care to hospice patients, communication is a key resource in relieving suffering and delivering comfort (Arnold, 2011). In many ways, communication has helped hospices achieve their palliative care goals, such as the incorporation of multidisciplinary teams that coordinate services across the domains of the biopsychosocial model of care. Two other resources that implement communication in hospice care delivery are hospice nurses and volunteers. Hospice nurses and volunteers communicate with patients and their families as well as with the other members of the interdisciplinary team and, in many ways, embody the hospice philosophy of care.

However, just as medicine is not inherently good or bad but a tool to be leveraged, communication can also serve to create barriers for hospice care. Modern hospices often fail to deliver culturally appropriate services to ethnic minorities such as African Americans and Asian Americans. Many physicians are slow to refer patients to hospice, thereby curtailing the benefits of palliative care to the patient. And, finally, the practice of collusion among families and professional caregivers is against the philosophy of hospice and may serve to increase patients' suffering.

COMMUNICATION ADVANTAGES IN HOSPICE CARE

Interdisciplinary Teams

In 1982, the Hospice Medicare Benefit (HMB) was introduced as a new cost structure for reimbursing physicians for services delivered to patients at the end of life. To qualify for HMB, hospices had to meet the conditions of participation, which include admitting only patients with a terminal illness diagnosis who are expected to live no more than six months. Another of the key requirements is the use of an interdisciplinary care team (IDT) and hospice volunteers in the delivery of hospice services (Connor, 2007–2008). In the biomedical model, the physician maintains the role of expert technician, with proprietary access to both the patient's body and medical science; the pathology of the body interacts with technology and the expertise of the physician. The physician then interprets the physical symptoms through the filters of technology and medicine and communicates the diagnosis and recommendation to the patient. The hospice requirement of IDTs shifts the responsibility of care from being solely that of the physician to that of the team. Although the majority of the communication in IDT team meetings is medical in nature (Wittenberg-Lyles, Gee, Oliver, & Demiris, 2009), the presence and interaction of professionals from other areas promote the biopsychosocial model of care better than any other clinical context.

The predominant focus on the hospice patient's physical needs is perhaps understandable when considered in relation to Maslow's hierarchy of needs (Maslow,

1943; for a more recent view of this position, see Zalenski & Raspa, 2006). Attention to the patient's comfort, especially as it applies to pain management, is paramount if one is to be able to focus on higher needs of emotional and spiritual care. Therefore, control of physical symptoms is prioritized, followed by attention to the patient's thoughts and feelings. Once emotional comfort is addressed, the patient may be able to wrestle with the meaning of existence, whether through religion or some other spiritual philosophy (Connor, 1998).

Wittenberg-Lyles and colleagues have contributed the most complete picture of communication in hospice IDT meetings. After coding 14 videotaped discussions of hospice cases, Wittenberg-Lyles et al. (2009) found that the communication in these meetings consisted of formal reporting, offering impressions of hospice patients and their families, and requesting clarification of information. In another ethnographic study, Wittenberg-Lyles (2005) described the integration of psychosocial information in hospice IDT meetings as occurring secondary to the medical update, in describing the goals of care for the patient, in discussing family issues, or when making a request for additional help. In a more recent study, Wittenberg-Lyles, Oliver, Demiris, and Regehr (2010) found that although collaboration is valued in IDT meetings, collaborative goals of interdependence and flexibility were perhaps perceived by team members more than they were actually enacted in meetings.

Although the use of IDTs in hospice care helps promote the psychosocial care of hospice patients, it is only a tool, not a panacea. Communication breakdowns can also impede the delivery of care, such in the case of restricted access of information in meetings when only one team member has possession of the patient's chart (Demiris, Washington, Oliver, & Wittenberg-Lyles, 2008). This lack of information may require members to repeat themselves or spend valuable meeting time requesting information from team members who are not present. Interpersonal power differentials can impinge on open communication between IDT members when non-medical professionals such as social workers and clergy feel marginalized in relation to physicians and medical directors (Ragan, Wittenberg-Lyles, Goldsmith, & Sanchez-Reilly, 2008). Role conflict can be an issue when multiple team members feel responsible for patients' psychosocial needs, but perhaps differ in their recommendations (Wittenberg-Lyles et al., 2008). These and other communication problems notwithstanding, even the imperfect meeting of IDT members who focus on the holistic care of hospice patients is superior to the alternative—disjointed visits to individual caregivers who have no communication with one another, or care provided by a physician trained solely in the biomedical model of health care.

Hospice Nurses

In the uniquely interdisciplinary context of hospice care, all members of the hospice team have the responsibility of conveying the philosophy of patient-centered, therapeutic care to hospice patients and their families. A good deal of time could be spent on each role of the hospice team and how well those who play these parts enact the biopsychosocial model. However, the focus of discussion here is on the hospice nurse, as the discipline of nursing has spent perhaps the most effort trying to understand how communication and medicine form a symbiotic partnership in the delivery of health care (Dobrina, Tenze, & Palese, 2014).

The holistic approach of hospice care is championed by hospice nurses through their communication with patients and their families and exemplified clearly in the data collected by Ellington, Reblin, Clayton, Berry, and Mooney (2012). In their study, although the largest portion of talk in home visits with patients and their families was, indeed, devoted to physical issues (21.81%; e.g., information provision), hospice nurses spent time discussing lifestyle issues (9.23%; e.g., responses to reminiscing), emotional concerns (8.70%; e.g., discussions related to patients' expressions of grief and/or anxiety), and psychosocial issues (8.09%; e.g., relationships). In addition to these discussions, hospice nurses spent 17.33% of their communication on building partnerships with patients and their families. This mix of physical, emotional, and social communication is not easily achieved, because often hospice patients are much more likely to disclose physical concerns than psychosocial ones, especially if they suffer with anxiety or depression. Unfortunately, despite nurses' best efforts, even the concerns that are disclosed by patients are often missed or misunderstood (Heaven & Maguire, 1997).

In comparison to most medical training, communication is a predominant focus in nurses' education (Egbert, Query, Quinlan, Savery, & Martinez, 2011). Nursing has even been defined as a therapeutic interpersonal process (Peplau, 1988). The focus on communication in nursing school is evidenced in professional practice, as hospice nurses with higher communication competence have been found to have better performance evaluations (Riggio & Taylor, 2000). In the case of hospice, nurses' communication skills are even more crucial. The communication of compassion for the many facets of the hospice patient is paramount at this stage of life. Compassionate communication for hospice workers consists of a process of recognizing, relating, and reacting to the needs of patients and their families (Way & Tracy, 2012) and is embodied in the training and practice of hospice nursing. That said, nurses' communication skills can be improved further through targeted communication training and interventions (Wilkinson, Perry, Blanchard, & Linsell, 2008).

Hospice Volunteers

The third major way that the holistic, biospychosocial nature of hospice is communicatively enacted is through the services of hospice volunteers. Volunteers are used in other health care roles, such as in nonprofit organizations and hospitals, but hospice volunteers are uniquely suited to provide the compassionate communication that hospice patients need. Compared with hospital volunteers, hospice volunteers are more empathic and likely to provide emotional support (Egbert & Parrott, 2003). Emotional support in the form of listening to the narratives of the hospice patient and family members is especially valuable (Stollick, 2002); "hospice volunteers support the capacity for relationship and the personalization of care in such a way that patient narratives can be better supported" (Pesut, Hooper, Lehbauer, & Dalhuisen, 2014, p. 75). Other roles that hospice volunteers perform include providing respite for family caregivers, serving as patient advocate (Savery & Egbert, 2010), performing basic patient care needs, and acting as a bridge between formal health care services and informal social support (Morris, Wilmot, Hill, Ockenden, & Payne, 2012). As a result of their experiences, hospice volunteers often become ambassadors for hospice and educators about end-of-life issues (Wittenberg-Lyles, 2006).

In addition to hospice volunteers possessing unique traits and abilities for their work with patients at end of life, training programs can equip hospice volunteers with necessary communication tools. Effective training programs for hospice volunteers directly address the importance of communication skills, such as empathic listening. However, communication training for hospice volunteers can go much further than this, incorporating concepts related to communication responsiveness and emotional intelligence (Worthington, 2008). Hospice volunteers can also be taught the value of building trust through personal sharing as well as modeling sensitive, vigilant, and flexible behavior (Coffman & Coffman, 1993). As in any effective training program, a variety of educational strategies should be employed to achieve training goals. Effective strategies include lecture, discussion, role-play, reflective writing, readings, multimedia presentations, games, and other creative learning activities.

The main thrust of hospice care is holistic, palliative care for the terminally ill patient and his or her family. Hospice care differs from the biomedical model of patient care in that its goal is to provide comfort and relieve patient suffering physically, emotionally, mentally, and spiritually. This mission is accomplished in many ways, with three of the most significant avenues highlighted here: the communication of interdisciplinary teams, hospice nursing, and volunteers. Additional aspects of hospice care could surely be highlighted as well, but the absence of any of these three pillars of hospice would cripple the ability of hospice to provide holistic patient care. The next section highlights three ways in which communication has not yet achieved the desired effects in hospice care.

COMMUNICATION CHALLENGES IN THE DELIVERY OF HOSPICE CARE

Similar to the previous section, although there are more than three ways in which communication has failed to deliver optimal hospice care, three factors stand out in the literature as particularly prominent obstacles. This section highlights how the use of collusion in perpetuating deception and denial about the end of life, lack of culturally sensitive communication and programs, and barriers to enrollment in hospice are particularly destructive to the biopsychosocial model of patient care.

Communication Avoidance and Collusion

Discussing bad news such as a terminal diagnosis is one of the most difficult communication tasks that physicians and nurses experience (Malloy, Virani, Kelly, & Munevar, 2010). However, attention to communication issues is sorely needed, as caregivers and patients need timely, accurate, and appropriate information delivered in a sensitive manner during this very vulnerable period. Focus group research has revealed that family caregivers desire more information to help them make informed decisions and reduce uncertainty (Royak-Schaler et al., 2006). However, although some caregivers expressed that they wished that terminal illness and hospice care be discussed earlier and more openly, others felt that physicians should not be blunt, especially in front of the patient (Royak-Schaler et al., 2006). Across 22 data-based studies, barriers to physician-patient communication in end-of-life care included lack of time and availability by the physician as well as the physician not speaking honestly and openly about terminal illness (Slort et al., 2011).

Communication breakdown during conversations between physicians and family members can be attributed both to physicians' lack of communication and family members' difficulty in receiving the bad news (Cherlin et al., 2005; Slort et al., 2011). Although nearly 20% of family caregivers reported that their primary physician never told them that the patient's illness was incurable, many family caregivers were ambivalent or did not want to know more about the patient's illness and life expectancy. This contradiction illustrates how family caregivers can vary in the amount of information they receive. Culture can also play a large role in how much information a family desires. Caregivers with roots in Korea and other Asian countries as well as many Latino families often want less information about the patient's condition, and may even request that the physician not reveal the diagnosis to the patient for fear it will destroy hope (de Haes & Teunissen, 2005).

The desire by families to spare the patient bad news about his or her condition raises an important ethical question: Does full disclosure of this information put the patient at risk for unnecessary psychological and emotional harm? Patients have a right to their own medical information; thus, without clear evidence that the patient wishes to remain unaware, physicians must disclose the information to the patient. Despite this obligation, many families end up entering into collusion with the health professionals, preferring to protect their family member (and, perhaps, themselves) from having to confront and discuss a terminal diagnosis (Faulkner, 1998). The practice of collusion and avoidance of communication is central to the cultural and religious belief system of many Latinos (Kreling, Selsky, Perret-Gentil, Huerta, & Mandelblatt, 2010). Latino family members may even become angry when physicians speak openly about a terminal diagnosis and hospice, causing them not to trust the physicians and other health care providers, which might put the patient's health in jeopardy.

Even when the information is provided by physicians, patients and families may engage in alternative defense mechanisms to protect themselves from processing the difficult news. Timmermans (1994) suggests that there are three categories of awareness in these situations: (1) suspended open awareness, whereby the patient/family members deny or do not understand that the patient will die, even when it is evident to others; (2) uncertain open awareness, whereby the patient/family members suspect the truth but choose instead to focus on the possibility of a good outcome and ignore the negative; and (3) active open awareness, whereby everyone speaks openly of the impending death and behaves accordingly. Patients and family members may fluctuate between these categories over time, depending on their ability to absorb the information, as well as the amount and quality of the information provided by physicians and nurses (Dunne, 2005).

Communication between patients/family members and medical specialists such as oncologists and surgeons is crucial because these specialists are often the ones who deliver a terminal diagnosis that could lead to hospice enrollment. Back et al. (2000) recommend that when giving bad news, physicians should find a private, quiet spot and allocate plenty of time for the interaction. Physicians should ask the patient or his or her family members how much is understood at this point, and how much they would like to know about the details of the patient's condition. If the patient clearly communicates that he or she does not wish to know, or wishes to know only a small amount, the physician is released from the obligation of full disclosure. The physician can proceed to provide information in a simple, concrete manner, avoiding the use of medical jargon or euphemisms about death. Finally, the physician should be prepared to respond with empathy to the emotional reactions after the news and broach the subject of hospice if appropriate. At this point, it is also recommended that the physician summarize what was discussed and move forward with the strategy that the patient/family members desire.

Lack of Cultural Sensitivity

As discussed above, there is substantial variation in how different cultural groups approach terminal illness. Although declining in many modern Asian cities, for some Asian Americans there is a strong traditional belief in filial piety, whereby the family has the responsibility to care for its sick members; thus, hospice care is seen as shirking one's duty to the family (Glass, Chen, Hwang, Ono, & Nahapetyan, 2010). Similarly, in Korean culture, Confucianism emphasizes family-centered traditions that include taking care of dying family members. Latino caregivers are more likely than white caregivers to have no previous knowledge of hospice, to avoid open discussions of death, to believe that hospice is an inferior health care option for poor people, and to want to make end-of-life decisions for the patient (Kreling et al., 2010). These negative attitudes toward hospice may contribute to the reasons Hispanic Americans were less likely than other ethnic groups to be discharged to facility-based hospice (Kirkendall, Shen, & Gan, 2014).

There are also differences between Caucasians and African Americans regarding hospice care. Historically, African Americans are less likely to have advance directives (Resnick, Schuur, Heineman, Stone, & Weissman, 2008). However, African Americans as a group also tend to be heterogeneous, as African American nursing home residents with cancer with a do-not-resuscitate (DNR) order enter hospice at a higher rate than do white nursing home cancer patients with a DNR (Lepore, Miller, & Gozalo, 2010). African Americans are more likely than whites to be admitted to hospice directly from the hospital or emergency department, suggesting that African Americans have less access to non–acute care settings such as a family doctor or medical specialist (Johnson, Kuchibhatla, & Tulsky, 2011). More exposure to non–acute health care may help increase awareness about hospice while there is still time for patients to benefit from it, as patients admitted to hospice from the hospital are more likely to die within one week of enrollment.

To improve the cultural sensitivity of hospice care, hospice programs must first increase awareness of hospice services in minority communities. For example, among Korean Americans, although younger, more educated individuals were more favorable toward using hospice services, these correlations were wiped out when prior awareness of hospice was accounted for (Jang, Chiriboga, Allen, Kwak, & Haley, 2010). Hospices must also work to accommodate family interests and cultural values in care provision (Taxis, Keiler, & Cruz, 2008). For many minority groups, including South Asians, communicating through family members or other people from their community hired as interpreters can be problematic when private health information and/or issues related to terminal illness are discussed

(Randhawa, Owens, Fitches, & Khan, 2003). To be more culturally sensitive, hospice services should employ interpreters when needed and engage staff members in training that promotes effective intercultural communication (Lyke & Colon, 2004; Ngo-Metzger, August, Srinivasan, Liao, & Meyskens, 2008). To the extent possible, hospice patients prefer that health care providers and hospice staff members be of the same gender and ethnicity as they are (Randhawa et al., 2003). However, this ideal is often very difficult to realize when hospice services themselves are already overly burdened and understaffed.

Barriers to Hospice Enrollment

The number of hospice patients has grown exponentially since 2000, with a 74% increase in the number of people served by hospice and 47% growth in the number of hospice programs (Meier, 2011). In 2012, an estimated 1.5 to 1.6 million Americans received hospice care (National Hospice and Palliative Care Organization, 2013). Hospice patients are much less likely to be readmitted to the hospital and die in the hospital as compared with non-hospice patients (Gozalo & Miller, 2007), saving up to $6,500 per patient, depending on the patient's length of hospice stay (Kelley, Deb, Du, Carlson, & Morrison, 2013). In addition, hospice patients receive better-quality care and, according to some studies, even live longer than non-hospice patients (Kelley et al., 2013; Meier, 2011). Interviews with families of hospice patients revealed that the longer patients were in hospice, the more services they received, and the greater the helpfulness of these services (Rickerson, Harrold, Kapo, Carroll, & Casarett, 2005).

However, despite the growing acceptance of hospice care, increases in the number of hospice care organizations, and significant reductions in cost, a number of barriers can restrict access to hospice care. The requirements for Medicare patients to enroll in hospice are that the patient have a terminal diagnosis (less than six months to live) and that the patient forgo curative or restorative treatment. Although these requirements seem simple, some treatments, such as chemotherapy, are used for both curative and palliative purposes, thus precluding some patients from admission to hospice. In some cases, to be admitted to hospice, patients must have a caregiver, be willing to forgo hospitalization, and/or forgo treatments such as chemotherapy, radiation, transfusions, or total parenteral nutrition. A study of California hospice programs found that 63% of responding hospice programs reported using at least one of these restrictive criteria in admissions, with 29% reporting using three or four restrictive criteria (Lorenz, Asch, Rosenfeld, Liu, & Ettner, 2004).

As a result of these restrictions, physicians often begin discussions of hospice with patients and their families very late in the dying process (Cherlin et al., 2005), often finding it hard to predict how long a patient might live (Casarett & Quill, 2007). A larger issue is the professional culture of medicine, in which the focus is on curing the patient by employing all tools and strategies afforded by modern medical technology. For many physicians, to admit a patient into hospice is to admit defeat. In addition, nursing home staff members often hold preconceived beliefs that hospice care provided in the nursing home does not add value to patient care or that hospice care is only for the "very end" (Welch, Miller, Martin, & Nanda, 2008). Nursing homes typically do not have formal procedures in place for periodically reassessing patients' terminal status or eligibility for hospice care. Instead, nursing homes rely on staff members to independently recognize decline in patients and initiate discussions of the hospice option with patients and family members on their own (Welch et al., 2008).

The timing of hospice admission is an important financial issue. As previously mentioned, hospice patients have lower rates of hospital utilization, which can reduce the number of invasive tests that they have to suffer (Gozalo & Miller, 2007). Hospices are reimbursed a set amount per day for each patient, regardless of the care the patient receives, making sicker patients who require more complex care a financial risk (Lorenz et al., 2004). To make matters worse, physicians are not paid for the time they spend counseling patients about hospice and palliative care. These circumstances have resulted in a trend whereby for-profit hospices selectively admit patients with longer life prognoses and lower average costs per day (Noe & Forgione, 2014). As costs are highest at the beginning and end of a patient's time in hospice, some for-profit hospices market themselves to non-terminal patients to maximize the amount they can bill Medicare (Laise, 2012). Medicare's spending on hospice programs has greatly increased in recent years, owing in part to the irregularities in hospice enrollment, along with the growth in the number of hospice patients. In response, the Patient Protection and Affordable Care Act of 2010 has stipulated several reforms to the hospice system (Meier, 2011), including investigations into several of these issues. It remains to be seen how these changes will affect the timing, cost, and availability of hospice care.

CONCLUSIONS

On September 17, 2014, the Institute of Medicine (IOM) issued the report *Dying in America: Improving Quality and Honoring Individual Preferences Near the End of Life*. This report articulates the importance of increased attention to palliative care as the number of older adults increases and becomes more culturally diverse, while at the same time health care costs continue to climb. Despite these trends, there remains a lack of palliative care specialists and a broken system of financial compensation. To deal with these issues, the IOM (2014) suggests developing resources for advance care planning and clinician-patient communication, a focus on "person-centered, family-oriented end-of-life care," and reform of health care policy to support coordination between medical and palliative health care delivery systems (p. 2).

As the IOM has identified in its report, although the philosophy of hospice champions the patient-centered, psychosocial model of health care, barriers to the realization of this philosophy abound. Also in the fall of 2014, a young woman by the name of Brittany Maynard made national news when she moved to Oregon to take advantage of the state's Death With Dignity Act. According to this law, terminally ill individuals can receive a prescription for a large dose of painkillers, allowing them to decide when and where their lives will end. Maynard was 29 years old and suffered from a form of brain cancer that would lead to a painful and difficult death within a short period of time. Although controversial, the Death With Dignity Act succeeds in putting the wishes of the terminally ill patients first—empowering the patient's personhood in life and in death.

Communication in hospice care should do no less. A model of communication for hospice care should, in all ways, privilege the patient and the patient's family. As a biopsychosocial-spiritual model would suggest, the patient should be cared for holistically, not just medically. The team-based approach to communication, one of the strengths of hospice care, should be leveraged in the quest for patient-based care. The result would not privilege any of the specialties incorporated in IDTs but instead would focus on team-building processes that function to protect the patient and family from stress, uncertainty, and pain (see Figure 1).

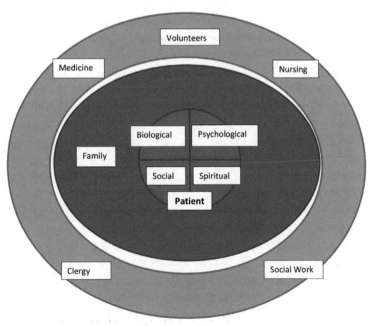

Figure 1. Protective Model of Communication in Hospice Care.

In a model such as the one proposed, the patient's voice is privileged above all. Although not every patient will be as certain of her desires as Brittany Maynard was, both professional and family caregivers are responsible for soliciting and empowering the patient's voice. Ragan, Wittenberg, and Hall (2003) suggest that clinicians and researchers can turn to patient narratives to improve the delivery of palliative health care services. This practice can help ensure that patients guide new initiatives using their experiences and understandings (Arnold, 2011). Turning to the patient to inform research and practice would also assist in the development of culturally appropriate palliative care services.

One way in which the model can be leveraged to improve communication in hospice care is through online communication tools such as interactive websites and tablet/smart phone applications. One example has already been developed that encompasses patient feedback, clinical evaluations, and educational materials (Dy et al., 2011). Online formats allow IDTs to access patient information simultaneously as well as solicit feedback from patients and caregivers. Another example is the use of videophone technology to increase interaction between family caregivers and hospice staff (Oliver, Demiris, Day, Courtney, & Porock, 2006).

In conclusion, hospice care is defined by the comfort it brings to those at the end of life. According to the psychosocial-spiritual model of health care, comfort is needed for the patient's body, mind, heart, and even spirit. Effective hospice care can be both delivered and thwarted by the communication of health care providers, family caregivers, and hospice patients. Many times, satisfaction with care at the end of life can be directly related to timely, effective communication with hospice staff (Royak-Schaler et al., 2006). As Arnold (2011) aptly puts it, "communication is a key currency for delivering optimal palliative care" (p. 1). As such, learning how to foster comfort through communication should be as much a priority of our health care system as traditional biomedical models of health care delivery.

REFERENCES

Arnold, B. I. (2011). Mapping hospice patients' perception and verbal communication of end-of-life needs: An exploratory mixed-methods inquiry. *BMC Palliative Care, 1*, 1–10.

Back, A. L., Buckman, R., Lenzi, R., Glober, G., Beale, E., & Kuelka, A. P. (2000). SPIKES—a six-step protocol for delivering bad news: Application to the patient with cancer. *Oncologist, 5*, 302–311.

Borrell-Carrió, F., Suchman, A. L., & Epstein, R. M. (2004). The biopsychosocial model 25 years later: Principles, practice, and scientific inquiry. *Annals of Family Medicine, 2*, 576–582.

Casarett, D. J., & Quill, T. E. (2007). "I'm not ready for hospice": Strategies for timely and effective hospice discussions. *Annals of Internal Medicine, 146*, 443–448.

Center to Advance Palliative Care. (2014). Defining palliative care. Retrieved from http://www.capc.org/building-a-hospital-based-palliative-care-program/case/definingpc

Cherlin, E., Fried, T., Prigerson, H. G., Schulman-Green, D., Johnson-Hurzeler, R., & Bradley, E. H. (2005). Communication between physicians and family caregivers about care at the end of life: When do discussions occur and what is said? *Journal of Palliative Medicine, 8*, 1176–1185.

Coffman, S. L., & Coffman, V. T. (1993). Communication training for hospice volunteers. *Omega, 27*, 155–163.

Connor, S. R. (1998). *Hospice: Practice, pitfalls, and promise.* Washington, DC: Taylor & Francis.

Connor, S. R. (2007–2008). Development of hospice and palliative care in the United States. *Omega: Journal of Death and Dying, 56*, 89–99.

de Haes, H., & Teunissen, S. (2005). Communication in palliative care: A review of the recent literature. *Current Opinion in Oncology, 17*, 345–350.

Demiris, G., Washington, K., Oliver, D. P., & Wittenberg-Lyles, E. (2008). A study of information flow in hospice interdisciplinary team meetings. *Journal of Interprofessional Care, 22*, 621–629.

Dobrina, R., Tenze, M., & Palese, A. (2014). An overview of hospice and palliative care nursing models and theories. *International Journal of Palliative Nursing, 20*, 75–81.

Dunne, K. (2005). Effective communication in palliative care. *Nursing Standard, 20*, 57–64.

Dy, S. M., Roy, J., Ott, G. E., McHale, M., Kennedy, C., Kutner, J. S., & Tien, A. (2011). Tell us: A web-based tool for improving communication among patients, families, and providers in hospice and palliative care through systematic data specification, collection, and use. *Journal of Pain and Symptom Management, 42*, 526–534.

Egbert, N., & Parrott, R. (2003). Empathy and social support for the terminally ill: Implications for recruiting and retaining hospice volunteers. *Communication Studies, 54*, 18–34.

Egbert, N., Query, J. L., Jr., Quinlan, M. M., Savery, C. A., & Martinez, A. R. (2011). (Re) viewing health communication and related interdisciplinary curricula: Towards a transdisciplinary perspective. In T. L. Thompson, J. Nussbaum, & R. L. Parrott (Eds.), *Handbook of health communication* (2nd ed., pp. 610–631). New York, NY: Taylor & Francis.

Ellington, L., Reblin, M., Clayton, M. F., Berry, P., & Mooney, K. (2012). Hospice nurse communication with patients with cancer and their family caregivers. *Journal of Palliative Medicine, 15*, 262–268.

Engel, G. L. (1977). The need for a new medical model: A challenge for biomedicine. *Science, 196*, 129–136.

Faulkner, A. (1998). ABC of palliative care: Communication with patients, families, and other professionals. *British Medical Journal, 316*, 130–132.

Glass, A. P., Chen, L-K., Hwang, E., Ono, Y., & Nahapetyan, L. (2010). A cross-cultural comparison of hospice development in Japan, South Korea, and Taiwan. *Journal of Cross-Cultural Gerontology, 25*, 1–19.

Gozalo, P. L., & Miller, S. C. (2007). Hospice enrollment and evaluation of its causal effect on hospitalization of dying nursing home patients. *Health Services Research, 42*, 587–610.

Havelka, M., Lučanin, J. D., & Lučanin, D. (2009). Biopsychosocial model: The integrated approach to health and disease. *Collegium Antropologicum, 1*, 303–310.

Heaven, C. M., & Maguire, P. (1997). Disclosure of concerns by hospice patients and their identification by nurses. *Palliative Medicine, 11*, 283–290.

Institute of Medicine. (2014, September). *Dying in America: Improving quality and honoring individual preferences near the end of life.* Retrieved November 16, 2014, from http://www.iom.edu/~/media/Files/Report%20Files/2014/EOL/Report%20Brief.pdf

Jang, Y., Chiriboga, D. A., Allen, J. Y., Kwak, J., & Haley, W. (2010). Willingness of older Korean-American adults to use hospice. *Journal of the American Geriatric Society, 58*, 352–356.

Johnson, K. S., Kuchibhatla, M., & Tulsky, J. A. (2011). Racial differences in location before hospice enrollment and association with hospice length of stay. *Journal of the American Geriatrics Society,* 59, 732–737.

Kaut, K. P. (2002). Religion, spirituality, and existentialism near the end of life: Implications for assessment and application. *American Behavioral Scientist, 46,* 220–234.

Kelley, A. S., Deb, P., Du, Q., Carlson, M. D., & Morrison, R. S. (2013). Hospice enrollment saves money for Medicare and improves care quality across a number of different lengths-of-stay. *Health Affairs, 32,* 552–561.

Kirkendall, A., Shen, J. J., & Gan, Y. (2014). Associations of race and other socioeconomic factors with post-hospitalization hospice care settings. *Ethnicity and Disease, 24,* 236–242.

Kreling, B., Selsky, C., Perret-Gentil, M., Huerta, E. E., & Mandelblatt, J. S. (2010). "The worst thing about hospice is that they talk about death": Contrasting hospice decisions and experience among immigrant Central and South American Latinos and U.S.-born White, non-Latino cancer caregivers. *Palliative Medicine, 24,* 427–434.

Laise, E. (2012, March). Should your loved one really be in hospice? *Kiplinger's Retirement Report,* 14–15.

Lepore, M. J., Miller, S. C., & Gozalo, P. (2010). Hospice use among urban Black and White U.S. nursing home decedents in 2006. *The Gerontologist, 51,* 251–260.

Lorenz, K. A., Asch, S. M., Rosenfeld, K. E., Liu, H., & Ettner, S. L. (2004). Hospice admission practices: Where does hospice fit in the continuum of care? *Journal of the American Geriatrics Society, 52,* 725–730.

Lyke, J., & Colon, M. (2004). Practical recommendation for ethnically and racially sensitive hospice services. *American Journal of Hospice and Palliative Medicine, 21,* 131–133.

Malloy, P., Virani, R., Kelly, K., & Munevar, C. (2010). Beyond bad news: Communication skills of nurses in palliative care. *Journal of Hospice and Palliative Nursing, 12,* 166–174.

Maslow. A. H. (1943). A theory of human motivation. *Psychological Review, 50,* 370–396.

Meier, D. E. (2011). Increased access to palliative care and hospice services: Opportunities to improve value in health care. *The Millbank Quarterly, 89,* 343–380.

Morris, S., Wilmot, A., Hill, M., Ockenden, N., & Payne, S. (2012). A narrative literature review of the contribution of volunteers in end-of-life care services. *Palliative Medicine, 27,* 428–436.

National Hospice and Palliative Care Organization. (2013). NHPCO's facts and figures: Hospice care in America. Retrieved November 11, 2014, from http://www.nhpco.org/sites/default/files/public/Statistics_Research/2013_Facts_Figures.pdf

Ngo-Metzger, Q., August, K. J., Srinivasan, M., Liao, S., & Meyskens, F. L. (2008). End-of-life care: Guidelines for patient-centered communication. *American Family Physician, 77,* 167–174.

Noe, K., & Forgione, D. A. (2014). Economic incentive in the hospice care setting: A comparison of for-profit and nonprofit providers. *Journal of Public Budgeting, Accounting, and Financial Management, 26,* 233–270.

Oliver, D. R., Demiris, G., Day, D., Courtney, K. L., & Porock, D. (2006). Telehospice support for elder caregivers of hospice patients: Two case studies. *Journal of Palliative Medicine, 9,* 264–267.

Peplau, H. (1988). *Interpersonal relations in nursing.* London, UK: Macmillan.

Pesut, B., Hooper, B., Lehbauer, S., & Dalhuisen, M. (2014). Promoting volunteer capacity in hospice palliative care: A narrative review. *American Journal of Hospice and Palliative Medicine, 3,* 69–78.

Ragan, S. L., Wittenberg-Lyles, E. M., Goldsmith, J., & Sanchez-Reilly, S. (2008). *Communication as comfort: Multiple voices in palliative care.* New York, NY: Routledge.

Ragan, S. L., Wittenberg, E., & Hall, H. T. (2003). The communication of palliative care for the elderly cancer patient. *Health Communication, 15*, 219–226.

Randhawa, G., Owens. A., Fitches, R., & Khan, Z. (2003). Communication in the development of culturally competent palliative care services in the U.K.: A case study. *International Journal of Palliative Nursing, 9*, 24–31.

Resnick, H. E., Schuur, J. D., Heineman, J., Stone, R., & Weissman, J. S. (2008). Advanced directives in nursing home residents aged > 65 years: United States 2004. *American Journal of Hospice and Palliative Care, 25*, 476–482.

Rickerson, E., Harrold, J., Kapo, J., Carroll, J. T., & Casarett, D. (2005). Timing of hospice referral and families' perceptions of services: Are earlier hospice referrals better? *Journal of the American Geriatrics Society, 53*, 819–823.

Riggio, R. E., & Taylor, S. J. (2000). Personality and communication skills as predictors of hospice nurse performance. *Journal of Business and Psychology, 15*, 351–359.

Royak-Schaler, R., Gadalla, S. M., Lemkau, J. P., Ross, D. D., Alexander, C., & Scott, D. (2006). Family perspectives on communication with healthcare providers during end-of-life cancer care. *Oncology Nursing Forum, 33*, 753–760.

Savery, C. A., & Egbert, N. (2010). Hospice volunteer as patient advocate: A trait approach. *Palliative and Supportive Care, 8*, 159–167.

Slort, W., Schweitzer, B. P., Blankerstein, A. H., Abarshi, E. A., Riphagen, I. I., Echteid, M. A.,… Deliens, L. (2011). Perceived barriers and facilitators for general practitioner-patient communication in palliative care: A systematic review. *Palliative Medicine, 25*, 613–629.

Stollick, M. (2002). Overcoming the tendency to lie to dying patients. *American Journal of Hospice and Palliative Care, 19*, 29–34.

Sulmasy, D. P. (2002). A biopsychosocial-spiritual model for the care of patients at the end of life. *The Gerontologist, 42*, 24–33.

Taxis, J. C., Keiler, T., & Cruz, V. (2008). Mexican Americans and hospice care: Culture, control, and communication. *Journal of Hospice and Palliative Nursing, 10*, 133–141.

Timmermans, S. (1994). Dying of awareness: The Theory of Awareness contexts revisited. *Sociology of Health & Illness, 16*, 322–339.

Tracy, T. F. (2014). Hospice care and a theology for patients at the end of life. *Dialog: A Journal of Theology, 53*, 259–267.

Way, D., & Tracy, S. J. (2012). Conceptualizing compassion as recognizing, relating and (re)acting: A qualitative study of compassionate communication at hospice. *Communication Monographs, 79*, 292–315.

Welch, L. C., Miller, S. C., Martin, E. W., & Nanda, A. (2008). Referral and timing of referral to hospice care in nursing homes: The significant role of staff members. *The Gerontologist, 48*, 477–484.

Wilkinson, S. Perry, R., Blanchard, K., & Linsell, L. (2008). Effectiveness of a three-day communication skills course on nurses' communication skills with cancer/palliative care patients: A randomized controlled trial. *Palliative Medicine, 22*, 365–375.

Wittenberg-Lyles, E. M. (2005). Information sharing in interdisciplinary team meetings: An evaluation of hospice team goals. *Qualitative Health Research, 15*, 1377–1391.

Wittenberg-Lyles, E. M. (2006). Narratives of hospice volunteers: Perspectives on death and dying. *Qualitative Research Reports in Communication, 7*, 51–56.

Wittenberg-Lyles, E. M., Gee, G. C., Oliver, D. P., & Demiris, G. (2009). What patients and families don't hear: Backstage communication in hospice interdisciplinary team meetings. *Journal of Housing for the Elderly, 23*, 92–105.

Wittenberg-Lyles, E. M., Oliver, D., Demiris, G., Baldwin, P., & Regehr, K. (2008). Communication dynamics in hospice teams: Understanding the role of the chaplain in interdisciplinary team collaboration. *Journal of Palliative Medicine, 11*, 1330–1335.

Wittenberg-Lyles, E. M., Oliver, D. P., Demiris, G., & Regehr, K. (2010). Interdisciplinary collaboration in hospice team meetings. *Journal of Interprofessional Care, 24*, 264–273.

Worthington, D. L. (2008). Communication skills training in a hospice volunteer training program. *Journal of Social Work in End-of-Life and Palliative Care, 4*, 17–37.

Zalenski, R. J., & Raspa, R. (2006). Maslow's hierarchy of needs: A framework for achieving human potential in hospice. *Journal of Palliative Care, 9*, 1120–1127.

CHAPTER ELEVEN

Bereavement AND Post-Death Adjustments: A Lifespan Approach TO Bereavement

PAIGE TOLLER

We will all grieve the death of a loved one at some point in our lives. As children and adolescents, we may experience the death of a beloved grandparent or pet. During adulthood, we will encounter "expected" deaths, such as the death of an elderly parent. As older adults, our lifelong friends and family members will die. During the course of a lifetime, some of us will experience tragic and life-changing deaths, such as the death of a child or the death of a spouse/romantic partner.

The death of a loved one is more than physical absence. Our relationship(s) with the deceased is (are) forever changed, as we can no longer enact familiar patterns of communication. The death of a loved one also changes how we see ourselves and the world around us. Indeed, the very purpose of grieving is to learn how to exist in the world without our deceased loved ones (Attig, 1996). Communication is at the heart of the grieving process as we create narratives and stories of loss to find meaning in our loved one's death (Neimeyer, 1999). Through rituals, conversation, storytelling, writing, and other forms of communication, we co-construct our stories of grief and loss (Neimeyer, Klass, & Dennis, 2014; Neimeyer, Prigerson, & Davies, 2002). Talking with others about a loved one's death validates our pain (Harvey, 2000) and helps us bear witness to our relationships with the deceased (Neimeyer & Thompson, 2014). To find meaning in our loved one's death we engage in a process of sense-making, benefit finding, and identity change (Gillies & Neimeyer, 2006). During this process, we may wrestle with unanswerable questions as our assumptions about the fairness and predictability of the world is challenged (Janoff-Bulman, & Berg, 1998). In time, we may come to view aspects of our loved one's death as beneficial or positive, such as a loved one's death giving us new priorities, or reminding us just how fragile life is (Gillies & Neimeyer, 2006). We may also come to see ourselves as stronger, more resilient, and more compassionate human beings (Gillies & Neimeyer, 2006). Conversely, we may experience a fractured and fragmented identity, as our loved one's death prevents us from enacting our familiar and desired social roles (Harvey, 2000). Deaths that are especially traumatic or defy the natural order of life, such as the death of a child, are particularly difficult to make sense of, as these types of death violate our expectations of how the world is supposed to work and who is to die first (Janoff-Bulman & Berg, 1998).

In this chapter, I frame my discussion of communication and grief using a lifespan approach (Nussbaum, 1989), as the meaning we give to a loved one's death is often shaped by where we are located in our lifespan. The first section of this chapter includes research on children's first death experiences as well as how children experience the death of a parent and sibling. The next section is focused on adults who have experienced the death(s) of a parent, spouse, or child. When talking about the death of a spouse, this section is divided into young adult/adulthood and older adulthood in order to highlight the similarities and differences between older and younger bereaved spouses.

CHILDHOOD/ADOLESCENT EXPERIENCES WITH DEATH

In the U.S. alone, 3 million children will experience the death of an immediate family member in a given year, and around 2.5 million children under the age of 18 have experienced the death of a parent (Social Security Administration, 2000; U.S. Census Bureau, 2000). For children, the death of a loved one represents the loss of a relationship and an attachment figure, and in some cases a loss in routine and stability (see Baker & Sedney, 2004). How a child experiences a loved one's death is often contingent on their cognitive development and chronological age. Most experts believe that children under the age of 6 or 7 cannot understand the irreversibility, inevitability, and universality of death. Children between 7 and 9 years old appear to understand that death is irreversible, but may still not understand that death is inevitable and universal. By age 10, children are believed to have developed a more "adult" understanding of death, realizing that death is final, permanent, and universal (see Robinson, this volume).

Despite their limited understanding of death, small children under the age of 6 will emotionally and behaviorally react to a loved one's death by acting aggressively toward others or clinging to a parent or caregiver (Baker & Sedney, 2004).

Elementary-aged children may respond to death by downplaying or hiding their emotions to appear more grown up. Children at this age may also experience guilt and believe that they somehow caused the death, although they may not vocalize this. Adolescents, like elementary-aged students, may also hide their grief to appear more mature or not to stand out from their peers. Some may cope with their grief by engaging in "risky" behavior, such as excessive drinking or running away from home.

To help children grieve the death of a loved one, Baker, Sedney, and Gross (1992) created a three-stage psychological task model. According to this, children need somehow to understand the finality of death as well as be given age-appropriate information about the cause of death relatively soon after the loss. During this time, children also need to be reassured that they are safe and that they will be taken care of. In the middle stages of their grief, children need to move beyond the intellectual or cognitive realization that their loved one is dead and work through the emotional pain that accompanies the death of a loved one. For instance, children must cope with the fact that they can no longer spend time with their loved one or that they will not see their loved one again. During this phase, children need to renegotiate their relationship with the deceased and find symbolic ways of staying connected to them. In later stages, the grieving child needs to develop a new identity that accounts for his or her experience and incorporates aspects of the deceased's memory, without becoming too dependent on the deceased's memory. During this time, children need to form new relationships with others, while continuing an ongoing connection or inner relationship with the deceased. Finally, children must manage the grief that periodically occurs, such as the pain that may resurge on holidays or anniversaries.

Parents and other significant family members can play a pivotal role in helping children accomplish these tasks and cope with their grief (Baker et al., 1992; Rosen, 2004). If parents do not talk with children about death, it may communicate to young, impressionable children that it is not okay within the family system to share feelings of grief and loss (Porterfield, Cain, & Saldinger, 2003). By creating meaningful rituals and telling stories about their loved one and his or her death, families can make sense of a loved one's death together (Bosticco & Thompson, 2005). When families engage in open and honest communication about their grief, they teach children that it is acceptable and safe for them to freely express their own grief emotions (see Rosen, 2004). Likewise, when families talk with each other about the lifestyle changes that may occur as a result of a loved one's death, children are better able to cope with and accept these changes. Open dialogue within the family system about death is important for children, as family systems that are more aware of emotions and encourage emotional expression may experience less intense grief over time (Schoka-Traylor, Hayslip, Kaminiski, & York, 2003).

Parental Death During Childhood

The vast majority of research examining childhood bereavement has focused on parental death, which can be traumatic for children. Parentally bereaved children may be at increased risk for depression, anxiety, poorer school performance, lower self-esteem, and behavioral problems (Dowdney, 2000; Hope & Hodge, 2006; Worden & Silverman, 1996). Nevertheless, many parentally bereaved children are resilient and cope with the death of a parent extraordinarily well, demonstrating little to no long-term emotional or psychological harm (Christ, Siegel, & Sperber, 1994; Kalter et al., 2002–2003; Silverman & Worden, 1992).

Research findings are mixed concerning whether children fare better if the death of a parent is anticipated or if it is sudden. Saldinger and her colleagues found that children who experience the anticipated death of a parent (i.e., due to long-term illness) demonstrated less psychological and emotional adjustment than do children whose parent dies suddenly (Saldinger, Cain, Kalter, & Lohnes, 1999). When a parent is terminally ill, a child is faced not only with the pending death of a parent but also the absence of a surviving parent who may be engrossed in the care of the ill spouse. Children can be negatively impacted by the dying parent's inability to be physically and emotionally available to them, and viewing a parent's physical and mental decline may frighten and confuse them. Children may also experience secondary traumatization, as they are faced with a physically and/or emotionally absent surviving parent, their own feelings of guilt and fear, and the potential loss of family security and predictability (Saldinger, Cain, & Porterfield, 2003). Despite a dying parent's difficulty in connecting with their child either physically or emotionally, or the inability to do so, children often desire intimacy with their ill parent. Unfortunately, the dying parent may not wish to be as involved with his or her children because of the progression of the disease or the lack of energy to engage with the child. To stay involved in their child's life, dying parents may create artifacts of remembrance, such as videos or letters; however, creating these acts of remembrance can be painful as it forces the dying parent and the family system to acknowledge his or her impending death.

There are benefits to anticipated deaths as children and surviving parents may have the opportunity to spend meaningful time with the dying parent as well as say their final goodbyes (Saldinger et al., 2004). Close or intimate relationships can be nurtured between a dying parent and his or her children; however, the dying parent must be able to confront his or her impending death, and both the parent and child must be comfortable spending time together during the dying process. If the dying parent does not acknowledge his or her impending death, and/or if both parent and child are uncomfortable spending time together, children can be further traumatized.

Adolescent children (ages 11 to 17) often experience parental death differently than do younger children. In a study examining parental death due to cancer, Christ and her colleagues found that unlike small children, adolescents are able to cognitively grasp their parent's illness and terminal condition, feel empathy toward their sick parent, and understand the ramifications the illness and death would have on their family structure (Christ et al., 1994). While a parent is terminally ill, adolescents may become more emotionally involved with their dying parent, even though many want to be more independent and disconnected from their family at this time. Adolescents may be expected to take on additional responsibilities at home, which can interfere with their extracurricular activities and other "normal" teen behavior. Adolescent girls, in particular, may be expected to take on extra household responsibilities as well as care for the ill parent. Adolescents may be angry at their ill parent for the burdens placed on them, while simultaneously feeling guilty about being angry at a dying parent.

Children and adolescents cope with and grieve parental death in a variety of ways. To stay connected to their deceased parent, bereaved children may perpetuate or continue aspects of their deceased parent's life and personality into their own lives (see Silverman, Baker, Cait, & Boerner, 2002–2003). Children may identify with qualities of the deceased parent (i.e., intelligent, adventurous) or take on a role previously occupied by the deceased parent, such as doing the housework the deceased formerly did. Using the concept of legacy, Silverman and her colleagues found that bereaved children who internalized negative legacies may be at higher risk for emotional and behavioral problems. For instance, children whose parent died of a lengthy illness expressed fear of dying of the same malady. Surviving parents who were able to reframe and redefine negative legacies into more positive perspectives helped their children better cope with their grief. Conversely, children whose parents were dismissive or did not recognize the impact of the legacy appeared to struggle with their parent's death emotionally.

How well a bereaved child copes with parental death may largely depend on how well the surviving parent is coping (Silverman & Worden, 1992,) and to what extent surviving parents are child centered when communicating about the parent's death with their children (Saldinger et al., 2004). To be child centered about a parent's death, surviving parents are encouraged to be aware of a child's loss-related needs, manage the degree of exposure a child has to the dying or deceased parent, include children in death-related rituals, and help children make meaning of their parent's death. Likewise, surviving parents can help their grieving children cope by encouraging the child to maintain a spiritual or emotional connection with the deceased parent, making sure their child is given age-appropriate information about the parent's death, encouraging the child to express his or her grief, creating and/or maintaining a consistent, stable environment for the child, and if needed, getting the child outside support or help, such as counseling

(Haine, Ayers, Sandler, & Wolchik, 2008; Haine, Wolchik, Sandler, Millsap, & Ayers, 2006). Unfortunately, it may be difficult for surviving parents to talk about and offer support to their children as they are simultaneously trying to cope with their *own* heartache, exhaustion, and overwhelming grief, resulting in less overall parental involvement with their children (Kalter et al., 2002–2003).

Sibling Death

In addition to the death of a parent, the death of a sibling is also traumatic for children. For instance, following the death of a sibling from cancer, preschool children can display anger and sadness, act out behaviorally, and have difficulty understanding the concept of death (Barrera, Alam, D'Agostino, Nicholas, & Schneiderman, 2013). In the Barrera et al. study, adolescent children whose sibling died struggled to engage in school, appeared to be fearful of death, did not share grief emotions with others, and engaged in "risky" behaviors such as drinking. To cope with their sibling's death, bereaved adolescents may engage in more social activities, share memories about their sibling with their parents, rely on friends for support, and seek out professional support (Hogan, De Santis, Demi, Cowles, & Ross, 1994). Among adolescents whose sibling committed suicide, many display symptoms of posttraumatic stress, experience feelings of guilt, and feel alone in their grief, as their parents are often immersed in their own pain and guilt (Dyregrov & Dyregrov, 2005). In addition, adolescents may have "inside" information about their sibling's suicide (i.e., forewarning) that they believe they need to keep from parents, which further compounds their own feelings of guilt and loneliness.

ADULT EXPERIENCES OF DEATH

Many children experience the death of a loved one as they are growing up, and some of these deaths are traumatic, such as the death of a sibling or parent. How our parents and other significant family members respond to a loved one's death can impact how we react to death during our adult years. As adults, we may expect certain deaths to occur, such as the death of an aging or elderly parent. These "expected" deaths are still painful and can be difficult to mourn. The death of a child or spouse during one's young adult/adulthood years is particularly traumatic and painful, as these deaths are usually not expected. I begin this section discussing how adults experience parental death. Following this, the death of a spouse is discussed, touching on both older adult conjugal bereavement (age 65 and older) and young adult/adulthood conjugal bereavement. This section is concluded by examining one of the most painful and difficult losses adults may deal with, which is the death of a child.

Parental Death During Adulthood

Thanks to medical advancements and increasing life expectancies, most individuals do not experience the death of a parent until they are middle aged or older. Although a parent's death may be expected, and in some cases timely, it is still a difficult and painful loss. The death of a parent is a significant life event for adult children. Even in situations in which the parent was elderly and in poor health, adult children may experience intense grief. Bereaved adult children may be more likely to experience increased alcohol use, psychological distress, and decreased physical health when compared with their non-bereaved peers (Umberson & Chen, 1994). Moss, Moss, Rubinstein, and Resch (1993) found that middle-aged daughters ranked the death of their elderly mother as "one of the hardest things they have ever had to deal with" (p. 8), and for these adult women, the more intense their grief was, the more they experienced health problems, and the less accepting they were of their mother's death.

A parent's death symbolically represents the passing of the family "torch" as adult children are left with the responsibility of passing on family values (see Petersen & Rafuls, 1998). After their parent dies, adult children may reprioritize their lives and engage more fully with their own spouses, partners, and children. Bereaved adult children may also be more conscious and deliberate when it comes to deciding what values and beliefs they want to pass on to their own children. For some adult children, the death of a parent may represent freedom, particularly if the child and parent had a conflictual or toxic relationship or if the adult child had been the primary caretaker for the elderly parent (Moss & Moss, 1983–1984).

How adult children respond to parental death may be contingent on their gender (Moss, Resch, & Moss, 1997) or the gender of the deceased parent. In a longitudinal study of nearly 10,000 bereaved adult children, Marks, Jun, and Song (2007) found that for adult women, maternal death had a stronger, more negative impact on them than did paternal death. Likewise, for adult sons, paternal death impacted them more negatively than did maternal death. For adult daughters, maternal death was linked to decreases in self-esteem, lower levels of control (i.e., personal mastery), and increased probability of binge drinking, and the death of both parents resulted in numerous negative outcomes, such as an increase in depressive symptoms, decreased happiness and self-esteem, and lower psychological wellness. For adult sons, paternal death resulted in an increase in depressive symptoms and lower psychological wellness, and the death of both parents resulted in decreased self-esteem, personal mastery, and psychological wellness, and increased their probability of binge drinking (Marks et al., 2007).

In a qualitative study of adults between the ages of 53 and 71 who experienced the death of both parents, Marshall (2004) found that adult children experienced a type of "double-grief" as they grieved both for the loss of their parent and for their surviving parent who had lost his or her partner or spouse. Many adult children felt that they had to hide or suppress their own grief in order to be strong for their surviving parent. These adult children were also concerned about the well-being of the surviving parent and felt they were responsible for making sure their newly bereaved parent could cope with this dramatic life change. When it came to the death of the surviving parent, participants in Marshall's study experienced the death quite differently, feeling they could finally grieve the death of both of their parents. Many also described themselves as "orphans" who gained a new sense of their own mortality.

To cope with and mourn their loss, bereaved adult children must also re-negotiate the relationship they had with their deceased parent (Moss & Moss, 1983–1984). For some adult children, this may involve carrying on family traditions and values or creating ongoing relational and spiritual bonds. The death of a parent may force bereaved adult children to reflect on their own mortality and finitude as they are faced with the reality that they are now the older generation. Unfortunately, because the death of an aging or elderly parent is viewed as expected and in some cases timely, adult children may mask or hide intense grief in order not to appear too bereaved. Because a parent's death is expected during adulthood, there may be a lack of support for adult children, particularly if the adult child's grief appears to be long or too intense.

Death of Spouse: Young Adult/Adulthood

Regardless of one's age, the death of a spouse represents the loss of a lover, friend, support system, and confidant. When a spouse dies, the surviving spouse often experiences deep shock and loneliness (Anderson & Dimond, 1994). The death of a spouse often means the death of life goals and/or future plans that the couple had together (see Bauer & Bonanno, 2001). Bereaved spouses may be faced with the daunting task of raising a family on their own, providing an income, and taking on new roles and responsibilities previously occupied by their spouse. Parenting following the death of a spouse is often difficult for surviving spouses, as they struggle to define what it means to be a single parent and to what degree they need to take on the parenting role of their deceased spouse (Glazer, Clark, Thomas, & Haxton, 2010). Surviving spouses with children may also lack confidence in their ability both to adapt to new parenting roles and nurture grieving children.

The death of a spouse also significantly impacts a surviving spouse's life expectancy. Bereaved spouses between the ages of 45 and 64 are significantly more likely to die of cardiovascular disease, coronary heart disease, stroke, cancer, alcoholism, suicide, and accidents than are their non-bereaved counterparts (Hart, Hole, Lawlor, Smith, & Lever, 2007). Likewise, widowed parents with young children who are on a limited income and have low levels of support may be at higher risk for depression and depression-like symptoms (see Worden & Silverman, 1996). Conjugally bereaved fathers often experience lower self-esteem as they may feel unprepared to step into the role of primary parent and meet the emotional needs of grieving children, all while taking on new household responsibilities.

When one's spouse is terminally ill, the marital relationship itself is significantly stressed. Both partners are often caught between hoping for a cure while simultaneously acknowledging the reality of the terminal diagnosis (see Saldinger & Cain, 2005). The "healthy" spouse is often exhausted from trying to care for the sick spouse and any children at home. Any intimacy the couple once had often diminishes, particularly when they struggle, as a couple, to talk about what each is feeling and experiencing during the final stages of the illness.

Family relationships are also substantially altered following the death of a spouse. In a study comparing bereaved families headed by either a widowed father or mother, Boerner and Silverman (2001) found that a mother's death resulted in greater disruption for the family even though fathers attempted to create new family patterns and routines. Fathers in this particular study were initially more focused on how their wife's death affected them, as opposed to how it impacted their children. As time passed, fathers became more aware of how their children were affected by their mother's death, but because they were also more likely to begin dating than were widowed mothers, the children of these widowed fathers felt their father was less available to them overall. The mothers in this study, conversely, demonstrated more awareness about how their husband's death affected their children and were much less likely to begin dating.

To cope with these drastic life changes, younger bereaved spouses may rely on their own immediate family and close friends for support and comfort (Kaunonen, Tarkka, Paunonen, & Laippala, 1999) as well as grief support groups (Glazer et al., 2010). Family members and friends who spend time, offer assistance, and allow grieving spouses to express their emotion are also very helpful and supportive to bereaved spouses (Kaunonen et al., 1999).

Death of Elderly Spouse

There are substantial similarities between the grief of older and younger bereaved spouses (see Anderson & Dimond, 1994). Both cohorts experience shock, disbelief, and sadness following their spouse's death. Both groups also report persistent loneliness following the first year after the death, and both groups often coped with their grief by engaging in activities (i.e., keeping busy) and relying on friends and family. However, younger bereaved spouses may experience more intense despair and feelings of chaos, possibly because younger surviving spouses are faced with enduring the loss of a spouse for a longer length of time, or because they believe their spouse was not able to enjoy a full, lengthy life. Conversely, older bereaved spouses may experience more physical symptoms of grief, such as fatigue, loss of appetite, and sleep disturbances.

Women age 65 and older are three times as likely to be widowed than are men of the same age, and around 73% of women 85 and older are widowed, compared with 35% of 85-year-old men (Federal Interagency Forum on Aging-Related Statistics, 2012), mainly because women tend to live longer and marry men who are older (Kinsella & Velkoff, 2001). As such, the majority of research focusing on conjugal bereavement among older adults relies heavily on the experiences of widowed women.

For both widowed men and women, depression following a spouse's death is a common occurrence (Bennett, Smith, & Hughes, 2005). Older bereaved spouses have reported experiencing persistent thoughts about dying, feeling hopeless about their future, and having feelings of worthlessness (e.g., Zisook & Shuchter, 1993). As a result, these individuals may be less likely to participate in social activities, engage in new relationships, and maintain current relationships with friends and family. Both widowed men and women are also more likely to have lower morale and less likely to engage in social activities than are their married counterparts (Bennett, 1998, 2005). Unfortunately, emotional support from family may decline over time (Powers, Bisconti, & Bergeman, 2014). It is not surprising, then, that both elderly men and women have described their experience of widowhood as lonely (Bennett & Victor, 2012). Conversely, the death of a spouse can result in positive outcomes for older adults. Bereaved older adults may experience a stronger and more empowered sense of self (Bennett, 2010; Bonanno, Mihalecz, & LeJune, 1999) or gain new perspective and priorities (Hogan, Greenfield, & Schmidt, 2001).

Death of Children

Clearly, the death of a spouse at any age is one of the most difficult and painful losses a person can endure (Arbuckle & de Vries, 1995); however, the death of one's own child is a painful loss that surpasses all others (Rando, 1991). Unlike the death of an aging or elderly parent, the death of a child is unexpected and untimely. A child's death defies the natural order of life, as parents of all ages do not expect to outlive their own children (Becvar, 2001). In actuality, the Centers for Disease Control and Prevention predicts that nearly 150,000 children and young adults will die each year in the U.S., leaving behind grieving parents and family members. This number does not include miscarriages, stillbirths, and the individuals over the age of 40 (The Compassionate Friends, 2006).

The death of an infant or young child is symbolically different from the death of an adult child (Rando, 1991), although the deaths of infants, children, and young adults are believed to be equally painful (see de Vries, Dalla Lana, & Falck,

1994). The death of an adult child symbolizes the loss of a relationship that parents had invested in over the years, whereas the death of an infant or young child symbolizes the loss of potential, hopes, and dreams. Frequently, parents of adult children and parents of perinatal children become "disenfranchised" grievers, in which they do not receive support and validation from others as most attention and support are given to the adult child's spouse or children (Doka, 1989; Rando, 1991).

To cope with their grief, bereaved parents may form continuing bonds with their deceased children, using ritual, storytelling, and memorializing to keep their child's memory alive to them (Grout & Romanoff, 2000; Klass, 1993, 1997; Toller, 2011). Oftentimes, talking with each other or their social network about their loss can be a source of healing and support for bereaved parents (e.g., Toller, 2011). However, communicating with their spouse can be difficult as each parent is simultaneously experiencing the death, and each may grieve in substantially different ways (Rando, 1991; Toller & Braithwaite, 2009). Communication between bereaved parents is further challenged by men's and women's tendencies to grieve and express emotion differently (Riches & Dawson, 2000). As a result, bereaved couples may find themselves avoiding communication with their spouse or restricting talk about certain topics related to the child's death.

Likewise, communicating with friends and family about their child's death is difficult for bereaved parents (Hastings, 2000; Toller, 2011). Family and friends may struggle to understand just how devastating and life altering a child's death is (Riches & Dawson, 2000), and the support bereaved parents expect to receive from family and friends is often absent as family and friends may avoid interacting with bereaved parents or make hurtful comments (Dyregrov, 2003–2004). As Rosenblatt (2000) suggested, a deep gap exists between bereaved parents and the rest of the world, as parents are engrossed in their grief, and friends and family view grief as the parents' responsibility to work through (Rosenblatt, 2000). It is no wonder that Riches and Dawson (2000) coined the phrase "an intimate loneliness" to describe the experience and feelings of bereaved parents (p. 74).

CONCLUSIONS

I framed my discussion of communication and grief using a lifespan approach. In the first section of this chapter, I discussed how children conceptualize and experience death, as well as how children are impacted by the death of a parent. In the next section, I focused on how adults experienced the death(s) of a parent, spouse, or child. By taking a lifespan approach in this chapter, both similarities and differences were identified across all types of death and all ages of the bereaved. First, the death of a loved one profoundly impacts not only an individual's sense of self, but also how they view the world and their place within it. For many bereaved individuals, the death of a loved one truly is a crisis of meaning, as they must figure out how to go on living without the one(s) they love. This process of "living with loss" is a painful, emotional, and exhausting journey that can span months, if not years. Finally, it is clear that communication is integral in the grieving process as mourners reflect on and make sense of their loss through talking, ritual, and other forms of verbal and nonverbal expression.

Although we know a great deal about how individuals experience and grieve the death of a loved one, there are still many unanswered questions and research areas that need to be explored. The bulk of grief research conducted in the U.S. is homogeneous and excludes the voices and experiences of minority groups and cultures. Our working models of grief and the grieving process are largely rooted in Western thought and present grief as a cognitive, internal process that occurs within the individual instead of a community. In general, researchers in psychology, communication, and other related fields know very little about how grief is experienced and expressed in collectivistic communities. As the world becomes even more interconnected through social media and other mediated platforms, researchers will, it is hoped, have opportunities to investigate and explore grief among various cultural groups.

Likewise, the shock and trauma that accompany the all-too-frequent occurrences of mass shootings in schools, movie theaters, and other public places need to be explored by grief researchers in order to provide public officials, community leaders, and other involved parties information and possibly assist them in coping with their grief. The very nature of these mass shootings, coupled with the extensive media coverage that subsequently occurs, has moved grief and loss from the private sphere to the public arena. We know very little about these affected communities, such as whether they grieve collectively, offer one another support, or engage in sense-making together. It is imperative that future grief research addresses these questions, as mass shootings result in numerous grieving families and traumatized citizens and survivors of all ages and cultures.

REFERENCES

Anderson, K. L., & Dimond, M. F. (1994). The experience of bereavement in older adults. *Journal of Advanced Nursing, 22*, 308–315.

Arbuckle, N. W., & de Vries, B. (1995). The long-term effects of later life spousal and parental bereavement on personal functioning. *Gerontologist, 35*, 637–647.

Attig, T. (1996). *How we grieve: Re-learning the world.* New York, NY: Oxford University Press.

Baker, J. E, & Sedney, M. A. (2004). How bereaved children cope with loss: An overview. In C. Corr & D. M. Corr (Eds.), *Handbook of childhood death and bereavement* (pp. 109–129). New York, NY: Springer.

Baker, J. E., Sedney, M. A., & Gross, E. (1992). Psychological tasks for bereaved children. *American Journal of Orthopsychiatry, 62*, 105–116.

Barrera, M., Alam, R., D'Agostino, N. M., Nicholas, D. B., & Schneiderman, G. (2013). Parental perceptions of siblings' grieving after a childhood cancer death: A longitudinal study. *Death Studies, 37*, 25–46.

Bauer, J. J., & Bonanno, G. (2001). Continuity amidst discontinuity: Bridging one's past and present in stories of conjugal bereavement. *Narrative Inquiry, 11*, 123–158.

Becvar, D. S. (2001). *In the presence of grief*. New York, NY: Guilford Press.

Bennett, K. M. (1998). Longitudinal changes in mental and physical health among elderly, recently widowed men. *Mortality, 3*, 265–273.

Bennett, K. M. (2005). Psychological wellbeing in later life: The longitudinal effects of marriage, widowhood, and marital status change. *International Journal of Geriatric Psychiatry, 20*, 280–284.

Bennett, K. M. (2010). "You can't just spend years with someone and just cast them aside": Augmented identity in older British widows. *Journal of Women and Aging, 22*, 204–217.

Bennett, K. M., Smith, P. T., & Hughes, G. M. (2005). Coping, depressive feelings and gender differences in late life widowhood. *Aging and Mental Health, 9*, 348–353.

Bennett, K. M., & Victor, C. (2012). "He wasn't in that chair": What loneliness means to widowed older people. *International Journal of Ageing and Later Life, 7*, 33–53.

Boerner, K., & Silverman, P. R. (2001). Gender specific coping patterns in widowed parents with dependent children. *Omega: Journal of Death and Dying, 43*, 201–216.

Bonanno, G. A., Mihalecz, M. C., & LeJune, J. T. (1999). The core emotion themes of conjugal loss. *Motivation and Emotion, 23*, 175–201.

Bosticco, C., & Thompson, T. L. (2005). Narratives and story-telling in coping with grief and bereavement. *Omega: Journal of Death and Dying, 51*, 1–16.

Christ, G. H., Siegel, K., & Sperber, D. (1994). Impact of parental terminal cancer on adolescents. *American Journal of Orthopsychiatry, 64*, 604–613.

The Compassionate Friends. (2006). *When a child dies*. Retrieved from http://www.compassionate friends.org/pdf/When_a_Child_Dies-2006_Final.pdf

de Vries, B., Dalla Lana, R., & Falck, V. T. (1994). Parental bereavement over the life course: A theoretical intersection and empirical review. *Omega: Journal of Death and Dying, 29*, 47–69.

Doka, K. J. (1989). Disenfranchised grief. In K. J. Doka (Ed.), *Disenfranchised grief: Recognizing hidden sorrow* (pp. 3–11). Lexington, KY: Lexington Books.

Dowdney, L. (2000). Annotation: Childhood bereavement following parental death. *Journal of Child Psychology and Psychiatry and Allied Disciplines, 41*, 819–830.

Dyregrov, K. (2003–2004). Micro-sociological analysis of social support following traumatic bereavement: Unhelpful and avoidant responses from the community. *Omega: Journal of Death and Dying, 48*, 23–44.

Dyregrov, K., & Dyregrov, A. (2005). Siblings after suicide—"the forgotten bereaved." *Suicide and Life-Threatening Behavior, 35*, 714–724.

Federal Interagency Forum on Aging-Related Statistics. (2012). Older Americans 2012: Key indicators of well-being. *Federal Interagency Forum on Aging-Related Statistics*. Washington, DC: U.S. Government Printing Office.

Gillies, J., & Neimeyer, R. A. (2006). Loss, grief, and the search for significance: Toward a model of meaning reconstruction in bereavement. *Journal of Constructivist Psychology, 19*, 31–65.

Glazer, H. R., Clark, M. D., Thomas, R., & Haxton, H. (2010). Parenting after the death of a spouse. *American Journal of Hospice and Palliative Medicine, 27*, 532–536.

Grout, L. A., & Romanoff, B. D. (2000). The myth of the replacement child: Parents' stories and practices after perinatal death. *Death Studies, 24*, 93–113.

Haine, R. A., Ayers, T. S., Sandler, I. N., & Wolchik, C. (2008). Evidence-based practices for parentally bereaved children and their families. *Professional Psychology: Research and Practice, 39*, 113–121.

Haine, R. A., Wolchik, S. A., Sandler, I. N., Millsap, R., & Ayers, T. S. (2006). Positive parenting as a protective resource for parentally bereaved children. *Death Studies, 30*, 1–28.

Hart, C. L., Hole, D. J., Lawlor, D. A., Smith, G. D., & Lever, T. F. (2007). Effect of conjugal bereavement on mortality of the bereaved spouse in participants of the Renfrew/Paisley study. *Journal of Epidemiological Community Health, 61*, 455–460.

Harvey, J. H. (2000). *Give sorrow words: Perspectives on loss and trauma*. Philadelphia, PA: Brunner/Mazel.

Hastings, S. (2000). Self-disclosure and identity management by bereaved parents. *Communication Studies, 51*, 352–371.

Hogan, N. S., De Santis, L., Demi, A. S., Cowles, K. V., & Ross, H. M. (1994). Things that help or hinder adolescent sibling bereavement. *Western Journal of Nursing, 16*, 132–153.

Hogan, N. S., Greenfield, D. B., & Schmidt, L. A. (2001). Testing the grief to personal growth model using structural equation modeling. *Death Studies, 26*, 615–634.

Hope, R. M., & Hodge, D. M. (2006). Factors affecting children's adjustment to the death of a parent: The social work professional's viewpoint. *Child and Adolescent Social Work Journal, 23*, 107–126.

Janoff-Bulman, R., & Berg, M. (1998). Disillusionment and the creating of values. In J. H. Harvey (Ed.), *Perspectives on loss* (pp. 35–47). New York, NY: Brunner/Mazel.

Kalter, N., Lohnes, K., Chasin, J., Cain, A. C., Dunning, S., & Rowan, J. (2002–2003). The adjustment of parentally bereaved children: I. Factors associated with short-term adjustment. *Omega, 46*, 15–34.

Kaunonen, M., Tarkka, M. T., Paunonen, M., & Laippala, P. (1999). Grief and social support after the death of a spouse. *Journal of Advanced Nursing, 30*, 1304–1311.

Kinsella, K., & Velkoff, V. A. (2001). *An aging world* (U.S. Census Bureau, Series P95/01-1). Washington, DC: U.S. Government Printing Office.

Klass, D. (1993). Solace and immortality: Bereaved parents' continuing bond with their children. *Death Studies, 17*, 343–368.

Klass, D. (1997). The deceased child in the psychic and social worlds of bereaved parents during the resolution of grief. *Death Studies, 21*, 147–175.

Marks, N. F., Jun, H., & Song, J. (2007). Death of parents and adult psychological and physical well-being. *Journal of Family Issues, 28*, 1611–1638.

Marshall, H. (2004). Midlife loss of parents: The transition from adult child to orphan. *Ageing International, 29*, 351–367.

Moss, M. S., & Moss, S. Z. (1983–1984). The impact of parental death on middle aged children. *Omega: Journal of Death and Dying, 14*, 65–75.

Moss, M., S., Moss, S. Z., Rubinstein, R., & Resch, N. (1993). Impact of elderly mother's death on middle age daughters. *International Journal of Aging and Human Development, 37*, 1–22.

Moss, M. S., Resch, N., & Moss, S. Z. (1997). The role of gender in middle-aged children's responses to parent death. *Omega: Journal of Death and Dying, 35*, 43–65.

Neimeyer, R. A. (1999). Narrative strategies in grief therapy. *Journal of Constructivist Psychology, 12*, 65–85.

Neimeyer, R. A., Klass, D., & Dennis, M. R. (2014). A social constructionist account of grief: Loss and the narration of meaning. *Death Studies, 38*, 485–498.

Neimeyer, R. A., Prigerson, H. G., & Davies, B. (2002). Mourning and meaning. *American Behavioral Scientist, 46*, 235–251.

Neimeyer, R. A., & Thompson, B. E. (2014). Meaning making and the art of grief therapy. In B. E. Thompson & R. A. Neimeyer (Eds.), *Grief and the expressive arts: Practices for creating meaning* (pp. 3–13). New York, NY: Routledge.

Nussbaum, J. F. (1989). Life-span communication: An introduction. In J. F. Nussbaum (Ed.), *Life-span communication: Normative processes* (pp. 1–4). Hillsdale, NJ: Lawrence Erlbaum.

Petersen, S., & Rafuls, S. E. (1998). Receiving the scepter: The generational transition and impact of parent death on adults. *Death Studies, 22*, 493–524.

Porterfield, K., Cain, A., & Saldinger, A. (2003). The impact of early loss history on parenting of bereaved children: A qualitative study. *Omega: Journal of Death and Dying, 47*, 203–220.

Powers, S. M., Bisconti, T. L., & Bergeman, C. S. (2014). Trajectories of social support and well-being across the first two years of widowhood. *Death Studies, 38*, 499–509.

Rando, T. A. (1991). Parental adjustment to the loss of a child. In D. Papadatou & C. Papadatos (Eds.), *Children and death* (pp. 233–253). New York, NY: Hemisphere.

Riches, G., & Dawson, P. (2000). *An intimate loneliness: Supporting bereaved parents and siblings.* Buckingham, UK: Open University Press.

Rosen, E. J. (2004). The family as healing resource. In C. Corr & D. M. Corr (Eds.), *Handbook of childhood death and bereavement* (pp. 223–243). New York, NY: Springer.

Rosenblatt, P. C. (2000). *Parent grief: Narratives of loss and relationship.* Philadelphia, PA: Brunner/Mazel.

Saldinger, A., & Cain, A. (2005). De-romanticizing anticipated death. *Journal of Psychosocial Oncology, 22*, 69–92.

Saldinger, A., Cain, A., Kalter, N., & Lohnes, K. (1999). Anticipating parental death in families with young children. *American Journal of Orthopsychiatry, 69*, 39–48.

Saldinger, A., Cain, A., & Porterfield, K. (2003). Managing traumatic strain in children anticipating parental death. *Psychiatry, 66*, 168–181.

Saldinger, A., Cain, A., Porterfield, K., & Lohnes, K. (2004). Facilitating attachment between school-aged children and a dying parent. *Death Studies, 28*, 915–940.

Schoka-Traylor, E., Hayslip, B., Kaminski, P. L., & York, C. (2003). Relationships between grief and family system characteristics: A cross lagged longitudinal analysis. *Death Studies, 27*, 575–601.

Silverman, P. R., Baker, J., Cait, C. A., & Boerner, K. (2002–2003). The effects of negative legacies on the adjustment of parentally bereaved children and adolescents. *Omega: Journal of Death and Dying, 46*, 335–352.

Silverman, P. R., & Worden, J. W. (1992). Children's reactions in the early months after the death of a parent. *American Journal of Orthopsychiatry, 62*, 93–104.

Social Security Administration. (2000). Retrieved from http://www.ssa.gov

Toller, P. W. (2005). Negotiation of dialectical contradictions by parents who have experienced the death of a child. *Journal of Applied Communication Research, 33*, 44–66.

Toller, P. W. (2011). Bereaved parents' experiences of supportive and unsupportive communication. *Southern Communication Journal, 76*, 17–34.

Toller, P. W., & Braithwaite, D. O. (2009). Grieving together and apart: Bereaved parents' contradictions of marital interaction. *Journal of Applied Communication Research, 37*(3), 257–277.

Umberson, D., & Chen, M. D. (1994). Effects of a parent's death on adult children: Relationship salience and reaction to loss. *American Sociological Review, 59*, 152–168.

U.S. Census Bureau. (2000). Retrieved from http://www.census. gov

Worden, J. W., & Silverman, P. R. (1993). Grief and depression in newly widowed parents with school-age children. *Omega: Journal of Death and Dying, 27*, 251–261.

Worden, J. W., & Silverman, P. R. (1996). Parental death and the adjustment of school-age children. *Omega: Journal of Death and Dying, 33*, 91–102.

Zisook, S., & Shuchter, S. R. (1993). Major depression associated with widowhood. *The American Journal of Geriatric Psychiatry, 1*, 316–326.

CHAPTER TWELVE

Ethical Issues IN End-of-Life Communication

CRAIG M. KLUGMAN

Mrs. Johnson is in hospice with advanced kidney cancer. Mira, her daughter with a troubled past, is her primary caregiver. When Mrs. Johnson loses consciousness, Mira calls 9-1-1 and, ignoring her mother's wishes, presses for all treatment possible. Mrs. Johnson is unconscious, uncomfortable, and in pain. The medical and nursing staff believe that interventions are causing discomfort with no hope for improvement. As Mrs. Johnson's kidneys fail and pain medication loses effectiveness, Mira demands dialysis and experimental treatments.

Mrs. Chang has been admitted to the hospital with severe abdominal pain, bloating, fatigue, weight loss, and constipation. She is an immigrant and speaks limited English. A biopsy is sent to the lab for diagnosis, with advanced ovarian cancer being the most likely finding. Her eldest son has asked the medical team not to inform his mother if the result is cancer. He explains that in their society it is considered a cruel burden to inform someone that she has a terminal disease and that all information and decisions should come to him, not his mother.

These opening scenarios are based on real clinical ethics consultations and serve as illustrations throughout this chapter. When health care providers are confronted with situations that have significant conflicts, they have been trained to call for an ethics consult—a group of highly trained individuals who help health care providers to work through intractable, non-medical problems.

For 40 years, bioethics scholars have written on end-of-life issues and clinical ethics consultants have been helping patients and families make end-of-life decisions by facilitating difficult conversations. The most common reason that an ethics consult is requested is for difficulty in patient–health care provider interactions. As much as 80% of clinical ethics consults come down to a lack of good communication (Forde & Vandvik, 2005; Kaldjian, Weir, & Duffy, 2005). Although consults are new to ethics, challenges to clinical information exchange have long been known in health communication (Bleakley, 2006; Solet, Norvell, Rutan, & Frankel, 2005). The American Society for Bioethics & Humanities (ASBH) has identified "communication" as a key competency for clinical ethics consultants for facilitating "a clinical ethics consultation meeting or participating in a care conference including active listening, reflective listening, reinterpretation of points of view or positions, and the ability to summarize narratives and points of view" (ASBH Clinical Ethics Task Force, 2009, p. 65). This is a superficial understanding of communication that neglects the value of theory in interpreting these difficult clinical scenarios.

This chapter examines the field of bioethics, specifically medical ethics and clinical ethics as they relate to end-of-life communications. An overview of scholarship on bioethical issues related to health communications will lead to a derivation of four principles for ethical health communication.

LAYING THE GROUNDWORK

In the *Nicomachean Ethics*, Aristotle defined "ethics" as the application of moral knowledge. Ethics is a practice born of habit of consistently making virtuous choices through the exercise of reason (Aristotle, 1962). Thus, it is not enough to know what the right thing is to do; one must do it. In modern terms, "ethics" has taken on several different meanings, depending on the setting.

- In regard to public policy and law, ethics means following laws that dictate appropriate and inappropriate behavior.
- In philosophy, ethics is the examination of how people make decisions regarding right and wrong.
- In medical ethics, it is about what one ought to do. Ethics tells us how we ought to behave in specific situations.
- In clinical ethics, it is the process of facilitating moral deliberation surrounding a practical decision.
- In bioethics, it is about identifying issues, debating meaning, and asking questions.

Bioethics

Bioethics as a field grew out of several social movements in the 1960s and 1970s. This is the era of the civil rights movement when a social shift empowered individuals to make their own decisions rather than giving that power to authorities (e.g., parents, the state, teachers, physicians). Several high-profile cases also become public, such as the Tuskegee Study of Untreated Syphilis in the Negro Male (1932–1972) and Harry Beecher's high-profile article on human subjects research abuse (Beecher, 1966). With the advent of artificial kidneys and shunts as well as organ transplantation, questions arose about the rationing and distribution of scarce medical resources and what constitutes death. The increasing complexity of medical technology left professionals and patients facing dilemmas that were unique in human history. Bioethics gained momentum when scholars from different disciplines (such as medicine, law, philosophy, and religious studies) discovered that they were interested in similar questions. Soon thereafter, centers and journals developed, leading to the establishment of this new field (Jonsen, 1998).

The term "bioethics" is believed to have been first used in 1971 by Van Rensselaer Potter, who imagined an ethics of the biosphere (Potter, 1971). Today, it is an umbrella term that refers to examining questions dealing with health, medicine, health research, technology, and business: "The broad terrain of the moral problems of the life sciences, ordinarily taken to encompass medicine, biology, and some important aspects of the environmental, population and social sciences" (Reich, 1995).

Under the umbrella of bioethics are numerous professionally based ethics of practice (see Figure 1). Medical ethics examines right and wrong in the practice of medicine. Nursing ethics focuses on the practice of nursing. Other subtypes include public health ethics, (bio) business ethics, health research ethics, and even health communication ethics. These specific types of ethics examine the issues surrounding a particular established profession.

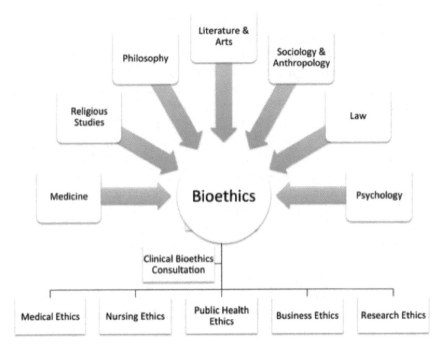

Figure 1. Bioethics and its relations.

Clinical Ethics

A unique contribution of bioethics has been the spawning of a new profession—clinical ethics. "Clinical ethics is a practical discipline that provides a structured approach for identifying, analyzing and resolving ethical issues in clinical medicine" (Jonsen, Siegler, & Winslade, 2002, p. 1). People who work in clinical ethics are most commonly found in hospitals and medical schools. ASBH has even developed a code of ethics and is currently reviewing a credentialing program for clinical ethicists (American Society for Bioethics & Humanities, 2011; White, Jankowski, & Shelton, 2014).

The Joint Commission requires hospitals to have a mechanism for handling ethics issues (The Joint Commission, 2013). Most often an institution will have an ethics committee (Fox, Myers, & Pearlman, 2007). These committees entered the public domain after being mentioned in the 1976 Karen Ann Quinlan ruling by the New Jersey Supreme Court (*Re Quinlan*, 1976). A recommendation for these committees also appeared in a 1982 report by a Presidential Commission.

The report suggested that a hospital-based ethics committee was an appropriate place to deal with difficult ethical decisions, as opposed to going through the courts (Presidential Commission for the Study of Ethical Problems in Medicine and Biomedical and Behavioral Research, 1982).

While there are no rules for the composition of such groups, usually they have 10 to 40 members representing a variety of professions (e.g., medicine, nursing, social work, chaplaincy, psychology, surgery, administration, risk management, legal affairs) and units in the hospital. Sometimes there is a community member. Notice that health communication is rarely an available service. The goal is to represent the variety of perspectives and diversity of expertise that is found throughout the institution.

Ethics committees can serve three main functions: policy, education, and consultation (Hester & Schonfeld, 2012). Policy work can include developing and reviewing hospital guidelines. Education takes the forms of member learning and acting as an ethics expert to other hospital units. The goals for consultation include "clarifying the situation and/or recommendations, ensuring effective communication among diverse groups, empowering clinical staff to assess and address ethical issues themselves, and recognizing patterns of consultation that may result in broader educational or policy implications" (Hester & Schonfeld, 2012, p. 3).

Consultations can be done by a full ethics committee (perhaps for addressing new issues or considering potential policy implications for the hospital), or by an individual consultant (if few people are available, or if there is a trained clinical ethics consultant available), or by a group (two or three individuals from a variety of disciplinary perspectives). Ethics consultations are most often requested by a member of the health care team (usually physicians, as nurses and residents are less likely to request them) or the family (Danis et al., 2008; Gacki-Smith & Gordon, 2005). After the consult service is invited to assist, there are five general steps:

1. Gather information (chart review, interview the care team, talk with the patient/family/friends).
2. Analyze (use understanding of ethical theories, health law, hospital policies, and community standards to identify and examine the issues in the case).
3. Negotiate options (identify the options, understand the positives and negatives for each perspective, hold family meetings, assess the viability of options, and make recommendations).
4. Document in the chart.
5. Evaluate the process and the outcome (following up with the health care team and family, ask them how useful the service was, reflect on ways to improve; Spike, 2012).

BIOETHICS TOOLBOX

In the analysis stage, the clinical ethicist will apply bioethics theories that can provide perspective and insight into how a decision could be made. These bioethical tools derive from philosophical theories about how one lives ethically. Although presented separately in this chapter, in any given clinical ethics case, the ethicist will use several different approaches.

Rules-Based

This tool draws on the work of Immanuel Kant (1724–1804), who believed that a person should make choices by following the moral law. That is, there are eternal laws in the universe that dictate right and wrong. An individual applies reason to discover these universal laws and is then obligated to follow them. In clinical ethics, this approach means that one needs at least to consider, if not follow, laws, rules, policies, and standards. In its purest form, consequences and emotions are ignored. What is right is following the rule.

For example, consider the opening scenario of Mrs. Chang. If the rule (in this case, law and hospital policy) is that patients must be fully informed of their diagnosis and treatment plans, then the right action is to refuse the son's request. That such a move might cause undue distress to Mrs. Chang or might make the family distrust the medical system is not a consideration because those are outcomes.

Utilitarianism/Consequentialism

This theory draws on the work of Jeremy Bentham (1748–1832), who was a social reformer interested in public policy. Bentham's idea was that the goal of any decision was to maximize pleasure and minimize pain in a population. The focus is on the consequences. Although Bentham created his theory for groups, in bioethics a utilitarian approach is one that aims for good or desired outcomes.

Referring to the other opening case, Mira Johnson demands dialysis and experimental treatments to help cure her mother. Most likely, such an action will increase Mrs. Johnson's pain. She is not a good candidate for dialysis or surgery. Any experiments would be a burden of probable pain and discomfort without possibility of improvement. The right action here is not to add any interventions. There is also a question of whether any current treatments should be withdrawn to decrease her pain.

Principlism

In 1977, Tom Beauchamp and James Childress published *Principles of Biomedical Ethics*, now in its seventh edition. These scholars proposed four principles to guide moral deliberation (Beauchamp & Childress, 2013):

- Autonomy—self-rule or governance. The right of an individual to make his or her own decisions
- Nonmaleficence—an obligation not to cause harm to others
- Beneficence—an obligation to attend to the welfare of patients by taking action to help them
- Justice—"fair, equitable and appropriate treatment in light of what is due or owed to persons" (Montello, 2014, p. 250)

Consider the opening scenarios. On one hand, for Mrs. Chang the request to deny her information may be a violation of autonomy. Nonmaleficence may be an issue if knowledge of a cancer diagnosis would cause her harm, as her son suggests. On the other hand, Mrs. Johnson had expressed her autonomous desires by being in hospice, but her surrogate decision maker has made other choices. One could argue that her autonomy is violated by the change in course of care. For the nursing staff, however, the issue is nonmaleficence—every intervention (other than comfort care) is causing pain without any benefit.

Ethic of Care

Psychology studies have found that men and women reason differently (Gilligan, 1982): men focus on rules and right action, while women focus more on relationships, caring, and nurturing. The ethic of care builds on this observation by stating the right action is one that embraces caring and nurturing. Unlike other ethical theories that focus on reasoning and dismiss emotion, ethics of care states that relationships matter and emotions are important.

In end-of-life cases, there usually comes a point when the patient is clearly going to die, and the focus shifts to how we help this family to move on from this event (Gauthier, 2008). For example, Mrs. Johnson had a terminal condition and no matter what was done, she was going to die. The feeding tube and ventilator were prolonging her dying, not her living. In talking with Mira, I asked her what she thought would happen with additional surgeries and treatments if they were possible. Her response was, "That my mom will open her eyes, tell me that she forgives me and that she loves me." Continued support was not in Mrs. Johnson's best interest, nor was it in the staff's interest, but we had to consider Mira's need to feel that she had done everything possible to earn forgiveness. Relationships matter.

Narrative Ethics

This theory holds that cases cannot be reduced to principles, standards, or rules. Instead, a person's current experience must be viewed as part of the continuing story of his or her life. The better decision is one that coheres with the patient's lifetime of choices (Gula, 2011). "A narrativist tries to capture the stories patients and families tell about the way they arrived at a particular predicament as well as the how of their moral decision-making at earlier important moments" (Montello, 2014, p. S3). The health care team is engaged as co-authors working with the patient to write a story consistent with the patient's life narrative.

Mira Johnson needs her mother to awaken because she needs forgiveness. Understanding this motivation provides a context for understanding why she has made certain choices for her mother. Mira had a history of drug use and time in juvenile hall, so she feels guilty about what she put her mother through. This explains Mira's motivation. The goal through this theory is to help Mira write her story in such a way that she can make the right choice for her mother (instead of for herself). Similarly, the request of Mrs. Chang's son can be better understood by learning what kind of woman she is and how she may have approached medical encounters in the past. It is important not to make assumptions about a person because he or she is a member of a cultural group. Understanding what her background and culture mean to Mrs. Chang is important in analyzing the story.

COMMUNICATION ISSUES IN BIOETHICS

A meta-analysis of studies in end-of-life communication show that several ethical issues repeatedly appear. These include patient-family-provider interactions, decision making and surrogate decision makers, advance care planning, exercising autonomy, informed consent, lack of training in end-of-life conversations, and dealing with emotions (both of patients and health care providers; DuVal, Sartorius, Clarridge, Gensler, & Danis, 2001; Fox et al., 2007; Galushko, Romotzky, & Voltz, 2012; McClung, Kamer, DeLuc, & Barber, 1996). In the field of bioethics broadly and clinical ethics specifically, concerns about communication have focused on a number of topics including health care providers relating to patients, federal regulations, conflicts of interest, and patients exercising their right of autonomy. This section examines clinical ethics issues that arise from communication challenges.

Advance Care Planning/Advance Directives

One of the most common communication needs in bioethics is seen with advance care planning and advance directives. Advance care planning is a process of conversations with trained facilitators, health care providers, surrogates, and families about future care goals. Advance care planning and advance directives substitute a present conversation for a future impossible one. Even this imperfect substitute happens rarely, less than a quarter of the time (Hofmann et al., 1997; Klugman & Tolwin, 2014). Often, physicians are reluctant to discuss end-of-life issues because of a lack of knowledge, understanding, and time (Morrison, Morrison, & Glickman, 1994). This reluctance finds its way into the medical school curriculum; thus, students believe they are not prepared to discuss end-of-life issues (Buss, Marx, & Sulmasy, 1998).

One of the first studies in bioethics that addressed this issue was the *Study to Understand Prognoses and Preferences for Outcomes and Risks of Treatments* (SUPPORT). One arm of this study trained nurses in how to have conversations about making prospective choices and had them talk with patients, families, and other care providers. The research found that special training did not increase or improve the use and application of the documents (Connors, 1995). Problems with this form of future communication have included a lack of knowledge when completing advance directives, a focus on procedures instead of values, and the difficulty of making choices for a future condition which can be difficult to imagine (Lynn, 1991; Tulsky, 2005; Vandecreek & Frankowski, 1996). There is also often a separation between face-to-face conversation and completing documentation. Ideally, the two would happen together, but studies show that the conversations rarely happen (Hahn, 2003).

Advance care planning includes not only choices about medical interventions but also people's values concerning quality of life, choosing a proxy decision maker, body disposal, and instructions on what kind of setting people want in the last hours of life (location, people present, sounds, sensations; Lang & Quill, 2004; Stump, Klugman, & Thornton, 2008). In the Mrs. Johnson scenario, the presence of an advance directive may have helped in conversations with Mira to demonstrate how she was not making the choices her mother wanted. Documented conversations about how Mrs. Johnson wanted to spend her final days may have changed the tone and type of discussions.

Conflicts of Interest

In a conflict of interest, an individual owes allegiance to more than one party. Consider the researcher who receives money from a pharmaceutical company and may feel some obligation to produce results proving that company's drugs are effective.

Studies show that physicians' prescribing habits are influenced by their exposure to pharmaceutical representatives (Harris, 2009). Physicians are more likely to prescribe a company's drugs in the time following a representative's visit. Physicians who prescribe a large amount of a particular drug get perks from the pharmaceutical companies such as paid lectures, preferential access to drugs in times of rationing, and patient access to clinical trials. The best interest of the patient may take a back seat to the potential personal and professional gain of the physician (Brody, 2006; Lo & Field, 2009).

The response to conflict of interest has been a requirement to report apparent conflicts of interest through the filing of a self-report form. Presumably, this self-report is reviewed to see whether action must be taken. In general, such conflicts should be avoided. But when they exist, it is rare that a conversation over a reported conflict of interest occurs. The question also arises whether revelation alone is sufficient to deal with the conflict, especially because disclosure to patients is rare.

Giving Bad News

One study found that medical professionals at all levels of training felt a lack of preparedness in giving patients and families bad news (Orgel, McCarter, & Jacobs, 2010). New curricula have been introduced into medical education to address this gap using didactic and practical sessions (with real family and standardized patients). In the classroom, a student may learn facts about patient retention of information once bad news is given, patient reactions, handling the emotional response, and protocols for delivery. One such formula is known as SPIKES and consists of creating a Setting (private location, who is present, sit down, be attentive, and listen), Perception (how the patient talks about the situation), Invitation (how much the patient wants to know), Knowledge (how much the patient already knows, a warning shot—"I'm afraid your test results are not what we had hoped"), Empathy (identify, acknowledge, and validate patient emotions), and Strategy (identify the next steps; Baile et al., 2000; Buckman, 2005).

Incidental Findings

Incidental findings are potentially relevant clinical observations that are unexpectedly discovered when performing unrelated clinical or research screenings (Illes et al., 2006). Such discoveries can come about as a result of a clinical test, participating in a research protocol, or using direct-to-consumer testing.

For example, while conducting a CT scan to look for the source of hip pain, a radiologist discovers a spinal tumor. Should such information be given to patients? If a research study finds that a person has a gene that makes her susceptible to a disease, does the non-physician researcher have an obligation to inform the non-patient subject (Appelbaum et al., 2014)? How can one gain the consent of patients and subjects for incidental findings—should they be told about every possible condition that might be discovered; should a plan for conveying such knowledge be made before the testing; should they not be told at all? Most researchers believe that subjects should be told about such findings (Klitzman et al., 2013) but they disagree on how much information should be shared (Appelbaum et al., 2014; Klitzman et al., 2013). A President's Commission has recommended that patients be told of the likelihood of incidental findings beforehand, perhaps as part of informed consent: "Open communication between practitioners and individuals, accessible and understandable documents and resources, and transparent processes in all three contexts [research, clinical, direct-to-consumer] help ensure that individuals understand risks and benefits before they consent" (Presidential Commission for the Study of Bioethical Issues, 2013, p. 5).

Informed Consent

Before being treated for an illness or enrolling in a research study, patients exercise their autonomy by giving their permission to participate. This practice is rooted in medical tradition, ethical theory (autonomy), and law (del Carmen & Joffe, 2005). Although the idea of informed consent may be simple in concept, studies show that the process of informed consent is challenging because health care providers are often insensitive to the consent conversations and lack empathy to comprehend the patient's point of view (Albrecht, Franks, & Ruckdeschel, 2005).

Truly informed consent requires that it be both volitional and informational. The volitional component holds that a person must have capacity—the ability to make, express, and explain rational choices—to exercise autonomy. If a person lacks capacity, then his or her autonomy must be given to someone else, a medical power of attorney or health care surrogate (American Medical Association, 2006). The informational component requires that patients (or surrogates) be given all information that a reasonable person would want to be able to make a decision. Such knowledge includes the process of the treatment or test, the benefits, the side effects and burdens, and the alternatives.

Privacy and Confidentiality

Confidentiality is the guarding of secret information. "Confidentiality refers to the boundaries surrounding secrets and to the process of guarding these boundaries" (Bok, 1983). Patients share information that they would not normally give to others with the assurance that the professional will use this knowledge to assist the patient and will hold such information secret. In health care, this includes not only conversations but also documentation of clinical encounters.

Privacy, conversely, is a person's legal right to have control over information about himself or herself and whether to share it (DeCew, 2013). In U.S. law, patients and subjects have privacy protection under the Health Insurance Portability and Accountability Act (HIPAA). This federal law also protects the confidentiality of any information that a person chooses to share with a health care provider. The regulations control how information is stored and with whom a provider may share the knowledge (U.S. Department of Health and Human Services, 2014). In ethics, confidentiality is considered to be sacrosanct with a few exceptions:

- Required breach when
    o Patient/subject reveals that he or she is an imminent threat to self or others
    o Reporting infections that could affect public health (e.g., infectious disease)
    o Child or elder abuse is suspected
    o Ordered by a court

- Permitted breach when
    o Health care provider needs to consult with a colleague on a specific relevant case
    o Information/patient made anonymous for evaluation, quality improvement, education, and research
    o Patient gives permission for information to be shared

When health care providers talk to their patients, it is expected that assurances of confidentiality will be made, but these exceptions should be noted. If a patient or subject asks that information not be shared and it falls under a required exception, the health care provider should inform that person that he or she cannot guarantee complete confidentiality.

Truth Telling

Truth telling is a foundational topic in ethics in that it underlays values and practices in breaking bad news, privacy, and even deception. Although the discussion here is from a bioethics perspective, it holds relevance for human communications as well.

Trust is at the heart of the provider-patient relationship. One element of trust is an expectation that truthful and accurate information will be shared. In one study, health care providers were found to underestimate the number of patients who wanted their health information and how much information they desired

(Sullivan, Menapace, & White, 2001). Such dilemmas represent as much as two-thirds of clinical ethics cases (Forde & Vandvik, 2005).

However, there may be times when telling the full truth may violate trust. Trust also hangs on the idea that a party with power and authority (the health care provider) will not use that information to cause harm (nonmaleficence) or to allow harm to happen (beneficence). Thus, there may be times when information should not be disclosed. The philosopher Sissela Bok holds that in general, patients should always be told the truth, except when such a disclosure would cause harm to the individual (Bok, 1989).

Consider the opening scenario of Mrs. Chang. The ethicist may explain that U.S. medical practice emphasizes autonomy, meaning that the patient has the right to decide. Asking the patient how much she wants to know and whether there is someone else who should also know allows the patient to decide to follow a cultural practice (or not to) and also honors the U.S. standard. Before disclosing her test results (and ideally before conducting the test), the physician should ask Mrs. Chang what she wants to know. The physician should speak to her alone and not include her son. The one exception would be if Mrs. Chang waived her legal and ethical right to know her information and named her son as a proxy.

ETHICAL PRINCIPLES

From the ethical theories and bioethical discourse on various issues discussed in this chapter, it is possible to derive principles of health communication at the end of life. Respect for persons holds that as a result of human dignity, people generally have self-governance. Transparency focuses on honesty and building trust. Supportiveness is about providing compassionate assistance and empathy to patients. Specificity acknowledges that all individuals are unique and have different capabilities and needs. The following four principles provide guidance for ethical health communication.

Respect for Persons

Health care interactions should maximize a patient's autonomy. Respect for persons means that an individual with cognitive capacity can make decisions and communicate that to others. For a health care provider, it means being aware of the level of language, the means of communication, and even whether value-laden words are used. Patients also have the right to assign their autonomy to others if they wish to avoid knowledge of a diagnosis or responsibility to make decisions. In cases in which capacity is diminished or absent, or when a public health crisis requires limiting autonomy, the goal should be to restrict autonomy as little as possible. Thus, advance care planning and appointing surrogate decision makers are key to ensuring that a patient's wishes are known. In addition, health care providers should recognize that silence—lack of instructions or consent—from a patient does not mean consent.

Transparency

Transparency means that communication is open, honest, and clear. Health care professionals should not keep secrets from patients/subjects. Such an effort is necessary to build rapport as well as to create and maintain trust. Conversations should be specific enough that they do not leave room for interpretation. For example, asking, "Do you want resuscitation?" is broad and does not give guidance on such related interventions as intubation and pressors, or even for how long CPR should be attempted and under what conditions. Should a do-not-resuscitate (DNR) order be maintained or lifted during a surgery if the cause of the need for CPR is reversible such as might occur from anesthesia? Broad questions do not permit room for discussing what is an acceptable quality of life, or under what conditions a person is willing to survive. Without such detail, family and care providers must interpret wishes without context (Lang & Quill, 2004).

That said, there are also some circumstances under which this virtue may need to be moderated. For instance, a patient may not want to know all of the information, or the patient may be at risk for harming self or others. In cases in which the patient's ability to deal with transparency is curtailed, a surrogate of the patient's choosing must hear it to be able to assist in decision making and providing emotional support.

Supportiveness

Health care providers must attend not only to the facts but also to the emotional experience of the patient. People are more than decisions; they are how they respond to news and how they feel about their options. Supportiveness holds that the goal in communication should be to assist the individual whether that be to deal with a diagnosis, to face tough choices, or to gain assistance in constructing the narrative of their life and death. Patients should always receive compassionate care in line with their values that supports their physical, mental, emotional, and spiritual well-being.

Specificity

Specificity is the concept that every patient and family is unique and thus communications must be tailored to their needs and capacities. This notion finds its roots in communication accommodation theory (Giles, Coupland, & Coupland, 1991). Providers should be aware of potential cultural and familial concerns, but not assume a particular patient will follow them. The health care provider will also have to use language at an appropriate level when communicating with the patient and family. Rarely will one approach or solution work for every patient and family.

CONCLUSIONS

In many ways, clinical ethics consultation answers the need mentioned by Watson, Hewett, and Gallois for a "patient care team with a superordinate identity, structured around the patient's condition rather than specialty roles" (Watson et al., 2012, p. 202). The ethics committee and consult team transcends professional silos and barriers to patient involvement. This practice uses an interdisciplinary ethics team to bring together a disparate set of patient care clinicians, family members, and the patient to focus on the needs, desires, and care of the patient through an exploration of options and open communication. This intergroup dynamic helps overcome traditional hospital communication problems.

This chapter has shown that there has been a lack of conversation between the fields of bioethics/clinical ethics and health communication even though both fields are interested in similar topics and issues. This lack of collaboration means that each side ends up rediscovering territory that the other has already explored. Giving bad news is a strong example of this duplicative effort as both fields have very different literatures on the topic. A bioethics perspective would hold that health communication is descriptive and thus not helpful in determining what ought to be (prescriptive). Many philosophers would say the environment of practice is irrelevant and thus they write about the clinic without ever stepping foot into one. A health communication scholar could say that the bioethicist is unrealistic, focusing on theoretical ideals rather than considering lived experiences. As an attempt to bridge this gap, the author has discussed the perspectives and language of bioethics in concept, as a clinical practice, as a set of tools used in decision making, and in exploring major communication issues inherent in clinical practice. The hope is to provide an opening for a prolonged dialogue between the two fields.

Watson et al. suggest that "better strategies for resolving intergroup conflict are essential" (2012, p. 301). Perhaps those better strategies can be found in clinical ethics. The tools and methods developed in this profession actively bring down silos, create open communication between clinical disciplines, and engage patients and families on a more equal footing with care providers to permit respectful, transparent, supportive, and specific communication. The practice of clinical ethics represents an opportunity for health communication research that may provide evidence of "communication interventions that promote cooperation between health professionals and reduce adverse impacts on patients" (Watson et al., 2012, p. 301). Except for the work of sociologists Renee Fox and Judith Swazey (2008), the study of clinical ethics is untapped and rich for exploration.

REFERENCES

Albrecht, T. L., Franks, M. M., & Ruckdeschel, J. C. (2005). Communication and informed consent. *Current Opinion in Oncology, 17*, 336–339.

American Medical Association. (2006). *Opinion 8.08 Informed Consent.* Retrieved from http://www. ama-assn.org/ama/pub/physician-resources/medical-ethics/code-medical-ethics/opinion808. page?

American Society for Bioethics & Humanities. (2011). Code of ethics and professional responsibilities for healthcare ethics consultants. Retrieved from http://www.asbh.org/publications/content/asbhpublications.html

Appelbaum, P. S., Waldman, C. R., Fyer, A., Klitzman, R., Parens, E., Martinez, J.,...Chung, W. K. (2014). Informed consent for return of incidental findings in genomic research. *Genetics in Medicine, 16*(5), 367–373. doi:10.1038/gim.2013.145

Aristotle. (1962). *Nicomachean ethics* (M. Ostwald, Trans.). Englewood Cliffs, NJ: Library of Liberal Arts.

ASBH Clinical Ethics Task Force. (2009). *Improving competencies in clinical ethics consultation: An education guide.* Glenview, IL: American Society for Bioethics & Humanities.

Baile, W. F., Buckman, R., Lenzi, R., Glober, G., Beale, E. A., & Kudelka, A. P. (2000). SPIKES—a six-step protocol for delivering bad news: Application to the patient with cancer. *Oncologist, 5*(4), 302–311.

Beauchamp, T. L., & Childress, J. F. (2013). *Principles of biomedical ethics* (7th ed.). New York, NY: Oxford University Press.

Beecher, H. K. (1966). Ethics and clinical research. *New England Journal of Medicine, 274*(24), 1354–1360.

Bleakley, A. (2006). You are who I say you are: The rhetorical construction of identity in the operating theater. *Journal of Workplace Learning, 18*, 414–425.

Bok, S. (1983). *Secrets: On the ethics and concealment of revelation.* New York, NY: Pantheon.

Bok, S. (1989). *Lying.* New York, NY: Vintage Books.

Brody, H. (2006). *Hooked: Ethics, the medical profession, and the pharmaceutical industry.* New York, NY: Rowman & Littlefield.

Buckman, R. A. (2005, March–April). Breaking bad news: The S-P-I-K-E-S strategy. *Community Oncology,* 138–142.

Buss, M. K., Marx, E. S., & Sulmasy, D. P. (1998). The preparedness of students to discuss end-of-life issues with patients. *Academic Medicine, 73*(4), 418–422.

Connors, A. F. (1995). A controlled trial to improve care for seriously ill hospitalized patients. *JAMA, 274*(20), 1591.

Danis, M., Farrar, A., Grady, C., Taylor, C., O'Donnell, P., Soeken, K., & Ulrich, C. (2008). Does fear of retaliation deter requests for ethics consultation? *Medicine, Health Care, and Philosophy, 11*(1), 27–34.

DeCew, J. (2013). Privacy. *The Stanford encyclopedia of philosophy.* Retrieved from http://plato.stan ford.edu/archives/fall2013/entries/privacy/

del Carmen, M. G., & Joffe, S. (2005). Informed consent for medical treatment and research: A review. *Oncologist, 10*(8), 636–641.

DuVal, G., Sartorius, L., Clarridge, B., Gensler, G., & Danis, M. (2001). What triggers requests for ethics consultations? *Journal of Medical Ethics, 27*(Suppl. 1), i24–i29.

Forde, R., & Vandvik, I. H. (2005). Clinical ethics, information, and communication: Review of 31 cases from a clinical ethics committee. *Journal of Medical Ethics, 31*(2), 73–77.

Fox, E., Myers, S., & Pearlman, R. A. (2007). Ethics consultation in United States hospitals: A national survey. *American Journal of Bioethics, 7*(2), 13–25.

Fox, R. C., & Swazey, J. P. (2008). *Observing bioethics.* New York, NY: Oxford University Press.

Gacki-Smith, J., & Gordon, E. J. (2005). Residents' access to ethics consultations: Knowledge, use, and perceptions. *Academic Medicine, 80*(2), 168–175.

Galushko, M., Romotzky, V., & Voltz, R. (2012). Challenges in end-of-life communication. *Current Opinion in Supportive Palliative Care, 6*(3), 355–364.

Gauthier, D. M. (2008). Challenges and opportunities: Communication near the end of life. *Medsurg Nursing, 15*(5), 291–296.

Giles, H., Coupland, N., & Coupland, J. (1991). Accommodation theory: Communication, context, and consequence. In H. Giles, J. Coupland, & N. Coupland (Eds.), *Contexts of accommodation* (pp. 1–68). New York, NY: Cambridge University Press.

Gilligan, C. (1982). *In a different voice: Psychological theory and women's development.* Cambridge, MA: Harvard University Press.

Gula, R. M. (2011). On writing the next chapter: Using narrative ethics in health care decisions. *Louvain Studies, 35,* 139–161.

Gunderson Health System. (2014). Respecting choices. Retrieved August 18, 2014, from http://www. gundersenhealth.org/respecting-choices

Hahn, M. E. (2003). Advance directives and patient-physician communication. *JAMA, 289*(1), 96.

Harris, G. (2009). Pharmaceutical representatives do influence physician behaviour. *Family Practice, 26*(3), 169–170.

Hester, D. M., & Schonfeld, T. (2012). Introduction to healthcare ethics committees. In D. M. Hester & T. Schonfeld (Eds.), *Guidance for healthcare ethics committees* (pp. 1–8). New York, NY: Cambridge University Press.

Hofmann, J. C., Wenger, N. S., Davis, R. B., Teno, J., Connors, A. F., Jr., Desbiens, N.,...Phillips, R. S. (1997). Patient preferences for communication with physicians about end-of-life decisions. SUPPORT Investigators. Study to Understand Prognoses and Preference for Outcomes and Risks of Treatment. *Annals of Internal Medicine, 127*(1), 1–12.

Illes, J., Kirschen, M. P., Edwards, E., Stanford, L. R., Bandettini, P., Cho, M. K.,...& Working Group on Incidental Findings in Brain Imaging, Research. (2006). Ethics: Incidental findings in brain imaging research. *Science, 311*(5762), 783–784. doi:10.1126/science.1124665

The Joint Commission. (2013). *Health care staffing services certification handbook.* Oakbrook Terrace, IL: Author.

Jonsen, A. R. (1998). *The birth of bioethics.* New York, NY: Oxford University Press.

Jonsen, A. R., Siegler, M., & Winslade, W. J. (2002). *Clinical ethics* (5th ed.). New York, NY: McGraw-Hill.

Kaldjian, L. C., Weir, R. F., & Duffy, T. P. (2005). A clinician's approach to clinical ethical reasoning. *Journal of General Internal Medicine, 20*(3), 306–311.

Klitzman, R., Appelbaum, P. S., Fyer, A., Martinez, J., Buquez, B., Wynn, J.,...Chung, W. K. (2013). Researchers' views on return of incidental genomic research results: Qualitative and quantitative findings. *Genetics in Medicine, 15*(11), 888–895.

Klugman, C. M., & Tolwin, N. M. (2014). *Evaluating prospective choices in an online advance directive program.* Unpublished manuscript, Department of Health Sciences, DePaul University, Chicago, IL.

Lang, F., & Quill, T. (2004). Making decisions with families at the end of life. *American Family Physician, 70*(4), 719–723.

Lo, B., & Field, M. J. (Eds.). (2009). *Conflict of interest in medical research, education, and practice.* Washington, DC: National Academies Press.

Lynn, J. (1991). Why I don't have a living will. *The Journal of Law, Medicine and Ethics, 19*(1–2), 101–104.

McClung, J. A., Kamer, R. S., DeLuc, M., & Barber, H. J. (1996). Evaluation of a medical ethics consultation service: Opinions of patients and health care providers. *American Journal of Medicine, 100*(4), 456–600.

Miyajo, N. T. (1993). The power of compassion: Truth-telling among American doctors in the care of dying patients. *Social Science and Medicine, 36*(3), 249–264.

Montello, M. (2014). Narrative ethics. *Hastings Center Report, 44*(Suppl. 1), S2–S6. doi:10.1002/hast.260

Morrison, R. S., Morrison, E. W., & Glickman, D. F. (1994). Physician reluctance to discuss advance directives: An empirical investigation of potential barriers. *Archives of Internal Medicine, 154*(20), 2311–2318.

Orgel, E., McCarter, R., & Jacobs, S. (2010). A failing medical educational model: A self-assessment by physicians at all levels of training of ability and comfort to deliver bad news. *Journal of Palliative Medicine, 13*(6), 677–683.

Parens, E., Appelbaum, P., & Chung, W. (2013). Incidental findings in the era of whole genome sequencing? *Hastings Center Report, 43*(4), 16–19.

Potter, V. R. (1971). *Bioethics: Bridge to the future.* Englewood Cliffs, NJ: Prentice-Hall.

Presidential Commission for the Study of Bioethical Issues. (2013). *Ethical management of incidental and secondary findings in the clinical, research, and direct-to-consumer contexts.* Washington, DC. Retrieved from http://bioethics.gov/sites/default/files/FINALAnticipateCommunicate_PCS BI_0.pdf

President's Commission for the Study of Ethical Problems in Medicine and Biomedical and Behavioral Research. (1982). *Making health care decisions: The ethical and legal implications of informed consent in the patient-practitioner relationship.* Washington, DC: Library of Congress. Retrieved from https://repository.library.georgetown.edu/bitstream/handle/10822/559354/making_health_care_decisions.pdf?sequence=1

Re Quinlan, 70 N.J. 10, 355 A.2d 647 (1976).

Reich, W. T. (1995). Bioethics. In W. T. Reich (Ed.), *Encyclopedia of bioethics* (2nd ed., p. 250). New York, NY: Macmillan.

Silva, C. H. M. D., Cunha, R. L. G., Tonaco, R. B., Cunha, M. T., Diniz, C. B., Domingos, G. G.,... Paula, R. L. (2003). Not telling the truth in the patient-physician relationship. *Bioethics, 17*(5–6), 417–424.

Solet, D. J., Norvell, J. M., Rutan, G. H., & Frankel, R. M. (2005). Lost in translation: Challenges and opportunities in physican-to-physician communication during patient handoffs. *Academic Medicine, 80,* 1094–1099.

Spike, J. (2012). Ethics consultation process. In D. M. Hester & T. Schonfeld (Eds.), *Guidance for healthcare ethics committees* (pp. 41–47). New York, NY: Cambridge University Press.

Stump, B. F., Klugman, C. M., & Thornton, B. (2008). Last hours of life: Encouraging end-of-life conversations. *Journal of Clinical Ethics, 19*(2), 150–159.

Sullivan, R. J., Menapace, L. W., & White, R. M. (2001). Truth-telling and patient diagnoses. *Journal of Medical Ethics, 27*(3), 192–197.

Surbone, A. (2008). Cultural aspects of communication in cancer care. *Supportive Care in Cancer, 16*(3), 235–240.

Tulsky, J. A. (2005). Beyond advance directives: Importance of communication skills at the end of life. *JAMA, 294*(3), 359–365. doi:10.1001/jama.294.3.359

U.S. Department of Health and Human Services. (2014). Health information privacy. Retrieved September 14, 2014, from http://www.hhs.gov/ocr/privacy/

Vandecreek, L., & Frankowski, D. (1996). Barriers that predict resistance to completing a living will. *Death Studies, 20*(1), 73–82.

Watson, B. M., Hewett, D. G., & Gallois, C. (2012). Intergroup communication and health care. In H. Giles (Ed.), *The handbook of intergroup communication* (pp. 293–305). New York, NY: Routledge.

White, B. D., Jankowski, J. B., & Shelton, W. N. (2014). Structuring a written examination to assess ASBH health care ethics consultation core knowledge competencies. *American Journal of Bioethics, 14*(1), 5–17.

Epilogue: Walking Through THE Door

ELAINE WITTENBERG-LYLES

JOY GOLDSMITH

SANDRA L. RAGAN

On any given day we busy ourselves with our families, the task of a daily commute, and overfilled workloads. Not until we cross a very noticeable or purposive threshold do we take stock of all of our labor, our commitments, and our role in the discourse that has become our life work. As long-time collaborators in the field of end-of-life communication, we are humbled by the development of end-of-life care as an area of study in health communication. This Epilogue provides us a meaningful opportunity to reflect on end-of-life communication in the communication discipline and to consider its place in the time we have ahead.

Our volume, *Communication as Comfort* (Ragan, Wittenberg-Lyles, Goldsmith, & Sanchez-Reilly, 2008), first provided a systematic investigation of communication issues in end-of-life care from a health communication perspective, offering an understanding of palliative care, palliative care communication, and end-of-life communication. We sought to clarify the confusion about the similarities and differences between palliative care and hospice, even among health care providers. As this practice of care grows, and as the governing bodies overseeing health care come to herald palliative care as a key intervention to buoy the fracturing health care system, palliative care programs are more clearly seen as *concentrating on relieving suffering and improving quality of life; they do not exclude or include a patient based on diagnosis or prognosis.* Hospice care is a subset of palliative care for individuals with a terminal diagnosis. Palliative care encapsulates hospice. Both include end-of-life communication.

For providers, communication about end of life involves the skills to provide an assessment of patient and family needs; flexible and fluid treatment interactions that include the ability to reframe medical jargon, procedures, and treatment; conflict navigation among family members; facilitated shared decision making; and the expression of support in decisions about care. End-of-life communication with patients and families results in better quality of life, reduced use of medical intervention near death, earlier hospice referrals, and care more consistent with patient preferences (Bernacki, Block, & American College of Physicians High Value Care Task Force, 2014). These skills are not extraneous for providers but are essential in their day-to-day practice. In fact, communication efforts such as the ones described here are considered to be a substantial portion of clinical care practice, not just a good idea. Because of this, palliative care provides a sea of opportunity for communication scholars to develop interventions and structures of practice that are proved to be successful.

Early discussions about communication at the end of life centered on whether or not patients understood their terminal condition. Protecting the patient from distress by avoiding communication about diagnosis and prognosis was seen as beneficent care. Research from this early era of end-of-life care was vital in identifying the omission, pretense, and failure of end-of-life communication that reduced the quality of life for the patient. As a result of these discoveries, communication was recognized as a cornerstone of quality care and has since been woven into current clinical practice guidelines for palliative care. In 2004, a major advance in palliative care was the clinical practice guidelines developed by a consortium of the leading palliative care organizations, the National Consensus Project for Quality Palliative Care (2004). These guidelines specified domains of care, and each domain revealed a strong reliance on quality communication.

The current volume provides a selective sampling of research on end-of-life communication, offering perspectives that feature the discipline of communication and its role in understanding the nuanced challenges of this communication context. We found the chapters by Thompson, Tullis, Foster and Keeley, and Pecchioni and White particularly useful in outlining how such end-of-life concepts as advance care planning—both physical (Thompson) and spiritual (Tullis)—conversations with the dying (Foster and Keeley), and family decision making (Pecchioni and White) are enhanced by considering these concepts within the broader context of health care communication. This volume and other works further establish end-of-life communication as a pivotal point in our lives that is worthy of study, examination, and most important, evidence-based resources to improve it (Wittenberg et al., in press; Wittenberg-Lyles, Goldsmith, Ferrell, & Ragan, 2012; Wittenberg-Lyles, Goldsmith, Ragan, & Sanchez-Reilly, 2010). In joining those who are studying this context, if we are to matter as a discipline and intend to address the needs of those for whom we write, we must research and write for those beyond our own academic audience; we have to integrate communication theories and methods into conversations with our interprofessional colleagues to be relevant, innovative, valid, worthwhile, meaningful, helpful, and useful.

MOVING BEYOND OURSELVES

Expansion of end-of-life communication research can occur in three specific areas. First, communication scholars can contribute to education about end-of-life communication for health care professionals. Patient simulation and interprofessional education have emerged in health care programs to teach communication. We should explore ways to join faculty working on interprofessional education about end-of-life care—and contribute to studies on patient simulation. Communication departments are known across colleges and institutions for practicing quality instruction. We can teach others to teach communication. We can help teach providers how to work together on teams, facilitate team problem solving, and practice leadership skills. We are uniquely trained to execute these and other pedagogical programs of training. But we will not be able to share our tools, theories, and methods unless we move into new paradigms of knowing, take on the challenge of new terminology, become part of other organizations, and partner with people who know things we know nothing about. These actions can be the most uncomfortable professional maneuvers imaginable but also the most gratifying, fruitful, and productive we have known.

Second, communication researchers can expand the scope of communication topics beyond breaking bad news. As Susan Eggly and colleagues so eloquently articulated nearly 10 years ago, bad news is only bad to the party who defines it that way. In the literature, the entire notion of "bad" is defined by the practitioner (Eggly et al., 2006). Beginning with our article describing the deficiencies in end-of-life communication about poor prognosis (Wittenberg-Lyles, Goldsmith, Sanchez-Reilly, & Ragan, 2008), we have said that end-of-life communication must be transactional. In a transactional model of communication, information is not deposited and then assessed for receipt; rather, it is mutually created through interaction with each participant influencing the other. Curriculum, instruction, interventions for family meetings, consultations about goals of care, transitions in care conversation, and shared decision making can be developed by communication scholars using a transactional model.

Finally, end-of-life communication research should focus on the development and testing of communication interventions. It is not enough to conduct research; researchers should consider practical applications of their findings (Sharf, 1999). Few exemplars of this approach can be found in our discipline. Rick Street and colleague provided seminal and system-changing research about patient-centered care that has served as a guide for other applied and engaged scholars (Epstein & Street, 2007). Only knowledge about communication intervention effectiveness will permit us to contribute substantially to change for care systems, for patients and families, and for health care teams.

Quality communication interventions are dependent on health care practice and payment incentives. These are not comfort zones for the typically trained communication scholar. But the threshold is there to walk over, to enter and mark a new horizon of research and practice opportunities. Knowledge about patient communication, family communication, and provider communication is in its infancy and without a clear connection to intervention development. *We should be doing this work.* Communication practices that meet health literacy needs and include various modes of delivery such as print and video are in our wheelhouse. *We should be doing this work.*

Although the communication field prepares scholars to advance science, build knowledge, understand deeply, measure with thoroughness, and ensure methodological rigor (Hannawa et al., 2014), it is time to move these skills beyond the communication threshold and join other academics and providers working to improve end-of-life care and experiences for patients and families. Since communication is inherently interdisciplinary, it is ironic that we have not done more to embrace other scholars and providers to promote and expand work in this area. Engaged scholarship requires evaluation and thinking outside of the "communication research" box to meet standards set in the health care context. To accomplish this, communication researchers must become less attached to form and more attached to knowing a multitude of forms, less married to standard (communication) writing practices and more eager to take up the challenge of writing for outlets we were never trained for, more committed to connecting with the actual audience, which may often mean letting go of communication-centric language and embracing language that our audience can drink in and use with abandon instead of a thesaurus.

CROSSING OVER INTO A NEW PLACE

More than a decade ago, Sandy Ragan asked one of us in her office and the other in an Indian restaurant to work with her on a book project. We both said yes. *Yes. We would write a book about end-of-life communication.* And with that offer to work on a book sealed, we began walking one step at a time to a new place that looks less and less like Communication Studies. The commitment to engage your research context will take you to that new place. Reflecting on the many steps we have taken, here is a brief look at some of what we have found on the other side of the door.

A cornerstone of our translational program of research is the COMFORT communication curriculum—a theoretically grounded curriculum for teaching palliative care communication (Ragan et al., 2008; Wittenberg-Lyles et al., 2012; Wittenberg-Lyles et al., 2010). COMFORT stands for C-Communication, O-Orientation and Opportunity, M-Mindful communication, F-Family, O-Openings, R-Relating, and T-Team and is detailed in a volume on communication in palliative nursing (Wittenberg-Lyles et al., 2012). It is organized in a clinical education format (assessment, plan, intervention, evaluation)—a format we had to learn and use in order to be useful to health care educators.

Health Communication is our iOS APP that presents free, easily accessed prompts to help health care professionals with end-of-life communication. Derived from the COMFORT curriculum, the "Communication Toolkit," "Difficult Scenarios," and "Plain Language Planner" provide more than 150 practical, evidence-based communication skills. Content within the *mobile-health* intervention is shaped for interprofessional team members who encounter specific challenges such as navigating team differences, complex family conflicts, varying health literacy needs, cultural humility, and difficult questions for which there are no simple answers.

Launched in late 2014, the *Palliative Care Communication Institute* (Palliative Care Communication Institute, 2014) provides a structure for us to organize the variety of tools and programs and trainings we launch. But more important, this website establishes a place that is recognizable for health care providers who are seeking communication tools that are theory driven and evidence based. The lessons we are learning about social media, trademarking, and points of dissemination are time consuming and invisible from the academy, but they are essential to enabling our work to reach its intended audience in a way that can be useful, practiced, and studied.

Looking forward is so much richer if we take time to look back at the many doors we have cracked open, peered past, and then—together—decided to walk through. All of them were needed. All of them were important. All of them will lead to whatever is still ahead. To move communication research about end-of-life communication forward, we must learn the language of health care and use it; we must spend time publicizing our work to health care professionals, patients, and families, and we must partner with other professionals. Challenging methodological issues need to be considered, including access to patients, families, and end-of-life care settings, accumulating patients and family members as participants, and securing grant monies to provide participant reimbursement and large-scale research. We have found that many of these labors are not part of an annual evaluation. But so many things that propel us forward are not measurable or countable in ways that will garner recognition. This is a point of divergence from the traditional structures of the academy. Yet we think this divergence has been worthwhile and gratifying to the degree that we would describe these benefits as immeasurable.

REFERENCES

Bernacki, R. E., Block, S. D., & American College of Physicians High Value Care Task Force. (2014). Communication about serious illness care goals: A review and synthesis of best practices. *JAMA Internal Medicine, 174*, 1994–2003.

Eggly, S., Penner, L., Albrecht, T., Cline, R., Foster, T., Naughton, M.,...Ruckdeshel, J. D. (2006). Discussing "bad news" in the outpatient oncology clinic: Rethinking current communication guidelines. *Journal of Clinical Oncology, 24*, 716–719.

Epstein, R., & Street, R. L. (2007). *Patient-centered communication in cancer care: Promoting healing and reducing suffering* (Publication No. 07-6225). Bethesda, MD: National Cancer Institute, National Institutes of Health.

Hannawa, A. F., Kreps, G. L., Paek, H. J., Schulz, P. J., Smith, S., & Street, R. L., Jr. (2014). Emerging issues and future directions of the field of health communication. *Health Communication, 29*, 955–961.

National Consensus Project for Quality Palliative Care. (2004). Clinical practice guidelines. Retrieved from http://www.nationalconsensusproject.org

Palliative Care Communication Institute. (2014). Retrieved from http://www.pccinstitute.com

Ragan, S., Wittenberg-Lyles, E. M., Goldsmith, J., & Sanchez-Reilly, S. (2008). *Communication as comfort: Multiple voices in palliative care*. New York, NY: Routledge.

Sharf, B. (1999). The present and future of health communication scholarship: Overlooked opportunities. *Health Communication, 11*, 195.

Wittenberg, E., Ferrell, B., Goldsmith, J., Ragan, S., Smith, T., Glachen, M., & Handzo, G. (in press). *Oxford textbook of communication in palliative care*. New York, NY: Oxford University Press.

Wittenberg-Lyles, E., Goldsmith, J., Ferrell, B., & Ragan, S. (2012). *Communication in palliative nursing*. New York, NY: Oxford University Press.

Wittenberg-Lyles, E., Goldsmith, J., Ragan, S., & Sanchez-Reilly, S. (2010). *Dying with comfort: Family illness narratives and early palliative care*. Cresskill, NJ: Hampton Press.

Wittenberg-Lyles, E., Goldsmith, J., Sanchez-Reilly, S., & Ragan, S. L. (2008). Communicating a terminal prognosis in a palliative care setting: Deficiencies in current communication training protocols. *Social Science and Medicine, 66*, 2356–2365.

About THE Editors AND Contributors

EDITORS

Jon F. Nussbaum is Professor of Communication Arts and Sciences and Human Development and Family Studies at the Pennsylvania State University.

Howard Giles is Professor of Communication at the University of California, Santa Barbara.

Amber K. Worthington is a doctoral candidate within the Department of Communication Arts and Sciences at the Pennsylvania State University.

CONTRIBUTORS

Marcia K. Carteret is Senior Instructor at the University of Colorado School of Medicine.

Nichole Egbert is Associate Professor of Communication Studies at Kent State University.

Elissa Foster is Associate Professor of Communication at DePaul University.

Kathleen A. Galvin is Professor of Communication Studies at Northwestern University.

Joy V. Goldsmith is Assistant Professor of Communication at the University of Memphis.

Jaber F. Gubrium is Professor and Chair of Communication at the University of Missouri.

Maureen P. Keeley is Professor of Communication Sciences at the Texas State University.

Craig M. Klugman is Professor and Chair of Health Sciences at DePaul University.

Loretta L. Pecchioni is Associate Professor of Communication Studies at the Louisiana State University.

Sandra Ragan is Professor Emeritus of Communication at the University of Oklahoma.

James D. Robinson is Professor of Communication at the University of Dayton.

Teresa Thompson is Professor of Communication at the University of Dayton.

Paige Toller is Associate Professor of Communication at the University of Nebraska, Omaha.

Jillian A. Tullis is Assistant Professor of Communication Studies at the University of San Diego.

Richard C. White is a doctoral student and graduate instructor of Communication Studies at the Louisiana State University.

Allison Whitney is a doctoral candidate within the Centre for the Study of Theory and Criticism at the University of Western Ontario.

Elaine Wittenberg-Lyles is Associate Professor at the City of Hope, Comprehensive Cancer Center.

Index

I

J

K

LIFESPAN
COMMUNICATION
Children, Families, and Aging

Thomas J. Socha, *General Editor*

From first words to final conversations, communication plays an integral and significant role in all aspects of human development and everyday living. The Lifespan Communication: Children, Families, and Aging series seeks to publish authored and edited scholarly volumes that focus on relational and group communication as they develop over the lifespan (infancy through later life). The series will include volumes on the communication development of children and adolescents, family communication, peer-group communication (among age cohorts), intergenerational communication, and later-life communication, as well as longitudinal studies of lifespan communication development, communication during lifespan transitions, and lifespan communication research methods. The series includes college textbooks as well as books for use in upper-level undergraduate and graduate courses.

Thomas J. Socha, Series Editor | *tsocha@odu.edu*
Mary Savigar, Acquisitions Editor | *mary.savigar@plang.com*

To order other books in this series, please contact our Customer Service Department at:

(800) 770-LANG (within the U.S.)
(212) 647-7706 (outside the U.S.)
(212) 647-7707 FAX

Or browse online by series at www.peterlang.com